HOLT
SCIENCE &
TECHNOLOGY

D0617314

Cells, Heredity, and Classification

HOLT, RINEHART AND WINSTON

A Harcourt Education Company

Orlando • **Austin** • New York • San Diego • Toronto • London

Acknowledgments

Contributing Authors

Linda Ruth Berg, Ph.D.
Adjunct Professor
Natural Sciences
St. Petersburg College
St. Petersburg, Florida

Barbara Christopher
Science Writer and Editor
Austin, Texas

Mark F. Taylor, Ph.D.
Associate Professor of Biology
Biology Department
Baylor University
Waco, Texas

Inclusion Specialist

Ellen McPeek Glisan
Special Needs Consultant
San Antonio, Texas

Safety Reviewer

Jack Gerlovich, Ph.D.
Associate Professor
School of Education
Drake University
Des Moines, Iowa

Academic Reviewers

Glenn Adelson
Instructor
Biology Undergraduate Program
Harvard University
Cambridge, Massachusetts

Joe W. Crim, Ph.D.
Professor and Head of Cellular Biology
Department of Cellular Biology
University of Georgia
Athens, Georgia

Jim Denbow, Ph.D.
Associate Professor of Archaeology
Department of Anthropology and Archaeology
The University of Texas at Austin
Austin, Texas

David Haig, Ph.D.
Professor of Biology
Organismic and Evolutionary Biology
Harvard University
Cambridge, Massachusetts

Laurie Santos, Ph.D.
Assistant Professor
Department of Psychology
Yale University
New Haven, Connecticut

Patrick K. Schoff, Ph.D.
Research Associate
Natural Resources Research Institute
University of Minnesota—Duluth
Duluth, Minnesota

Richard P. Vari
Research Scientist and Curator
Division of Fishes
National Museum of Natural History
Washington, D.C.

Teacher Reviewers

Diedre S. Adams
Physical Science Instructor
West Vigo Middle School
West Terre Haute, Indiana

Sarah Carver
Science Teacher
Jackson Creek Middle School
Bloomington, Indiana

Hilary Cochran
Science Teacher
Indian Crest Junior High School
Souderton, Pennsylvania

Karen Dietrich, S.S.J., Ph.D.
Principal and Biology Instructor
Mount Saint Joseph Academy
Flourtown, Pennsylvania

Debra S. Kogelman, MAed.
Science Teacher
University of Chicago Laboratory Schools
Chicago, Illinois

Elizabeth Rustad
Science Teacher
Higley School District
Gilbert, Arizona

Helen P. Schiller
Instructional Coach
The School District of Greenville County
Greenville, South Carolina

Stephanie Snowden
Science Teacher
Canyon Vista Middle School
Austin, Texas

Angie Williams
Teacher
Riversprings Middle School
Crawfordville, Florida

Lab Development

Diana Scheidle Bartos
Research Associate
School of Mines
Golden, Colorado

Carl Benson
General Science Teacher
Plains High School
Plains, Montana

Charlotte Blassingame
Technology Coordinator
White Station Middle School
Memphis, Tennessee

Marsha Carver
Science Teacher and Department Chair
McLean County High School
Calhoun, Kentucky

C Cells, Heredity, and Classification

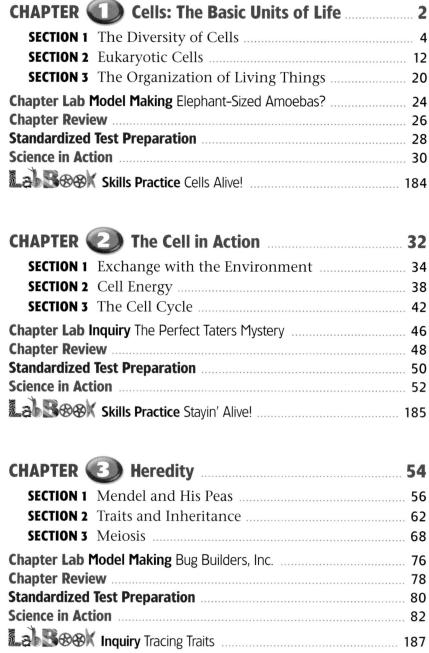

Contents

Skills Development

PRE-READING ACTIVITY

FOLDNOTES

Graphic Organizer

START-UP ACTIVITY

Quick Lab

SCHOOL to HOME

READING STRATEGY

Brainstorming

Discussion

Mnemonics

Paired Summarizing

Prediction Guide

Reading Organizer—Concept Map

Reading Organizer—Flowchart

Reading Organizer—Outline

Reading Organizer—Table

INTERNET ACTIVITY

Connection to . . .

Science in Action

Contents

How to Use Your Textbook

Your Roadmap for Success with Holt Science and Technology

Reading Warm-Up

A Reading Warm-Up at the beginning of every section provides you with the section's objectives and key terms. The objectives tell you what you'll need to know after you finish reading the section.

Key terms are listed for each section. Learn the definitions of these terms because you will most likely be tested on them. Each key term is highlighted in the text and is defined at point of use and in the margin. You can also use the glossary to locate definitions quickly.

STUDY TIP Reread the objectives and the definitions to the key terms when studying for a test to be sure you know the material.

Get Organized

A Reading Strategy at the beginning of every section provides tips to help you organize and remember the information covered in the section. Keep a science notebook so that you are ready to take notes when your teacher reviews the material in class. Keep your assignments in this notebook so that you can review them when studying for the chapter test.

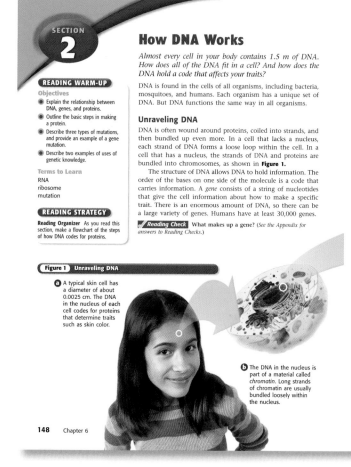

SECTION 2

How DNA Works

Almost every cell in your body contains 1.5 m of DNA. How does all of the DNA fit in a cell? And how does the DNA hold a code that affects your traits?

DNA is found in the cells of all organisms, including bacteria, mosquitoes, and humans. Each organism has a unique set of DNA. But DNA functions the same way in all organisms.

Unraveling DNA

DNA is often wound around proteins, coiled into strands, and then bundled up even more. In a cell that lacks a nucleus, each strand of DNA forms a loose loop within the cell. In a cell that has a nucleus, the strands of DNA and proteins are bundled into chromosomes, as shown in **Figure 1.**

The structure of DNA allows DNA to hold information. The order of the bases on one side of the molecule is a code that carries information. A *gene* consists of a string of nucleotides that give the cell information about how to make a specific trait. There is an enormous amount of DNA, so there can be a large variety of genes. Humans have at least 30,000 genes.

Reading Check What makes up a gene? (*See the Appendix for answers to Reading Checks.*)

READING WARM-UP

Objectives
- Explain the relationship between DNA, genes, and proteins.
- Outline the basic steps in making a protein.
- Describe three types of mutations, and provide an example of a gene mutation.
- Describe two examples of uses of genetic knowledge.

Terms to Learn
RNA
ribosome
mutation

READING STRATEGY

Reading Organizer As you read this section, make a flowchart of the steps of how DNA codes for proteins.

Figure 1 Unraveling DNA

a A typical skin cell has a diameter of about 0.0025 cm. The DNA in the nucleus of each cell codes for proteins that determine traits such as skin color.

b The DNA in the nucleus is part of a material called *chromatin.* Long strands of chromatin are usually bundled loosely within the nucleus.

148 Chapter 6

Be Resourceful — Use the Web

Internet Connect

boxes in your textbook take you to resources that you can use for science projects, reports, and research papers. Go to scilinks.org, and type in the SciLinks code to get information on a topic.

Visit go.hrw.com

Find worksheets, **Current Science**® magazine articles online, and other materials that go with your textbook at **go.hrw.com.** Click on the textbook icon and the table of contents to see all of the resources for each chapter.

An Example of a Substitution

A mutation, such as a substitution, can be harmful because it may cause a gene to produce the wrong protein. Consider the DNA sequence GAA. When copied as mRNA, this sequence gives the instructions to place the amino acid glutamic acid into the growing protein. If a mistake happens and the original DNA sequence is changed to GTA, the sequence will code for the amino acid valine instead.

This simple change in an amino acid can cause the disease *sickle cell anemia*. Sickle cell anemia affects red blood cells. When valine is substituted for glutamic acid in a blood protein, as shown in **Figure 4**, the red blood cells are changed into a sickle shape.

The sickle cells are not as good at carrying oxygen as normal red blood cells are. Sickle cells are also likely to get stuck in blood vessels and cause painful and dangerous clots.

Reading Check What causes sickle cell anemia?

SCHOOL to HOME
An Error in the Message
The sentence below is the result of an error similar to a DNA mutation. The original sentence was made up of three-letter words, but an error was made in this copy. Explain the idea of mutations to your parent. Then, work together to find the mutation, and write the sentence correctly.
THE IGB ADC ATA TET HEB IGR EDR AT.
ACTIVITY

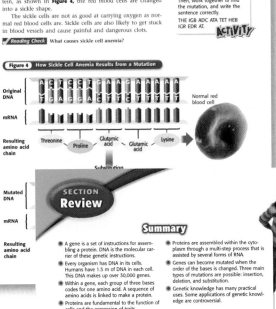

Figure 4 How Sickle Cell Anemia Results from a Mutation

Original DNA
mRNA
Resulting amino acid chain — Threonine, Proline, Glutamic acid, Glutamic acid, Lysine

Normal red blood cell

Substitution

Mutated DNA
mRNA
Resulting amino acid chain

SECTION Review

Summary

- A gene is a set of instructions for assembling a protein. DNA is the molecular carrier of these genetic instructions.
- Every organism has DNA in its cells. Humans have 1.5 m of DNA in each cell. This DNA makes up over 30,000 genes.
- Within a gene, each group of three bases codes for one amino acid. A sequence of amino acids is linked to make a protein.
- Proteins are fundamental to the function of cells and the expression of traits.
- Proteins are assembled within the cytoplasm through a multi-step process that is assisted by several forms of RNA.
- Genes can become mutated when the order of the bases is changed. Three main types of mutations are possible: insertion, deletion, and substitution.
- Genetic knowledge has many practical uses. Some applications of genetic knowledge are controversial.

Using Key Terms

1. Use each of the following terms in the same sentence: *ribosome* and *RNA*.

2. In your own words, write a definition for the term *mutation*.

Understanding Key Ideas

3. Explain the relationship between genes and proteins.

4. List three possible types of mutations.

5. Which type of mutation causes sickle cell anemia?
   a. substitution
   b. insertion
   c. deletion
   d. mutagen

Math Skills

6. A set of 23 chromosomes in a human cell contains 3.2 billion pairs of DNA bases in sequence. On average, about how many pairs of bases are in each chromosome?

Critical Thinking

7. Applying Concepts In which cell type might a mutation be passed from generation to generation? Explain.

8. Making Comparisons How is genetic engineering different from natural reproduction?

Interpreting Graphics

The illustration below shows a sequence of bases on one strand of a DNA molecule. Use the illustration below to answer the questions that follow.

9. How many amino acids are coded for by the sequence on one side (A) of this DNA strand?

10. What is the order of bases on the complementary side of the strand (B), from left to right?

11. If a G were inserted as the first base on the top side (A), what would the order of bases be on the complementary side (B)?

For a variety of links related to this chapter, go to www.scilinks.org
Topic: Genetic Engineering
SciLinks code: HSM0654

155

Use the Illustrations and Photos

Art shows complex ideas and processes. Learn to analyze the art so that you better understand the material you read in the text.

Tables and graphs display important information in an organized way to help you see relationships.

A picture is worth a thousand words. Look at the photographs to see relevant examples of science concepts that you are reading about.

Answer the Section Reviews

Section Reviews test your knowledge of the main points of the section. Critical Thinking items challenge you to think about the material in greater depth and to find connections that you infer from the text.

STUDY TIP When you can't answer a question, reread the section. The answer is usually there.

Do Your Homework

Your teacher may assign worksheets to help you understand and remember the material in the chapter.

STUDY TIP Don't try to answer the questions without reading the text and reviewing your class notes. A little preparation up front will make your homework assignments a lot easier. Answering the items in the Chapter Review will help prepare you for the chapter test.

Holt Online Learning

Visit Holt Online Learning
If your teacher gives you a special password to log onto the Holt Online Learning site, you'll find your complete textbook on the Web. In addition, you'll find some great learning tools and practice quizzes. You'll be able to see how well you know the material from your textbook.

CNN Student News

Visit CNN Student News
You'll find up-to-date events in science at **cnnstudentnews.com**.

SAFETY FIRST!

Exploring, inventing, and investigating are essential to the study of science. However, these activities can also be dangerous. To make sure that your experiments and explorations are safe, you must be aware of a variety of safety guidelines. You have probably heard of the saying, "It is better to be safe than sorry." This is particularly true in a science classroom where experiments and explorations are being performed. Being uninformed and careless can result in serious injuries. Don't take chances with your own safety or with anyone else's.

The following pages describe important guidelines for staying safe in the science classroom. Your teacher may also have safety guidelines and tips that are specific to your classroom and laboratory. Take the time to be safe.

Safety Rules!

Start Out Right

Always get your teacher's permission before attempting any laboratory exploration. Read the procedures carefully, and pay particular attention to safety information and caution statements. If you are unsure about what a safety symbol means, look it up or ask your teacher. You cannot be too careful when it comes to safety. If an accident does occur, inform your teacher immediately regardless of how minor you think the accident is.

If you are instructed to note the odor of a substance, wave the fumes toward your nose with your hand. Never put your nose close to the source.

Safety Symbols

All of the experiments and investigations in this book and their related worksheets include important safety symbols to alert you to particular safety concerns. Become familiar with these symbols so that when you see them, you will know what they mean and what to do. It is important that you read this entire safety section to learn about specific dangers in the laboratory.

Eye protection

Clothing protection

Hand safety

Heating safety

Electric safety

Chemical safety

Animal safety

Sharp object

Plant safety

x

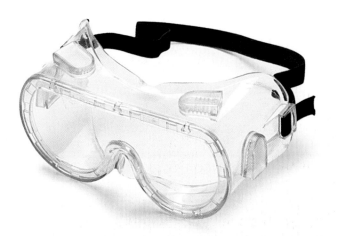

Eye Safety

Wear safety goggles when working around chemicals, acids, bases, or any type of flame or heating device. Wear safety goggles any time there is even the slightest chance that harm could come to your eyes. If any substance gets into your eyes, notify your teacher immediately and flush your eyes with running water for at least 15 minutes. Treat any unknown chemical as if it were a dangerous chemical. Never look directly into the sun. Doing so could cause permanent blindness.

Avoid wearing contact lenses in a laboratory situation. Even if you are wearing safety goggles, chemicals can get between the contact lenses and your eyes. If your doctor requires that you wear contact lenses instead of glasses, wear eye-cup safety goggles in the lab.

Safety Equipment

Know the locations of the nearest fire alarms and any other safety equipment, such as fire blankets and eyewash fountains, as identified by your teacher, and know the procedures for using the equipment.

Neatness

Keep your work area free of all unnecessary books and papers. Tie back long hair, and secure loose sleeves or other loose articles of clothing, such as ties and bows. Remove dangling jewelry. Don't wear open-toed shoes or sandals in the laboratory. Never eat, drink, or apply cosmetics in a laboratory setting. Food, drink, and cosmetics can easily become contaminated with dangerous materials.

Certain hair products (such as aerosol hair spray) are flammable and should not be worn while working near an open flame. Avoid wearing hair spray or hair gel on lab days.

Sharp/Pointed Objects

Use knives and other sharp instruments with extreme care. Never cut objects while holding them in your hands. Place objects on a suitable work surface for cutting.

Be extra careful when using any glassware. When adding a heavy object to a graduated cylinder, tilt the cylinder so the object slides slowly to the bottom.

Heat

Wear safety goggles when using a heating device or a flame. Whenever possible, use an electric hot plate as a heat source instead of using an open flame. When heating materials in a test tube, always angle the test tube away from yourself and others. To avoid burns, wear heat-resistant gloves whenever instructed to do so.

Electricity

Be careful with electrical cords. When using a microscope with a lamp, do not place the cord where it could trip someone. Do not let cords hang over a table edge in a way that could cause equipment to fall if the cord is accidentally pulled. Do not use equipment with damaged cords. Be sure that your hands are dry and that the electrical equipment is in the "off" position before plugging it in. Turn off and unplug electrical equipment when you are finished.

Chemicals

Wear safety goggles when handling any potentially dangerous chemicals, acids, or bases. If a chemical is unknown, handle it as you would a dangerous chemical. Wear an apron and protective gloves when you work with acids or bases or whenever you are told to do so. If a spill gets on your skin or clothing, rinse it off immediately with water for at least 5 minutes while calling to your teacher.

Never mix chemicals unless your teacher tells you to do so. Never taste, touch, or smell chemicals unless you are specifically directed to do so. Before working with a flammable liquid or gas, check for the presence of any source of flame, spark, or heat.

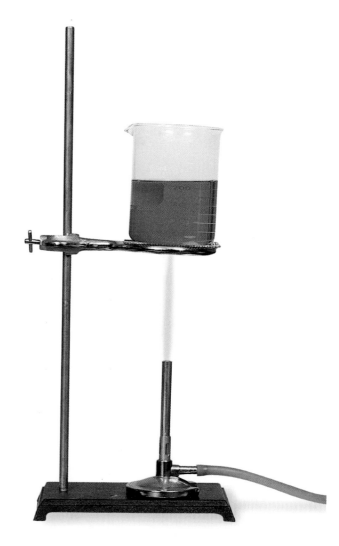

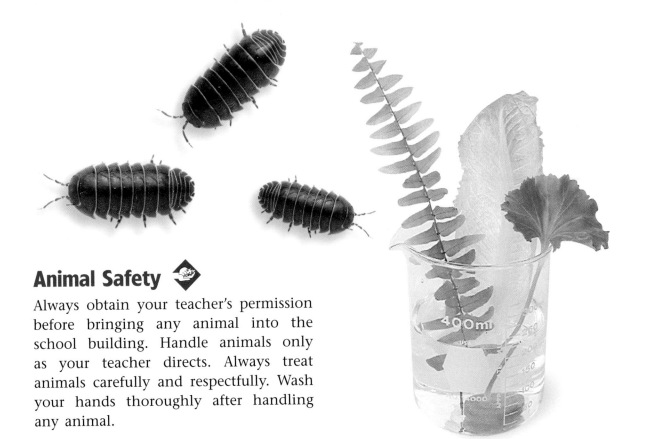

Animal Safety

Always obtain your teacher's permission before bringing any animal into the school building. Handle animals only as your teacher directs. Always treat animals carefully and respectfully. Wash your hands thoroughly after handling any animal.

Plant Safety

Do not eat any part of a plant or plant seed used in the laboratory. Wash your hands thoroughly after handling any part of a plant. When in nature, do not pick any wild plants unless your teacher instructs you to do so.

Glassware

Examine all glassware before use. Be sure that glassware is clean and free of chips and cracks. Report damaged glassware to your teacher. Glass containers used for heating should be made of heat-resistant glass.

Cells: The Basic Units of Life

About the PHOTO

Harmful bacteria may invade your body and make you sick. But wait—your white blood cells come to the rescue! In this image, a white blood cell (the large, yellowish cell) reaches out its pseudopod to destroy bacteria (the purple cells). The red discs are red blood cells.

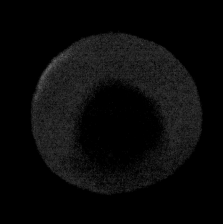

PRE-READING ACTIVITY

FOLDNOTES **Key-Term Fold** Before you read the chapter, create the FoldNote entitled "Key-Term Fold" described in the **Study Skills** section of the Appendix. Write a key term from the chapter on each tab of the key-term fold. Under each tab, write the definition of the key term.

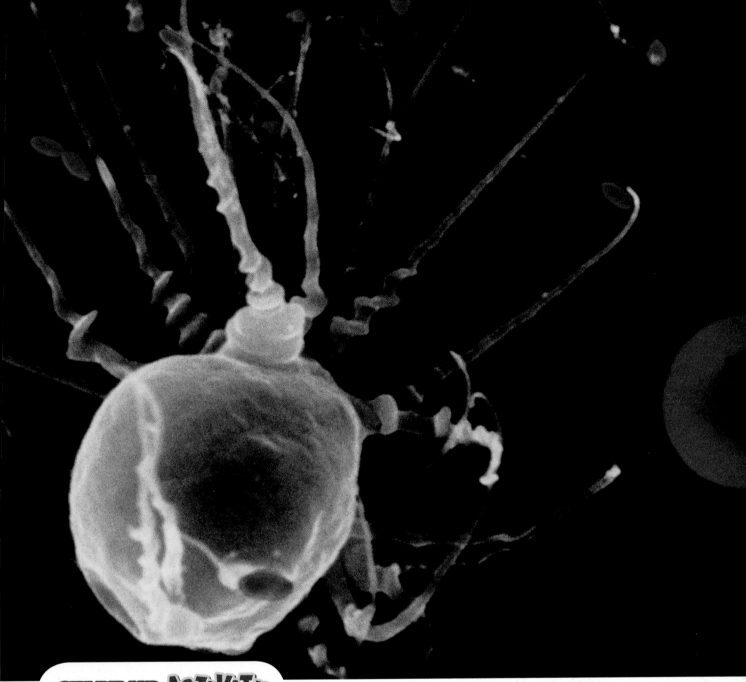

What Are Plants Made Of?

All living things, including plants, are made of cells. What do plant cells look like? Do this activity to find out.

Procedure

1. Tear off a **small leaf** from near the tip of an **Elodea sprig.**

2. Using **forceps,** place the whole leaf in a **drop of water** on a **microscope slide.**

3. Place a **coverslip** on top of the water drop by putting one edge of the coverslip on the slide near the water drop. Next, lower the coverslip slowly so that the coverslip does not trap air bubbles.

4. Place the slide on your **microscope.**

5. Using the lowest-powered lens first, find the plant cells. When you can see the cells under the lower-powered lens, switch to a higher-powered lens.

6. Draw a picture of what you see.

Analysis

1. Describe the shape of the *Elodea* cells. Are all of the cells in the *Elodea* the same?

2. Do you think human cells look like *Elodea* cells? How do you think they are different? How might they be similar?

The Diversity of Cells

Most cells are so small they can't be seen by the naked eye. So how did scientists find cells? By accident, that's how! The first person to see cells wasn't even looking for them.

All living things are made of tiny structures called cells. A **cell** is the smallest unit that can perform all the processes necessary for life. Because of their size, cells weren't discovered until microscopes were invented in the mid-1600s.

Cells and the Cell Theory

Robert Hooke was the first person to describe cells. In 1665, he built a microscope to look at tiny objects. One day, he looked at a thin slice of cork. Cork is found in the bark of cork trees. The cork looked like it was made of little boxes. Hooke named these boxes *cells,* which means "little rooms" in Latin. Hooke's cells were really the outer layers of dead cork cells. Hooke's microscope and his drawing of the cork cells are shown in **Figure 1.**

Hooke also looked at thin slices of living plants. He saw that they too were made of cells. Some cells were even filled with "juice." The "juicy" cells were living cells.

Hooke also looked at feathers, fish scales, and the eyes of houseflies. But he spent most of his time looking at plants and fungi. The cells of plants and fungi have cell walls. This makes them easy to see. Animal cells do not have cell walls. This absence of cell walls makes it harder to see the outline of animal cells. Because Hooke couldn't see their cells, he thought that animals weren't made of cells.

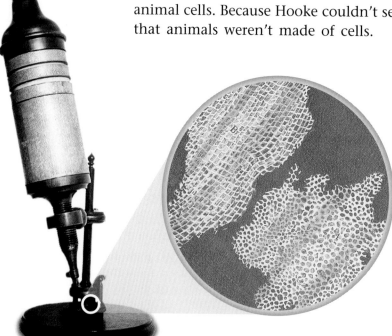

Figure 1 *Hooke discovered cells using this microscope. Hooke's drawing of cork cells is shown to the right of his microscope.*

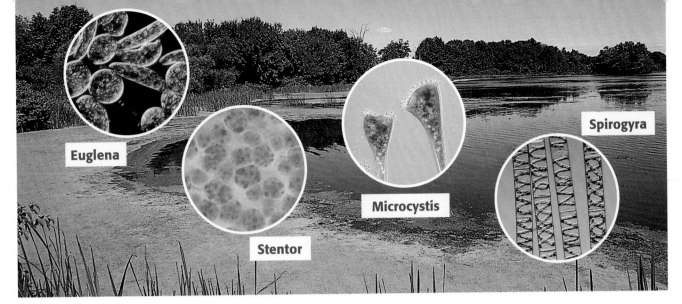

Euglena

Stentor

Microcystis

Spirogyra

Finding Cells in Other Organisms

In 1673, Anton van Leeuwenhoek (LAY vuhn HOOK), a Dutch merchant, made his own microscopes. Leeuwenhoek used one of his microscopes to look at pond scum. Leeuwenhoek saw small organisms in the water. He named these organisms *animalcules,* which means "little animals." Today, we call these single-celled organisms protists (PROH tists). Pond scum and some of the protists it contains are shown in **Figure 2.**

Leeuwenhoek also looked at animal blood. He saw differences in blood cells from different kinds of animals. For example, blood cells in fish, birds, and frogs are oval. Blood cells in humans and dogs are round and flat. Leeuwenhoek was also the first person to see bacteria. And he discovered that yeasts that make bread dough rise are single-celled organisms.

The Cell Theory

Almost 200 years passed before scientists concluded that cells are present in all living things. Scientist Matthias Schleiden (mah THEE uhs SHLIE duhn) studied plants. In 1838, he concluded that all plant parts were made of cells. Theodor Schwann (TAY oh dohr SHVAHN) studied animals. In 1839, Schwann concluded that all animal tissues were made of cells. Soon after that, Schwann wrote the first two parts of what is now known as the *cell theory*.

- All organisms are made of one or more cells.
- The cell is the basic unit of all living things.

Later, in 1858, Rudolf Virchow (ROO dawlf FIR koh), a doctor, stated that all cells could form only from other cells. Virchow then added the third part of the cell theory.

- All cells come from existing cells.

Reading Check What are the three parts of the cell theory?
(See the Appendix for answers to Reading Checks.)

Figure 2 *The green area at the edge of the pond is a layer of pond scum. This pond scum contains organisms called* protists, *such as those shown above.*

cell in biology, the smallest unit that can perform all life processes; cells are covered by a membrane and have DNA and cytoplasm

CONNECTION TO Physics

Microscopes The microscope Hooke used to study cells was much different from microscopes today. Research different kinds of microscopes, such as light microscopes, scanning electron microscopes (SEMs), and transmission electron microscopes (TEMs). Select one type of microscope. Make a poster or other presentation to show to the class. Describe how the microscope works and how it is used. Be sure to include images.

ACTIVITY

Cell Size

Most cells are too small to be seen without a microscope. It would take 50 human cells to cover the dot on this letter *i*.

A Few Large Cells

Most cells are small. A few, however, are big. A chicken egg, shown in **Figure 3,** is one big cell. The egg can be this large because it does not have to take in more nutrients.

Figure 3 *The white and yolk of this chicken egg are part of a single cell.*

Many Small Cells

There is a physical reason why most cells are so small. Cells take in food and get rid of wastes through their outer surface. As a cell gets larger, it needs more food and produces more waste. Therefore, more materials pass through its outer surface.

As the cell's volume increases, its surface area grows too. But the cell's volume grows faster than its surface area. If a cell gets too large, the cell's surface area will not be large enough to take in enough nutrients or pump out enough wastes. So, the area of a cell's surface—compared with the cell's volume—limits the cell's size. The ratio of the cell's outer surface area to the cell's volume is called the *surface area–to–volume ratio,* which can be calculated by using the following equation:

$$\textit{surface area–to–volume ratio} = \frac{\textit{surface area}}{\textit{volume}}$$

✓ Reading Check Why are most cells small?

MATH FOCUS

Surface Area–to–Volume Ratio Calculate the surface area–to–volume ratio of a cube whose sides measure 2 cm.

Step 1: Calculate the surface area.

surface area of cube = number of sides ×
area of side

surface area of cube = 6 × (2 cm × 2 cm)

surface area of cube = 24 cm²

Step 2: Calculate the volume.

volume of cube = side × side × side

volume of cube = 2 cm × 2 cm × 2 cm

volume of cube = 8 cm³

Step 3: Calculate the surface area–to–volume ratio.

$$\textit{surface area–to–volume ratio} = \frac{\textit{surface area}}{\textit{volume}} = \frac{24}{8} = \frac{3}{1}$$

Now It's Your Turn

1. Calculate the surface area–to–volume ratio of a cube whose sides are 3 cm long.

2. Calculate the surface area–to–volume ratio of a cube whose sides are 4 cm long.

3. Of the cubes from questions 1 and 2, which has the greater surface area–to–volume ratio?

4. What is the relationship between the length of a side and the surface area–to–volume ratio of a cell?

Parts of a Cell

Cells come in many shapes and sizes. Cells have many different functions. But all cells have the following parts in common.

The Cell Membrane and Cytoplasm

All cells are surrounded by a cell membrane. The **cell membrane** is a protective layer that covers the cell's surface and acts as a barrier. It separates the cell's contents from its environment. The cell membrane also controls materials going into and out of the cell. Inside the cell is a fluid. This fluid and almost all of its contents are called the *cytoplasm* (SIET oh PLAZ uhm).

Organelles

Cells have organelles that carry out various life processes. **Organelles** are structures that perform specific functions within the cell. Different types of cells have different organelles. Most organelles are surrounded by membranes. For example, the algal cell in **Figure 4** has membrane-bound organelles. Some organelles float in the cytoplasm. Other organelles are attached to membranes or other organelles.

Reading Check What are organelles?

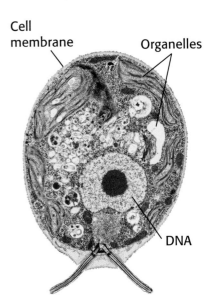

Figure 4 *This green alga has organelles. The organelles and the fluid surrounding them make up the cytoplasm.*

Genetic Material

All cells contain DNA (**deoxyribonucleic acid**) at some point in their life. *DNA* is the genetic material that carries information needed to make new cells and new organisms. DNA is passed on from parent cells to new cells and controls the activities of a cell. **Figure 5** shows the DNA of a bacterium.

In some cells, the DNA is enclosed inside an organelle called the **nucleus.** For example, your cells have a nucleus. In contrast, bacterial cells do not have a nucleus.

In humans, mature red blood cells lose their DNA. Red blood cells are made inside bones. When red blood cells are first made, they have a nucleus with DNA. But before they enter the bloodstream, red blood cells lose their nucleus and DNA. They survive with no new instructions from their DNA.

cell membrane a phospholipid layer that covers a cell's surface; acts as a barrier between the inside of a cell and the cell's environment

organelle one of the small bodies in a cell's cytoplasm that are specialized to perform a specific function

nucleus in a eukaryotic cell, a membrane-bound organelle that contains the cell's DNA and that has a role in processes such as growth, metabolism, and reproduction

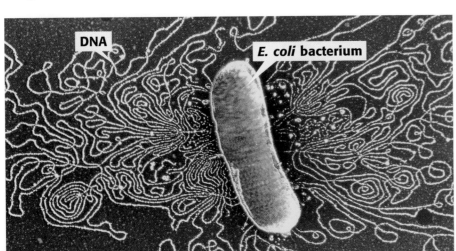

Figure 5 *This photo shows an* Escherichia coli *bacterium. The bacterium's cell membrane has been treated so that the cell's DNA is released.*

7

Quick Lab

Bacteria in Your Lunch?

Most of the time, you don't want bacteria in your food. Many bacteria make toxins that will make you sick. However, some foods—such as yogurt—are supposed to have bacteria in them! The bacteria in these foods are not dangerous.

In yogurt, masses of rod-shaped bacteria feed on the sugar (lactose) in milk. The bacteria convert the sugar into lactic acid. Lactic acid causes milk to thicken. This thickened milk makes yogurt.

1. Using a **cotton swab,** put a **small dot of yogurt** on a **microscope slide.**

2. Add a **drop of water.** Use the cotton swab to stir.

3. Add a **coverslip.**

4. Use a **microscope** to examine the slide. Draw what you observe.

prokaryote an organism that consists of a single cell that does not have a nucleus

Two Kinds of Cells

All cells have cell membranes, organelles, cytoplasm, and DNA in common. But there are two basic types of cells—cells without a nucleus and cells with a nucleus. Cells with no nucleus are *prokaryotic* (proh KAR ee AHT ik) *cells*. Cells that have a nucleus are *eukaryotic* (yoo KAR ee AHT ik) *cells*. Prokaryotic cells are further classified into two groups: *eubacteria* (yoo bak TIR ee uh) and *archaebacteria* (AHR kee bak TIR ee uh).

Prokaryotes: Eubacteria and Archaebacteria

Eubacteria and archaebacteria are prokaryotes (pro KAR ee OHTS). **Prokaryotes** are single-celled organisms that do not have a nucleus or membrane-bound organelles.

Eubacteria

The most common prokaryotes are eubacteria (or just *bacteria*). Bacteria are the world's smallest cells. These tiny organisms live almost everywhere. Bacteria do not have a nucleus, but they do have DNA. A bacteria's DNA is a long, circular molecule, shaped sort of like a rubber band. Bacteria have no membrane-covered organelles. But they do have ribosomes. *Ribosomes* are tiny, round organelles made of protein and other material.

Bacteria also have a strong, weblike exterior cell wall. This wall helps the cell retain its shape. A bacterium's cell membrane is just inside the cell wall. Together, the cell wall and cell membrane allow materials into and out of the cell.

Some bacteria live in the soil and water. Others live in, or on, other organisms. For example, you have bacteria living on your skin and teeth. You also have bacteria living in your digestive system. These bacteria help the process of digestion. A typical bacterial cell is shown in **Figure 6.**

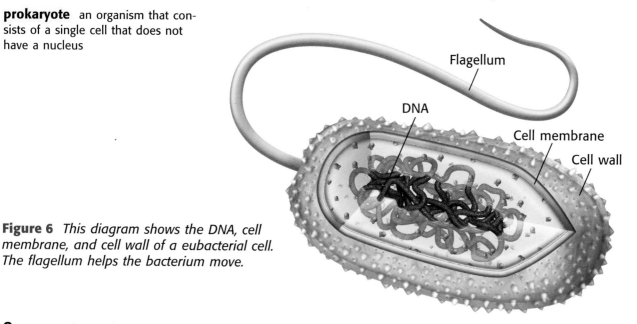

Figure 6 *This diagram shows the DNA, cell membrane, and cell wall of a eubacterial cell. The flagellum helps the bacterium move.*

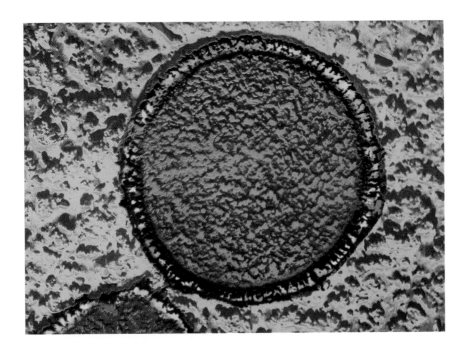

Figure 7 *This photograph, taken with an electron microscope, is of an archaebacterium that lives in the very high temperatures of deep-sea volcanic vents. The photograph has been colored so that the cell wall is green and the cell contents are pink.*

Archaebacteria

The second kind of prokaryote are the archaebacteria. These organisms are also called *archaea* (ahr KEE uh). Archaebacteria are not as common as bacteria, but they are similar to bacteria in some ways. For example, both are single-celled organisms. Both have ribosomes, a cell membrane, and circular DNA. And both lack a nucleus and membrane-bound organelles. But archaebacteria are different from bacteria. For example, archaebacterial ribosomes are different from eubacterial ribosomes.

Archaebacteria are similar to eukaryotic cells in some ways, too. For example, archaebacterial ribosomes are more like the ribosomes of eukaryotic cells. But archaebacteria also have some features that no other cells have. For example, the cell wall and cell membranes of archaebacteria are different from the cell walls of other organisms. And some archaebacteria live in places where no other organisms could live.

Three types of archaebacteria are *heat-loving, salt-loving,* and *methane-making.* Methane is a kind of gas frequently found in swamps. Heat-loving and salt-lovng archaebacteria are sometimes called extremophiles. *Extremophiles* live in places where conditions are extreme. They live in very hot water, such as in hot springs, or where the water is extremely salty. **Figure 7** shows one kind of methane-making archaebacteria that lives deep in the ocean near volcanic vents. The temperature of the water from those vents is extreme: it is above the boiling point of water at sea level.

✓ Reading Check What is one difference between eubacteria and archaebacteria?

CONNECTION TO Social Studies

Where Do They Live?
While most archaebacteria live in extreme environments, scientists have found that archaebacteria live almost everywhere. Do research about archaebacteria. Select one kind of archaebacteria. Create a poster showing the geographical location where the organism lives, describing its physical environment, and explaining how it survives in its environment.

ACTIVITY

Eukaryotic Cells and Eukaryotes

Eukaryotic cells are the largest cells. Most eukaryotic cells are still microscopic, but they are about 10 times larger than most bacterial cells. A typical eukaryotic cell is shown in **Figure 8.**

Unlike bacteria and archaebacteria, eukaryotic cells have a nucleus. The nucleus is one kind of membrane-bound organelle. A cell's nucleus holds the cell's DNA. Eukaryotic cells have other membrane-bound organelles as well. Organelles are like the different organs in your body. Each kind of organelle has a specific job in the cell. Together, organelles, such as the ones shown in **Figure 8,** perform all the processes necessary for life.

All living things that are not bacteria or archaebacteria are made of one or more eukaryotic cells. Organisms made of eukaryotic cells are called **eukaryotes.** Many eukaryotes are multicellular. *Multicellular* means "many cells." Multicellular organisms are usually larger than single-cell organisms. So, most organisms you see with your naked eye are eukaryotes. There are many types of eukaryotes. Animals, including humans, are eukaryotes. So are plants. Some protists, such as amoebas, are single-celled eukaryotes. Other protists, including some types of green algae, are multicellular eukaryotes. Fungi are organisms such as mushrooms or yeasts. Mushrooms are multicellular eukaryotes. Yeasts are single-celled eukaryotes.

Reading Check How are eukaryotes different from prokaryotes?

eukaryote an organism made up of cells that have a nucleus enclosed by a membrane; eukaryotes include animals, plants, and fungi, but not archaebacteria or eubacteria

Figure 8 **Organelles in a Typical Eukaryotic Cell**

Golgi complex
Nucleus
Mitochondrion
Lysosome
Endoplasmic reticulum
Ribosome
Cell membrane
Organelles
Nucleus

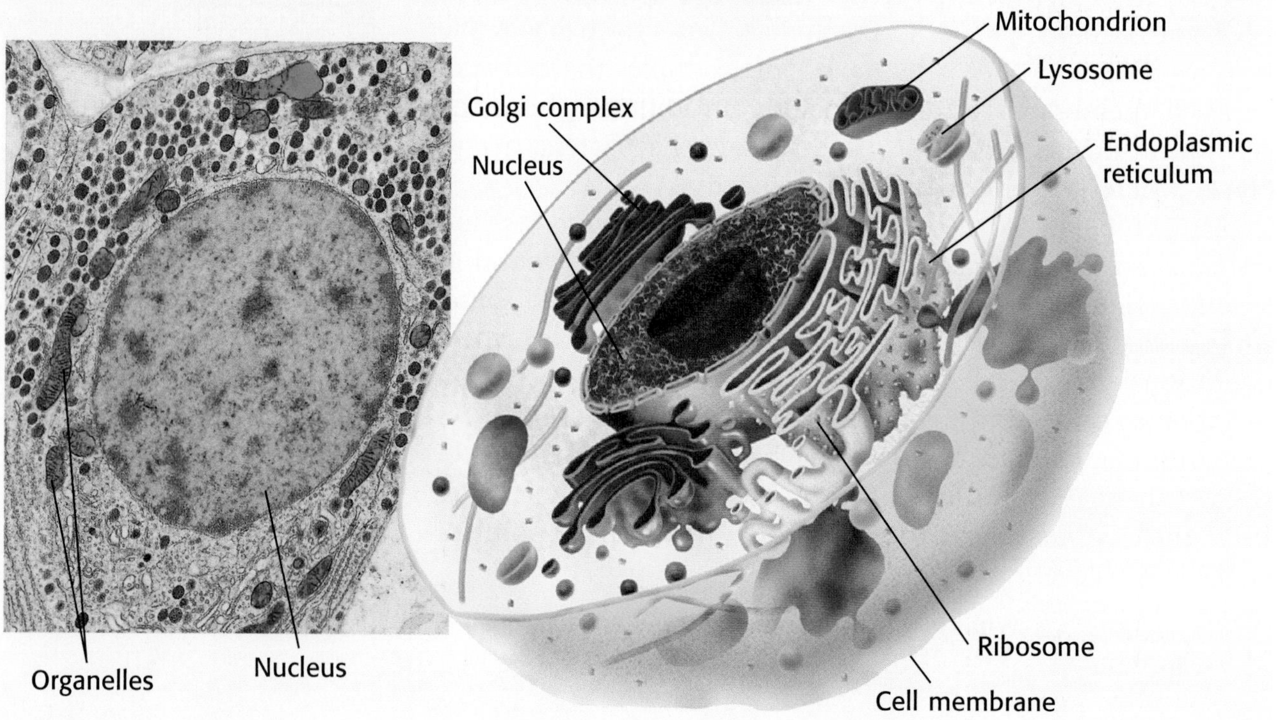

Summary

- Cells were not discovered until microscopes were invented in the 1600s.
- Cell theory states that all organisms are made of cells, the cell is the basic unit of all living things, and all cells come from other cells.
- All cells have a cell membrane, cytoplasm, and DNA.
- Most cells are too small to be seen with the naked eye. A cell's surface area–to–volume ratio limits the size of a cell.

- The two basic kinds of cells are prokaryotic cells and eukaryotic cells. Eukaryotic cells have a nucleus and membrane-bound organelles. Prokaryotic cells do not.
- Prokaryotes are classified as archaebacteria and eubacteria.
- Archaebacterial cell walls and ribosomes are different from the cell walls and ribosomes of other organisms.
- Eukaryotes can be single-celled or multicellular.

Using Key Terms

1. In your own words, write a definition for the term *organelle*.

2. Use the following terms in the same sentence: *prokaryotic, nucleus,* and *eukaryotic.*

Understanding Key Ideas

3. Cell size is limited by the
   a. thickness of the cell wall.
   b. size of the cell's nucleus.
   c. cell's surface area–to-volume ratio.
   d. amount of cytoplasm in the cell.

4. What are the three parts of the cell theory?

5. Name three structures that every cell has.

6. Give two ways in which archaebacteria are different from bacteria.

Critical Thinking

7. **Applying Concepts** You have discovered a new single-celled organism. It has a cell wall, ribosomes, and long, circular DNA. Is it a eukaryote or a prokaryote cell? Explain.

8. **Identifying Relationships** One of your students brings you a cell about the size of the period at the end of this sentence. It is a single cell, but it also forms chains. What characteristics would this cell have if the organism is a eukaryote? If it is a prokaryote? What would you look for first?

Interpreting Graphics

The picture below shows a particular organism. Use the picture to answer the questions that follow.

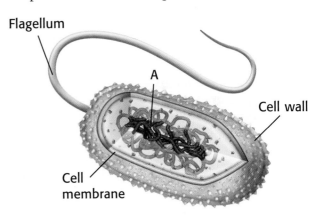

Flagellum

A

Cell wall

Cell membrane

9. What type of organism does the picture represent? How do you know?

10. Which structure helps the organism move?

11. What part of the organism does the letter *A* represent?

Eukaryotic Cells

Most eukaryotic cells are small. For a long time after cells were discovered, scientists could not see what was going on inside cells. They did not know how complex cells are.

Now, scientists know a lot about eukaryotic cells. These cells have many parts that work together and keep the cell alive.

Cell Wall

Some eukaryotic cells have cell walls. A **cell wall** is a rigid structure that gives support to a cell. The cell wall is the outermost structure of a cell. Plants and algae have cell walls made of cellulose (SEL yoo LOHS). *Cellulose* is a complex sugar that most animals can't digest.

The cell walls of plant cells allow plants to stand upright. In some plants, the cells must take in water for the cell walls to keep their shape. When such plants lack water, the cell walls collapse and the plant droops. **Figure 1** shows a cross section of a plant cell and a close-up of the cell wall.

Fungi, including yeasts and mushrooms, also have cell walls. Some fungi have cell walls made of *chitin* (KIE tin). Other fungi have cell walls made from a chemical similar to chitin. Eubacteria and archaebacteria also have cell walls, but those walls are different from plant or fungal cell walls.

✓ Reading Check What types of cells have cell walls? (*See the Appendix for answers to Reading Checks.*)

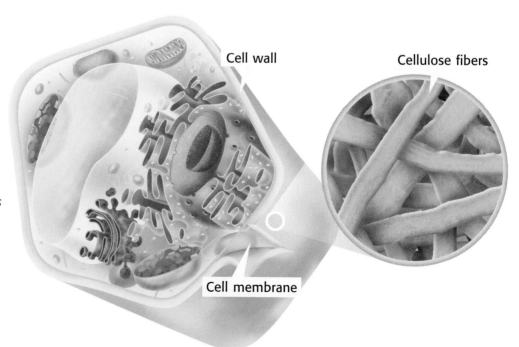

Cell wall

Cellulose fibers

Cell membrane

Figure 1 *The cell walls of plant cells help plants retain their shape. Plant cell walls are made of cellulose.*

Cell Membrane

All cells have a cell membrane. The *cell membrane* is a protective barrier that encloses a cell. It separates the cell's contents from the cell's environment. The cell membrane is the outermost structure in cells that lack a cell wall. In cells that have a cell wall, the cell membrane lies just inside the cell wall.

The cell membrane contains proteins, lipids, and phospholipids. *Lipids,* which include fats and cholesterol, are a group of compounds that do not dissolve in water. The cell wall has two layers of phospholipids (FAHS fo LIP idz), shown in **Figure 2.** A *phospholipid* is a lipid that contains phosphorus. Lipids are "water fearing," or *hydrophobic.* Lipid ends of phospholipids form the inner part of the membrane. Phosphorus-containing ends of the phospholipids are "water loving," or *hydrophilic.* These ends form the outer part of the membrane.

Some of the proteins and lipids control the movement of materials into and out of the cell. Some of the proteins form passageways. Nutrients and water move into the cell, and wastes move out of the cell, through these protein passageways.

✓ Reading Check What are two functions of a cell membrane?

CONNECTION TO Language Arts

WRITING SKILL **The Great Barrier** In your **science journal,** write a science fiction story about tiny travelers inside a person's body. These little explorers need to find a way into or out of a cell to solve a problem. You may need to do research to find out more about how the cell membrane works. Illustrate your story.

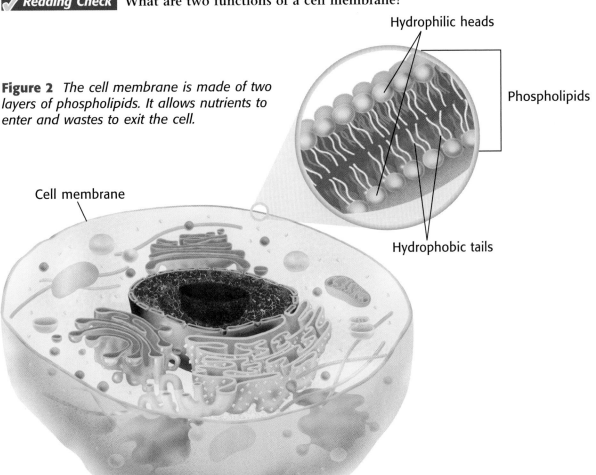

Figure 2 *The cell membrane is made of two layers of phospholipids. It allows nutrients to enter and wastes to exit the cell.*

Hydrophilic heads

Phospholipids

Hydrophobic tails

Cell membrane

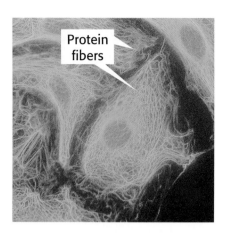

Figure 3 *The cytoskeleton, made of protein fibers, helps a cell retain its shape and move its organelles.*

Cytoskeleton

The *cytoskeleton* (SIET oh SKEL uh tuhn) is a web of proteins in the cytoplasm. The cytoskeleton, shown in **Figure 3,** acts as both a muscle and a skeleton. It keeps the cell's membranes from collapsing. The cytoskeleton also helps some cells move.

The cytoskeleton is made of three types of protein. One protein is a hollow tube. The other two are long, stringy fibers. One of the stringy proteins is also found in muscle cells.

✓ Reading Check What is the cytoskeleton?

Nucleus

All eukaryotic cells have the same basic membrane-bound organelles, starting with the nucleus. The *nucleus* is a large organelle in a eukaryotic cell. It contains the cell's DNA, or genetic material. DNA contains the information on how to make a cell's proteins. Proteins control the chemical reactions in a cell. They also provide structural support for cells and tissues. But proteins are not made in the nucleus. Messages for how to make proteins are copied from the DNA. These messages are then sent out of the nucleus through the membranes.

The nucleus is covered by two membranes. Materials cross this double membrane by passing through pores. **Figure 4** shows a nucleus and nuclear pores. The nucleus of many cells has a dark area called the nucleolus (noo KLEE uh luhs). The *nucleolus* stores materials that will be used to make ribosomes.

Figure 4 *The nucleus contains the cell's DNA. Pores, shown in the diagram at right, allow materials to pass from the nucleus to the cytoplasm.*

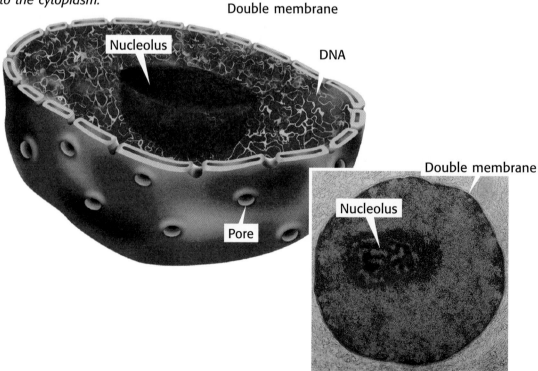

Ribosomes

Organelles that make proteins are called **ribosomes.** Ribosomes are the smallest of all organelles. And there are more ribosomes in a cell than there are any other organelles. Some ribosomes float freely in the cytoplasm. Others are attached to membranes or the cytoskeleton. Unlike most organelles, ribosomes are not covered by a membrane.

Proteins are made within the ribosomes. Proteins are made of amino acids. An *amino acid* is any one of about 20 different organic molecules that are used to make proteins. All cells need proteins to live. All cells have ribosomes.

Endoplasmic Reticulum

Many chemical reactions take place in a cell. Many of these reactions happen on or in the endoplasmic reticulum (EN doh PLAZ mik ri TIK yuh luhm). The **endoplasmic reticulum,** or ER, is a system of folded membranes in which proteins, lipids, and other materials are made. The ER is shown in **Figure 5.**

The ER is the internal delivery system of the cell. Its folded membrane contains many tubes and passageways. Substances move through the ER to different places within the cell.

Endoplasmic reticulum is either rough ER or smooth ER. The part of the ER covered in ribosomes is rough ER. Rough ER is usually found near the nucleus. Ribosomes on rough ER make many of the cell's proteins. The ER delivers these proteins throughout the cell. ER that lacks ribosomes is smooth ER. The functions of smooth ER include making lipids and breaking down toxic materials that could damage the cell.

ribosome cell organelle composed of RNA and protein; the site of protein synthesis

endoplasmic reticulum a system of membranes that is found in a cell's cytoplasm and that assists in the production, processing, and transport of proteins and in the production of lipids

Figure 5 *The endoplasmic reticulum (ER) is a system of membranes. Rough ER is covered with ribosomes. Smooth ER does not have ribosomes.*

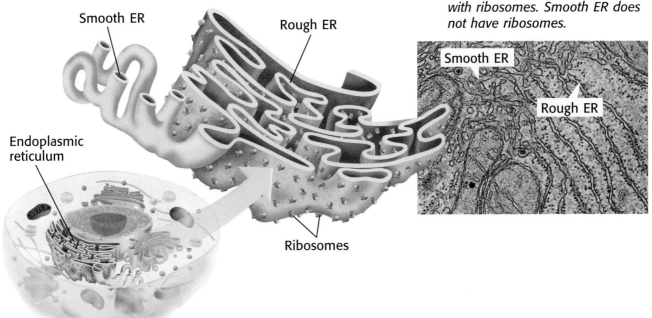

Smooth ER

Rough ER

Endoplasmic reticulum

Ribosomes

Smooth ER

Rough ER

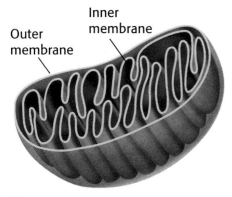

Outer membrane
Inner membrane

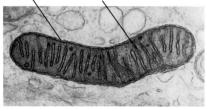

Outer membrane
Inner membrane

Figure 6 *Mitochondria break down sugar and make ATP. ATP is produced on the inner membrane.*

mitochondrion in eukaryotic cells, the cell organelle that is surrounded by two membranes and that is the site of cellular respiration

Figure 7 *Chloroplasts harness and use the energy of the sun to make sugar. A green pigment—chlorophyll—traps the sun's energy.*

Mitochondria

A mitochondrion (MIET oh KAHN dree uhn) is the main power source of a cell. A **mitochondrion** is the organelle in which sugar is broken down to produce energy. Mitochondria are covered by two membranes, as shown in **Figure 6.** Energy released by mitochondria is stored in a substance called *ATP* (**a**denosine **tri**phosphate). The cell then uses ATP to do work. ATP can be made at several places in a cell. But most of a cell's ATP is made in the inner membrane of the cell's mitochondria.

Most eukaryotic cells have mitochondria. Mitochondria are the size of some bacteria. Like bacteria, mitochondria have their own DNA, and mitochondria can divide within a cell.

✓ **Reading Check** Where is most of a cell's ATP made?

Chloroplasts

Animal cells cannot make their own food. Plants and algae are different. They have chloroplasts (KLAWR uh PLASTS) in some of their cells. *Chloroplasts* are organelles in plant and algae cells in which photosynthesis takes place. Like mitochondria, chloroplasts have two membranes and their own DNA. A chloroplast is shown in **Figure 7.** *Photosynthesis* is the process by which plants and algae use sunlight, carbon dioxide, and water to make sugar and oxygen.

Chloroplasts are green because they contain *chlorophyll,* a green pigment. Chlorophyll is found inside the inner membrane of a chloroplast. Chlorophyll traps the energy of sunlight, which is used to make sugar. The sugar produced by photosynthesis is then used by mitochondria to make ATP.

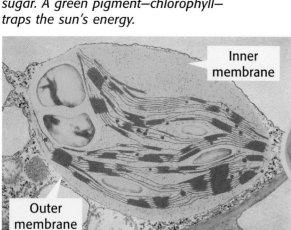

Inner membrane

Outer membrane

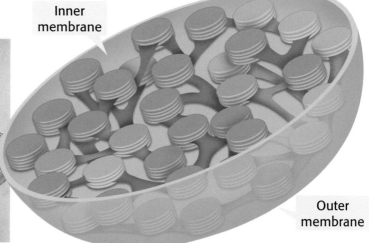

Inner membrane

Outer membrane

Golgi Complex

The organelle that packages and distributes proteins is called the **Golgi complex** (GOHL jee KAHM PLEKS). It is named after Camillo Golgi, the Italian scientist who first identified the organelle.

The Golgi complex looks like ER, as shown in **Figure 8.** Lipids and proteins from the ER are delivered to the Golgi complex. There, the lipids and proteins may be modified to do different jobs. The final products are enclosed in a piece of the Golgi complex's membrane. This membrane pinches off to form a small bubble. The bubble transports its contents to other parts of the cell or out of the cell.

Cell Compartments

The bubble that forms from the Golgi complex's membrane is a vesicle. A **vesicle** (VES i kuhl) is a small sac that surrounds material to be moved into or out of a cell. All eukaryotic cells have vesicles. Vesicles also move material within a cell. For example, vesicles carry new protein from the ER to the Golgi complex. Other vesicles distribute material from the Golgi complex to other parts of the cell. Some vesicles form when part of the cell membrane surrounds an object outside the cell.

Golgi complex cell organelle that helps make and package materials to be transported out of the cell

vesicle a small cavity or sac that contains materials in a eukaryotic cell

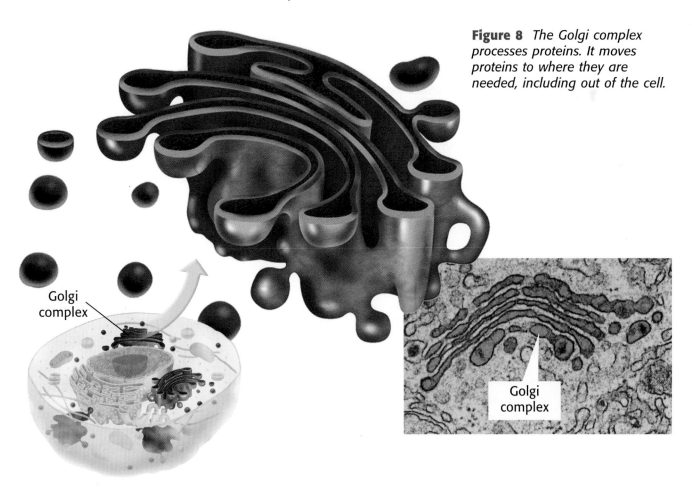

Figure 8 *The Golgi complex processes proteins. It moves proteins to where they are needed, including out of the cell.*

Golgi complex

Golgi complex

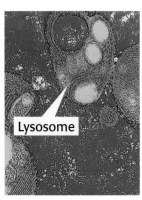

Figure 9
Lysosomes digest materials inside a cell. In plant and fungal cells, vacuoles often perform the same function.

Lysosome

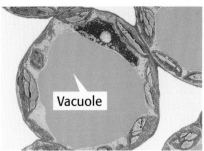

Vacuole

lysosome a cell organelle that contains digestive enzymes

Cellular Digestion

Lysosomes (LIE suh SOHMZ) are vesicles that are responsible for digestion inside a cell. **Lysosomes** are organelles that contain digestive enzymes. They destroy worn-out or damaged organelles, get rid of waste materials, and protect the cell from foreign invaders. Lysosomes, which come in a wide variety of sizes and shapes, are shown in **Figure 9.**

Lysosomes are found mainly in animal cells. When eukaryotic cells engulf particles, they enclose the particles in vesicles. Lysosomes bump into these vesicles and pour enzymes into them. These enzymes digest the particles in the vesicles.

Reading Check Why are lysosomes important?

Vacuoles

A *vacuole* (VAK yoo OHL) is a large vesicle. In plant and fungal cells, some vacuoles act like large lysosomes. They store digestive enzymes and aid in digestion within the cell. Other vacuoles in plant cells store water and other liquids. Vacuoles that are full of water, such as the one in **Figure 9,** help support the cell. Some plants wilt when their vacuoles lose water. **Table 1** shows some organelles and their functions.

Table 1 Organelles and Their Functions	
Nucleus the organelle that contains the cell's DNA and is the control center of the cell	**Chloroplast** the organelle that uses the energy of sunlight to make food
Ribosome the organelle in which amino acids are hooked together to make proteins	**Golgi complex** the organelle that processes and transports proteins and other materials out of cell
Endoplasmic reticulum the organelle that makes lipids, breaks down drugs and other substances, and packages proteins for Golgi complex	**Vacuole** the organelle that stores water and other materials
Mitochondria the organelle that breaks down food molecules to make ATP	**Lysosome** the organelle that digests food particles, wastes, cell parts, and foreign invaders

Summary

- Eukaryotic cells have organelles that perform functions that help cells remain alive.
- All cells have a cell membrane. Some cells have a cell wall. Some cells have a cytoskeleton.
- The nucleus of a eukaryotic cell contains the cell's genetic material, DNA.
- Ribosomes are the organelles that make proteins. Ribosomes are not covered by a membrane.

- The endoplasmic reticulum (ER) and the Golgi complex make and process proteins before the proteins are transported to other parts of the cell or out of the cell.
- Mitochondria and chloroplasts are energy-releasing organelles.
- Lysosomes are organelles responsible for digestion within a cell. In plant cells, organelles called *vacuoles* store cell materials and sometimes act like large lysosomes.

Using Key Terms

1. In your own words, write a definition for each of the following terms: *ribosome, lysosome,* and *cell wall.*

Understanding Key Ideas

2. Which of the following are found mainly in animal cells?
   a. mitochondria
   b. lysosomes
   c. ribosomes
   d. Golgi complexes

3. What is the function of a Golgi complex? What is the function of the endoplasmic reticulum?

Critical Thinking

4. **Making Comparisons** Describe three ways in which plant cells differ from animal cells.

5. **Applying Concepts** Every cell needs ribosomes. Explain why.

6. **Predicting Consequences** A certain virus attacks the mitochondria in cells. What would happen to a cell if all of its mitochondria were destroyed?

7. **Expressing Opinions** Do you think that having chloroplasts gives plant cells an advantage over animal cells? Support your opinion.

Interpreting Graphics

Use the diagram below to answer the questions that follow.

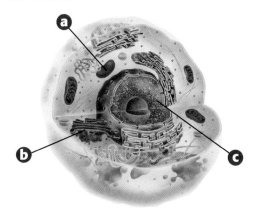

8. Is this a diagram of a plant cell or an animal cell? Explain how you know.

9. What organelle does the letter *b* refer to?

Developed and maintained by the
National Science Teachers Association

For a variety of links related to this chapter, go to www.scilinks.org

Topic: Eukaryotic Cells
SciLinks code: HSM0541

The Organization of Living Things

In some ways, organisms are like machines. Some machines have just one part. But most machines have many parts. Some organisms exist as a single cell. Other organisms have many—even trillions—of cells.

Most cells are smaller than the period that ends this sentence. Yet, every cell in every organism performs all the processes of life. So, are there any advantages to having many cells?

The Benefits of Being Multicellular

You are a *multicellular organism*. This means that you are made of many cells. Multicellular organisms grow by making more small cells, not by making their cells larger. For example, an elephant is bigger than you are, but its cells are about the same size as yours. An elephant just has more cells than you do. Some benefits of being multicellular are the following:

- **Larger Size** Many multicellular organisms are small. But they are usually larger than single-celled organisms. Larger organisms are prey for fewer predators. Larger predators can eat a wider variety of prey.

- **Longer Life** The life span of a multicellular organism is not limited to the life span of any single cell.

- **Specialization** Each type of cell has a particular job. Specialization makes the organism more efficient. For example, the cardiac muscle cell in **Figure 1** is a specialized muscle cell. Heart muscle cells contract and make the heart pump blood.

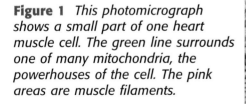 **Reading Check** List three advantages of being multicellular. *(See the Appendix for answers to Reading Checks.)*

READING WARM-UP

Objectives

- List three advantages of being multicellular.
- Describe the four levels of organization in living things.
- Explain the relationship between the structure and function of a part of an organism.

Terms to Learn

tissue	organism
organ	structure
organ system	function

READING STRATEGY

Paired Summarizing Read this section silently. In pairs, take turns summarizing the material. Stop to discuss ideas that seem confusing.

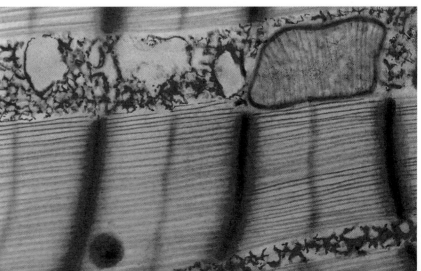

Figure 1 *This photomicrograph shows a small part of one heart muscle cell. The green line surrounds one of many mitochondria, the powerhouses of the cell. The pink areas are muscle filaments.*

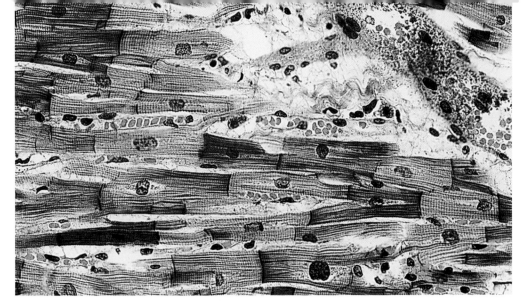

Figure 2 *This photomicrograph shows cardiac muscle tissue. Cardiac muscle tissue is made up of many cardiac cells.*

Cells Working Together

A **tissue** is a group of cells that work together to perform a specific job. The material around and between the cells is also part of the tissue. The cardiac muscle tissue, shown in **Figure 2,** is made of many cardiac muscle cells. Cardiac muscle tissue is just one type of tissue in a heart.

Animals have four basic types of tissues: nerve tissue, muscle tissue, connective tissue, and protective tissue. In contrast, plants have three types of tissues: transport tissue, protective tissue, and ground tissue. Transport tissue moves water and nutrients through a plant. Protective tissue covers the plant. It helps the plant retain water and protects the plant against damage. Photosynthesis takes place in ground tissue.

Tissues Working Together

A structure that is made up of two or more tissues working together to perform a specific function is called an **organ.** For example, your heart is an organ. It is made mostly of cardiac muscle tissue. But your heart also has nerve tissue and tissues of the blood vessels that all work together to make your heart the powerful pump that it is.

Another organ is your stomach. It also has several kinds of tissue. In the stomach, muscle tissue makes food move in and through the stomach. Special tissues make chemicals that help digest your food. Connective tissue holds the stomach together, and nervous tissue carries messages back and forth between the stomach and the brain. Other organs include the intestines, brain, and lungs.

Plants also have different kinds of tissues that work together as organs. A leaf is a plant organ that contains tissue that traps light energy to make food. Other examples of plant organs are stems and roots.

tissue a group of similar cells that perform a common function

organ a collection of tissues that carry out a specialized function of the body

A Pet Protist

Imagine that you have a tiny box-shaped protist for a pet. To care for your pet protist properly, you have to figure out how much to feed it. The dimensions of your protist are roughly 25 μ × 20 μ × 2 μ. If seven food particles per second can enter through each square micrometer of surface area, how many particles can your protist eat in 1 min?

Reading Check What is an organ?

Organs Working Together

organ system a group of organs that work together to perform body functions

organism a living thing; anything that can carry out life processes independently

structure the arrangement of parts in an organism

function the special, normal, or proper activity of an organ or part

A group of organs working together to perform a particular function is called an **organ system.** Each organ system has a specific job to do in the body.

For example, the digestive system is made up of several organs, including the stomach and intestines. The digestive system's job is to break down food into small particles. Other parts of the body then use these small particles as fuel. In turn, the digestive system depends on the respiratory and cardiovascular systems for oxygen. The cardiovascular system, shown in **Figure 3,** includes organs and tissues such as the heart and blood vessels. Plants also have organ systems. They include leaf systems, root systems, and stem systems.

✓ **Reading Check** List the levels of organization in living things.

Organisms

Anything that can perform life processes is an **organism.** An organism made of a single cell is called a *unicellular organism.* Bacteria, most protists, and some kinds of fungi are unicellular. Although some of these organisms live in colonies, the organisms are still unicellular. They are unicellular because all of the cells in the colony are the same. Each cell must carry out all life processes. In contrast, even the simplest multicellular organisms have specialized cells. Complex organisms are composed of cells, tissues, organs, and organ systems that perform specialized functions.

Figure 3 **Levels of Organization in the Cardiovascular System**

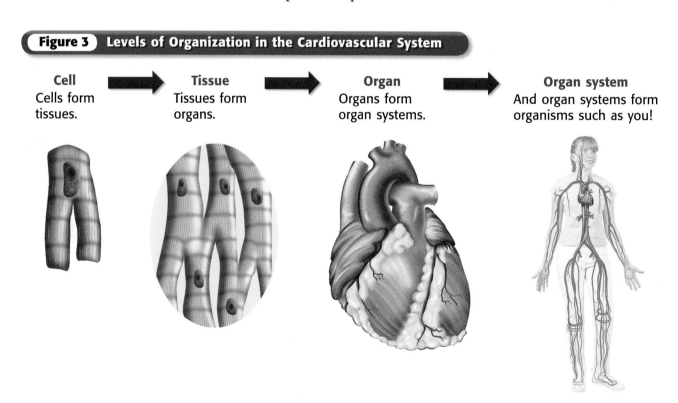

Cell
Cells form tissues.

Tissue
Tissues form organs.

Organ
Organs form organ systems.

Organ system
And organ systems form organisms such as you!

Structure and Function

In organisms, structure and function are related. **Structure** is the arrangement of parts in an organism. It includes the shape of a part and the material of which the part is made. **Function** is the job the part does. For example, the structure of the lungs is a large, spongy sac. In the lungs, there are millions of tiny air sacs called *alveoli*. Blood vessels wrap around the alveoli, as shown in **Figure 4.** Oxygen from air in the alveoli enters the blood. Blood then brings oxygen to body tissues. Also, in the alveoli, carbon dioxide leaves the blood and is exhaled.

The structures of alveoli and blood vessels enables them to perform a function. Together, they bring oxygen to the body and get rid of its carbon dioxide.

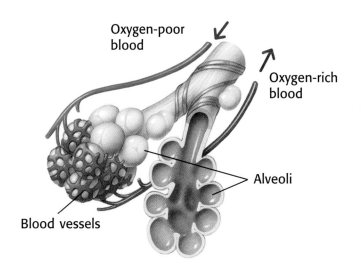

Figure 4 The Structure and Function of Alveoli

Oxygen-poor blood

Oxygen-rich blood

Alveoli

Blood vessels

SECTION Review

Summary

- Advantages of being multicellular are larger size, longer life, and cell specialization.
- Four levels of organization are cell, tissue, organ, and organ system.
- A *tissue* is a group of cells working together. An *organ* is two or more tissues working together. An *organ system* is two or more organs working together.
- In organisms, a part's structure and function are related.

Using Key Terms

1. Use each of the following terms in a separate sentence: *tissue, organ,* and *function.*

Understanding Key Ideas

2. What are the four levels of organization in living things?
   a. cell, multicellular, organ, organ system
   b. single cell, multicellular, tissue, organ
   c. larger size, longer life, specialized cells, organs
   d. cell, tissue, organ, organ system

Math Skills

3. One multicellular organism is a cube. Each of its sides is 3 cm long. Each of its cells is 1 cm^3. How many cells does it have? If each side doubles in length, how many cells will it then have?

Critical Thinking

4. **Applying Concepts** Explain the relationship between structure and function. Use alveoli as an example. Be sure to include more than one level of organization.

5. **Making Inferences** Why can multicellular organisms be more complex than unicellular organisms? Use the three advantages of being multicellular to help explain your answer.

SCiLINKS®

NSTA
Developed and maintained by the
National Science Teachers Association

For a variety of links related to this chapter, go to www.scilinks.org

Topic: Organization of Life
SciLinks code: HSM1080

Model-Making Lab

OBJECTIVES

Explore why a single-celled organism cannot grow to the size of an elephant.

Create a model of a cell to illustrate the concept of surface area–to-volume ratio.

MATERIALS

- calculator (optional)
- cubic cell patterns
- heavy paper or poster board
- sand, fine
- scale or balance
- scissors
- tape, transparent

SAFETY

Elephant-Sized Amoebas?

An amoeba is a single-celled organism. Like most cells, amoebas are microscopic. Why can't amoebas grow as large as elephants? If an amoeba grew to the size of a quarter, the amoeba would starve to death. To understand how this can be true, build a model of a cell and see for yourself.

Procedure

1 Use heavy paper or poster board to make four cube-shaped cell models from the patterns supplied by your teacher. Cut out each cell model, fold the sides to make a cube, and tape the tabs on the sides. The smallest cell model has sides that are each one unit long. The next larger cell has sides of two units. The next cell has sides of three units, and the largest cell has sides of four units. These paper models represent the cell membrane, the part of a cell's exterior through which food and wastes pass.

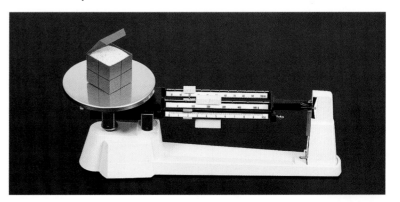

		Data Table for Measurements				Key to Formula Symbols
Length of side	Area of one side (A = S × S)	Total surface area of cube cell (TA = S × S × 6)	Volume of cube cell (V = S × S × S)	Mass of filled cube cell		S = the length of one side
1 unit	1 unit²	6 unit²	1 unit³			A = area
2 unit						6 = number of sides
3 unit						V = volume
4 unit						TA = total area

DO NOT WRITE IN BOOK

2 Copy the data table shown above. Use each formula to calculate the data about your cell models. Record your calculations in the table. Calculations for the smallest cell have been done for you.

3 Carefully fill each model with fine sand until the sand is level with the top edge of the model. Find the mass of the filled models by using a scale or a balance. What does the sand in your model represent?

4 Record the mass of each filled cell model in your Data Table for Measurements. (Always remember to use the appropriate mass unit.)

Analyze the Results

1 **Constructing Tables** Make a data table like the one shown at right.

2 **Organizing Data** Use the data from your Data Table for Measurements to find the ratios for each of your cell models. For each of the cell models, fill in the Data Table for Ratios .

Draw Conclusions

3 **Interpreting Information** As a cell grows larger, does the ratio of total surface area to volume increase, decrease, or stay the same?

4 **Interpreting Information** As a cell grows larger, does the total surface area–to-mass ratio increase, decrease, or stay the same?

5 **Drawing Conclusions** Which is better able to supply food to all the cytoplasm of the cell: the cell membrane of a small cell or the cell membrane of a large cell? Explain your answer.

6 **Evaluating Data** In the experiment, which is better able to feed all of the cytoplasm of the cell: the cell membrane of a cell that has high mass or the cell membrane of a cell that has low mass? You may explain your answer in a verbal presentation to the class, or you may choose to write a report and illustrate it with drawings of your models.

	Data Table for Ratios	
Length of side	Ratio of total surface area to volume	Ratio of total surface area to mass
1 unit		
2 unit		
3 unit		
4 unit		

DO NOT WRITE IN BOOK

Chapter Review

USING KEY TERMS

Complete each of the following sentences by choosing the correct term from the word bank.

cell	organ
cell membrane	prokaryote
organelles	eukaryote
cell wall	tissue
structure	function

1 A(n) ___ is the most basic unit of all living things.

2 The job that an organ does is the ___ of that organ.

3 Ribosomes and mitochondria are types of ___.

4 A(n) ___ is an organism whose cells have a nucleus.

5 A group of cells working together to perform a specific function is a(n) ___.

6 Only plant cells have a(n) ___.

UNDERSTANDING KEY IDEAS

Multiple Choice

7 Which of the following best describes an organ?

   a. a group of cells that work together to perform a specific job

   b. a group of tissues that belong to different systems

   c. a group of tissues that work together to perform a specific job

   d. a body structure, such as muscles or lungs

8 The benefits of being multicellular include

   a. small size, long life, and cell specialization.

   b. generalized cells, longer life, and ability to prey on small animals.

   c. larger size, more enemies, and specialized cells.

   d. longer life, larger size, and specialized cells.

9 In eukaryotic cells, which organelle contains the DNA?

   a. nucleus   **c.** smooth ER

   b. Golgi complex   **d.** vacuole

10 Which of the following statements is part of the cell theory?

   a. All cells suddenly appear by themselves.

   b. All cells come from other cells.

   c. All organisms are multicellular.

   d. All cells have identical parts.

11 The surface area–to-volume ratio of a cell limits

   a. the number of organelles that the cell has.

   b. the size of the cell.

   c. where the cell lives.

   d. the types of nutrients that a cell needs.

12 Two types of organisms whose cells do not have a nucleus are

   a. prokaryotes and eukaryotes.

   b. plants and animals.

   c. eubacteria and archaebacteria.

   d. single-celled and multicellular organisms.

Short Answer

13 Explain why most cells are small.

14 Describe the four levels of organization in living things.

15 What is the difference between the structure of an organ and the function of the organ?

16 Name two functions of a cell membrane.

17 What are the structure and function of the cytoskeleton in a cell?

CRITICAL THINKING

18 Concept Mapping Use the following terms to create a concept map: *cells, organisms, Golgi complex, organ systems, organs, nucleus, organelle,* and *tissues.*

19 Making Comparisons Compare and contrast the functions of the endoplasmic reticulum and the Golgi complex.

20 Identifying Relationships Explain how the structure and function of an organism's parts are related. Give an example.

21 Evaluating Hypotheses One of your classmates states a hypothesis that all organisms must have organ systems. Is your classmate's hypothesis valid? Explain your answer.

22 Predicting Consequences What would happen if all of the ribosomes in your cells disappeared?

23 Expressing Opinions Scientists think that millions of years ago the surface of the Earth was very hot and that the atmosphere contained a lot of methane. In your opinion, which type of organism, a eubacterium or an archaebacterium, is the older form of life? Explain your reasoning.

INTERPRETING GRAPHICS

Use the diagram below to answer the questions that follow.

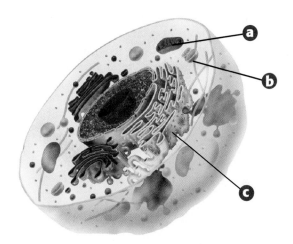

24 What is the name of the structure identified by the letter *a*?

25 Which letter identifies the structure that digests food particles and foreign invaders?

26 Which letter identifies the structure that makes proteins, lipids, and other materials and that contains tubes and passageways that enable substances to move to different places in the cell?

READING

Read each of the passages below. Then, answer the questions that follow each passage.

Passage 1 Exploring caves can be dangerous but can also lead to interesting discoveries. For example, deep in the darkness of Cueva de Villa Luz, a cave in Mexico, are slippery formations called *snottites*. They were named snottites because they look just like a two-year-old's runny nose. If you use an electron microscope to look at them, you see that snottites are bacteria; thick, sticky fluids; and small amounts of minerals produced by the bacteria. As tiny as they are, these bacteria can build up snottite structures that may eventually turn into rock. Formations in other caves look like hardened snottites. The bacteria in snottites are acidophiles. Acidophiles live in environments that are highly acidic. Snottite bacteria produce sulfuric acid and live in an environment that is similar to the inside of a car battery.

1. Which statement best describes snottites?
   A Snottites are bacteria that live in car batteries.
   B Snottites are rock formations found in caves.
   C Snottites were named for a cave in Mexico.
   D Snottites are made of bacteria, sticky fluids, and minerals.

2. Based on this passage, which conclusion about snottites is most likely to be correct?
   F Snottites are found in caves everywhere.
   G Snottite bacteria do not need sunlight.
   H You could grow snottites in a greenhouse.
   I Snottites create other bacteria in caves.

3. What is the main idea of this passage?
   A Acidophiles are unusual organisms.
   B Snottites are strange formations.
   C Exploring caves is dangerous.
   D Snottites are large, slippery bacteria.

Passage 2 The world's smallest mammal may be a bat about the size of a jelly bean. The scientific name for this tiny animal, which was unknown until 1974, is *Craseonycteris thonglongyai*. It is so small that it is sometimes called the *bumblebee bat*. Another name for this animal is the *hog-nosed bat*. Hog-nosed bats were given their name because one of their distinctive features is a piglike muzzle. Hog-nosed bats differ from other bats in another way: they do not have a tail. But, like other bats, hog-nosed bats do eat insects that they catch in mid-air. Scientists think that the bats eat small insects that live on the leaves at the tops of trees. Hog-nosed bats live deep in limestone caves and have been found in only one country, Thailand.

1. According to the passage, which statement about hog-nosed bats is most accurate?
   A They are the world's smallest animal.
   B They are about the size of a bumblebee.
   C They eat leaves at the tops of trees.
   D They live in hives near caves in Thailand.

2. Which of the following statements describes distinctive features of hog-nosed bats?
   F The bats are very small and eat leaves.
   G The bats live in caves and have a tail.
   H The bats live in Thailand and are mammals.
   I The bats have a piglike muzzle and no tail.

3. From the information in this passage, which conclusion is most likely to be correct?
   A Hog-nosed bats are similar to other bats.
   B Hog-nosed bats are probably rare.
   C Hog-nosed bats can sting like a bumblebee.
   D Hog-nosed bats probably eat fruit.

The diagrams below show two kinds of cells. Use these cell diagrams to answer the questions that follow.

Cell 1

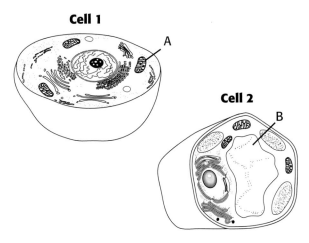

Cell 2

1. What is the name of the organelle labeled *A* in Cell 1?

  A endoplasmic reticulum

  B mitochondrion

  C vacuole

  D nucleus

2. What type of cell is Cell 1?

  F a bacterial cell

  G a plant cell

  H an animal cell

  I a prokaryotic cell

3. What is the name and function of the organelle labeled *B* in Cell 2?

  A The organelle is a vacuole, and it stores water and other materials.

  B The organelle is the nucleus, and it contains the DNA.

  C The organelle is the cell wall, and it gives shape to the cell.

  D The organelle is a ribosome, where proteins are put together.

4. What type of cell is Cell 2? How do you know?

  F prokaryotic; because it does not have a nucleus

  G eukaryotic; because it does not have a nucleus

  H prokaryotic; because it has a nucleus

  I eukaryotic; because it has a nucleus

Read each question below, and choose the best answer.

1. What is the surface area–to-volume ratio of the rectangular solid shown in the diagram below?

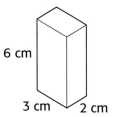

6 cm

3 cm   2 cm

  A 0.5:1

  B 2:1

  C 36:1

  D 72:1

2. Look at the diagram of the cell below. Three molecules of food per cubic unit of volume per minute are required for the cell to survive. One molecule of food can enter through each square unit of surface area per minute. What will happen to this cell?

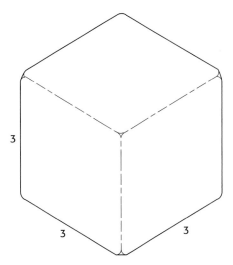

3

3   3

  F The cell is too small, and it will starve.

  G The cell is too large, and it will starve.

  H The cell is at a size that will allow it to survive.

  I There is not enough information to determine the answer.

Science in Action

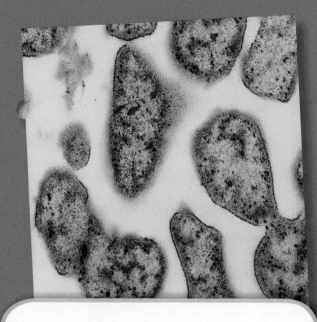

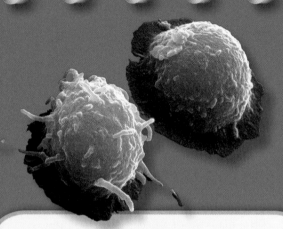

Scientific Discoveries

Discovery of the Stem Cell

What do Parkinson's disease, diabetes, aplastic anemia, and Alzheimer's disease have in common? All of these diseases are diseases for which stem cells may provide treatment or a cure. Stem cells are unspecialized cells from which all other kinds of cells can grow. And research on stem cells has been going on almost since microscopes were invented. But scientists have been able to culture, or grow, stem cells in laboratories for only about the last 20 years. Research during these 20 years has shown scientists that stem cells can be useful in treating—and possibly curing—a variety of diseases.

Weird Science

Extremophiles

Are there organisms on Earth that can give scientists clues about possible life elsewhere? Yes, there are! These organisms are called *extremophiles,* and they live where the environment is extreme. For example, some extremophiles live in the hot volcanic thermal vents deep in the ocean. Other extremophiles live in the extreme cold of Antarctica. But these organisms do not live only in extreme environments. Research shows that extremophiles may be abundant in plankton in the ocean. And not all extremophiles are archaebacteria; some extremophiles are eubacteria.

Language Arts ACTIVITY

WRITING SKILL Imagine that you are a doctor who treats diseases such as Parkinson's disease. Design and create a pamphlet or brochure that you could use to explain what stem cells are. Include in your pamphlet a description of how stem cells might be used to treat one of your patients who has Parkinson's disease. Be sure to include information about Parkinson's disease.

Social Studies ACTIVITY

Choose one of the four types of extremophiles. Do some research about the organism you have chosen and make a poster showing what you learned about it, including where it can be found, under what conditions it lives, how it survives, and how it is used.

Caroline Schooley

Microscopist Imagine that your assignment is the following: Go outside. Look at 1 ft^2 of the ground for 30 min. Make notes about what you observe. Be prepared to describe what you see. If you look at the ground with just your naked eyes, you may quickly run out of things to see. But what would happen if you used a microscope to look? How much more would you be able to see? And how much more would you have to talk about? Caroline Schooley could tell you.

Caroline Schooley joined a science club in middle school. That's when her interest in looking at things through a microscope began. Since then, Schooley has spent many years studying life through a microscope. She is a microscopist. A *microscopist* is someone who uses a microscope to look at small things. Microscopists use their tools to explore the world of small things that cannot be seen by the naked eye. And with today's powerful electron microscopes, microscopists can study things we could never see before, things as small as atoms.

Math ACTIVITY

An average bacterium is about 0.000002 m long. A pencil point is about 0.001 m wide. Approximately how many bacteria would fit on a pencil point?

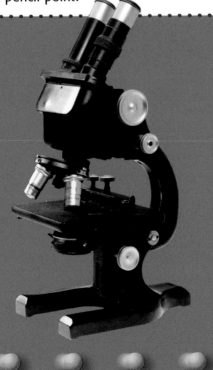

To learn more about these Science in Action topics, visit **go.hrw.com** and type in the keyword **HL5CELF**.

Current Science

Check out Current Science® articles related to this chapter by visiting go.hrw.com. Just type in the keyword HL5CS03.

2

The Cell in Action

About the PHOTO

This adult katydid is emerging from its last immature, or nymph, stage. As the katydid changed from a nymph to an adult, every structure of its body changed. To grow and change, an organism must produce new cells. When a cell divides, it makes a copy of its genetic material.

PRE-READING ACTIVITY

FOLDNOTES **Tri-Fold** Before you read the chapter, create the FoldNote entitled "Tri-Fold" described in the **Study Skills** section of the Appendix. Write what you know about the actions of cells in the column labeled "Know." Then, write what you want to know in the column labeled "Want." As you read the chapter, write what you learn about the actions of cells in the column labeled "Learn."

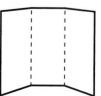

Cells in Action

Yeast are single-celled fungi that are an important ingredient in bread. Yeast cells break down sugar molecules to release energy. In the process, carbon dioxide gas is produced, which causes bread dough to rise.

Procedure

1. Add **4 mL of a sugar solution** to **10 mL of a yeast-and-water mixture.** Use a **stirring rod** to thoroughly mix the two liquids.

2. Pour the stirred mixture into a small test tube.

3. Place a slightly **larger test tube** over the **small test tube.** The top of the small test tube should touch the bottom of the larger test tube.

4. Hold the test tubes together, and quickly turn both test tubes over. Place the test tubes in a test-tube rack.

5. Use a **ruler** to measure the height of the fluid in the large test tube. Wait 20 min, and then measure the height of the liquid again.

Analysis

1. What is the difference between the first height measurement and the second height measurement?

2. What do you think caused the change in the fluid's height?

SECTION 1

Exchange with the Environment

diffusion the movement of particles from regions of higher density to regions of lower density

What would happen to a factory if its power were shut off or its supply of raw materials never arrived? What would happen if the factory couldn't get rid of its garbage?

Like a factory, an organism must be able to obtain energy and raw materials and get rid of wastes. An organism's cells perform all of these functions. These functions keep cells healthy so that they can divide. Cell division allows organisms to grow and repair injuries.

The exchange of materials between a cell and its environment takes place at the cell's membrane. To understand how materials move into and out of the cell, you need to know about diffusion.

What Is Diffusion?

What happens if you pour dye on top of a layer of gelatin? At first, it is easy to see where the dye ends and the gelatin begins. But over time, the line between the two layers will blur, as shown in **Figure 1.** Why? Everything, including the gelatin and the dye, is made up of tiny moving particles. Particles travel from where they are crowded to where they are less crowded. This movement from areas of high concentration (crowded) to areas of low concentration (less crowded) is called **diffusion** (di FYOO zhuhn). Dye particles diffuse from where they are crowded (near the top of the glass) to where they are less crowded (in the gelatin). Diffusion also happens within and between living cells. Cells do not need to use energy for diffusion.

Figure 1 *The particles of the dye and the gelatin slowly mix by diffusion.*

Figure 2 **Osmosis**

1 The side that holds only pure water has the higher concentration of water particles.

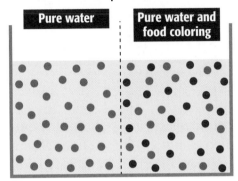

| Pure water | Pure water and food coloring |

2 During osmosis, water particles move to where they are less concentrated.

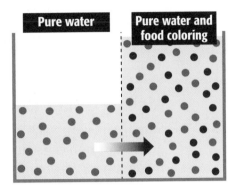

| Pure water | Pure water and food coloring |

Diffusion of Water

The cells of organisms are surrounded by and filled with fluids that are made mostly of water. The diffusion of water through cell membranes is so important to life processes that it has been given a special name—**osmosis** (ahs MOH sis).

Water is made up of particles, called *molecules*. Pure water has the highest concentration of water molecules. When you mix something, such as food coloring, sugar, or salt, with water, you lower the concentration of water molecules. **Figure 2** shows how water molecules move through a membrane that is semipermeable (SEM i PUHR mee uh buhl). *Semipermeable* means that only certain substances can pass through. The picture on the left in **Figure 2** shows liquids that have different concentrations of water. Over time, the water molecules move from the liquid with the high concentration of water molecules to the liquid with the lower concentration of water molecules.

The Cell and Osmosis

Osmosis is important to cell functions. For example, red blood cells are surrounded by plasma. Plasma is made up of water, salts, sugars, and other particles. The concentration of these particles is kept in balance by osmosis. If red blood cells were in pure water, water molecules would flood into the cells and cause them to burst. When red blood cells are put into a salty solution, the concentration of water molecules inside the cell is higher than the concentration of water outside. This difference makes water move out of the cells, and the cells shrivel up. Osmosis also occurs in plant cells. When a wilted plant is watered, osmosis makes the plant firm again.

✓ Reading Check Why would red blood cells burst if you placed them in pure water? (*See the Appendix for answers to Reading Checks.*)

osmosis the diffusion of water through a semipermeable membrane

Bead Diffusion

1. Put three groups of **colored beads** on the bottom of a **plastic bowl.** Each group should be made up of five beads of the same color.

2. Stretch some **clear plastic wrap** tightly over the top of the bowl. Gently shake the bowl for 10 seconds while watching the beads.

3. How is the scattering of the beads like the diffusion of particles? How is it different from the diffusion of particles?

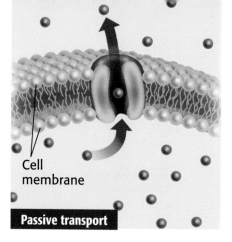
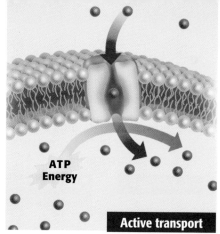

Figure 3 *In passive transport, particles travel through proteins to areas of lower concentration. In active transport, cells use energy to move particles, usually to areas of higher concentration.*

Cell membrane

ATP Energy

Passive transport

Active transport

Moving Small Particles

Small particles, such as water and sugars, cross the cell membrane through passageways called *channels*. These channels are made up of proteins in the cell membrane. Particles travel through these channels by either passive or active transport. The movement of particles across a cell membrane without the use of energy by the cell is called **passive transport**, and is shown in **Figure 3.** During passive transport, particles move from an area of high concentration to an area of low concentration. Diffusion and osmosis are examples of passive transport.

A process of transporting particles that requires the cell to use energy is called **active transport.** Active transport usually involves the movement of particles from an area of low concentration to an area of high concentration.

passive transport the movement of substances across a cell membrane without the use of energy by the cell

active transport the movement of substances across the cell membrane that requires the cell to use energy

endocytosis the process by which a cell membrane surrounds a particle and encloses the particle in a vesicle to bring the particle into the cell

Moving Large Particles

Small particles cross the cell membrane by diffusion, passive transport, and active transport. Large particles move into and out of the cell by processes called *endocytosis* and *exocytosis*.

Endocytosis

The active-transport process by which a cell surrounds a large particle and encloses the particle in a vesicle to bring the particle into the cell is called **endocytosis** (EN doh sie TOH sis). *Vesicles* are sacs formed from pieces of cell membrane. **Figure 4** shows a cell taking up a large particle through endocytosis.

Figure 4 **Endocytosis**

❶ The cell comes into contact with a particle.

❷ The cell membrane begins to wrap around the particle.

❸ Once the particle is completely surrounded, a vesicle pinches off.

This photo shows the end of *endocytosis,* which means "within the cell."

Figure 5   Exocytosis

1 Large particles that must leave the cell are packaged in vesicles.

2 The vesicle travels to the cell membrane and fuses with it.

3 The cell releases the particle to the outside of the cell.

Exocytosis means "outside the cell."

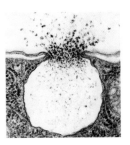

Exocytosis

When a large particle leaves the cell, the cell uses an active-transport process called **exocytosis** (EK soh sie TOH sis). During exocytosis, a vesicle forms around a large particle within the cell. The vesicle carries the particle to the cell membrane. The vesicle then fuses with the cell membrane and releases the particle to the outside of the cell. Exocytosis is shown in **Figure 5**.

exocytosis the process in which a cell releases a particle by enclosing the particle in a vesicle that then moves to the cell surface and fuses with the cell membrane

✓ **Reading Check** What is exocytosis?

SECTION Review

Summary

● Diffusion is the movement of particles from an area of high concentration to an area of low concentration.

● Osmosis is the diffusion of water through a semipermeable membrane.

● Cells move small particles by diffusion, which is an example of passive transport, and by active transport.

● Large particles enter the cell by endocytosis, and exit the cell by exocytosis.

Using Key Terms

For each pair of terms, explain how the meanings of the terms differ.

1. *diffusion* and *osmosis*

2. *active transport* and *passive transport*

3. *endocytosis* and *exocytosis*

Understanding Key Ideas

4. The movement of particles from a less crowded area to a more crowded area requires

   a. sunlight.   **c.** a membrane.

   b. energy.   **d.** osmosis.

5. What structures allow particles to move through cell membranes?

Math Skills

6. The area of particle 1 is 2.5 mm². The area of particle 2 is 0.5 mm². The area of particle 1 is how many times as big as the area of particle 2?

Critical Thinking

7. **Predicting Consequences** What would happen to a cell if its channel proteins were damaged and unable to transport particles? What would happen to the organism if many of its cells were damaged in this way? Explain your answer.

8. **Analyzing Ideas** Why does active transport require energy?

SCILINKS®   **NSTA**

Developed and maintained by the National Science Teachers Association

For a variety of links related to this chapter, go to www.scilinks.org

Topics: Diffusion; Osmosis
SciLinks code: HSM0406; HSM1090

Cell Energy

Why do you get hungry? Feeling hungry is your body's way of telling you that your cells need energy.

All cells need energy to live, grow, and reproduce. Plant cells get their energy from the sun. Many animal cells get the energy they need from food.

From Sun to Cell

Nearly all of the energy that fuels life comes from the sun. Plants capture energy from the sun and change it into food through a process called **photosynthesis.** The food that plants make supplies them with energy. This food also becomes a source of energy for the organisms that eat the plants.

Photosynthesis

Plant cells have molecules that absorb light energy. These molecules are called *pigments*. Chlorophyll (KLAWR uh FIL), the main pigment used in photosynthesis, gives plants their green color. Chlorophyll is found in chloroplasts.

Plants use the energy captured by chlorophyll to change carbon dioxide and water into food. The food is in the form of the simple sugar glucose. Glucose is a carbohydrate. When plants make glucose, they convert the sun's energy into a form of energy that can be stored. The energy in glucose is used by the plant's cells. Photosynthesis also produces oxygen. Photosynthesis is summarized in **Figure 1.**

photosynthesis the process by which plants, algae, and some bacteria use sunlight, carbon dioxide, and water to make food

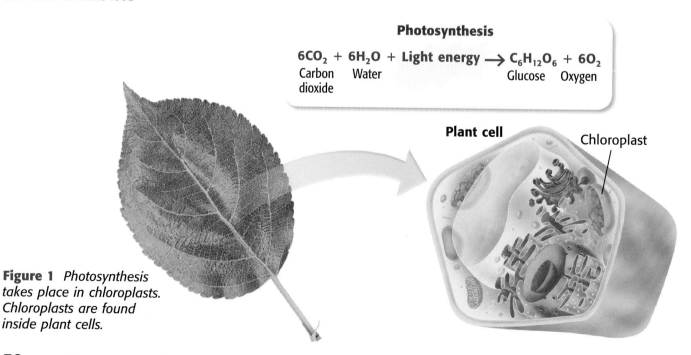

Photosynthesis

$$6CO_2 + 6H_2O + \text{Light energy} \longrightarrow C_6H_{12}O_6 + 6O_2$$

Carbon dioxide   Water   Glucose   Oxygen

Plant cell

Chloroplast

Figure 1 *Photosynthesis takes place in chloroplasts. Chloroplasts are found inside plant cells.*

Getting Energy from Food

Animal cells have different ways of getting energy from food. One way, called **cellular respiration,** uses oxygen to break down food. Many cells can get energy without using oxygen through a process called **fermentation.** Cellular respiration will release more energy from a given food than fermentation will.

Cellular Respiration

The word *respiration* means "breathing," but cellular respiration is different from breathing. Breathing supplies the oxygen needed for cellular respiration. Breathing also removes carbon dioxide, which is a waste product of cellular respiration. But cellular respiration is a chemical process that occurs in cells.

Most complex organisms, such as the cow in **Figure 2,** obtain energy through cellular respiration. During cellular respiration, food (such as glucose) is broken down into CO_2 and H_2O, and energy is released. Most of the energy released maintains body temperature. Some of the energy is used to form adenosine triphosphate (ATP). ATP supplies energy that fuels cell activities.

Most of the process of cellular respiration takes place in the cell membrane of prokaryotic cells. But in the cells of eukaryotes, cellular respiration takes place mostly in the mitochondria. The process of cellular respiration is summarized in **Figure 2.** Does the equation in the figure remind you of the equation for photosynthesis? **Figure 3** on the next page shows how photosynthesis and respiration are related.

Reading Check What is the difference between cellular respiration and breathing? (*See the Appendix for answers to Reading Checks.*)

cellular respiration the process by which cells use oxygen to produce energy from food

fermentation the breakdown of food without the use of oxygen

Figure 2 *The mitochondria in the cells of this cow will use cellular respiration to release the energy stored in the grass.*

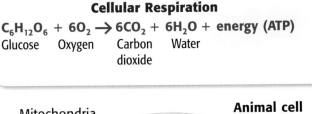

Cellular Respiration

$$C_6H_{12}O_6 + 6O_2 \rightarrow 6CO_2 + 6H_2O + \text{energy (ATP)}$$

Glucose   Oxygen   Carbon dioxide   Water

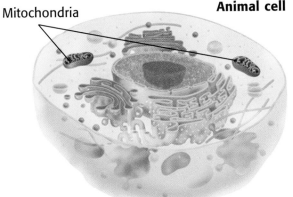

Mitochondria   **Animal cell**

Figure 3 **The Connection Between Photosynthesis and Respiration**

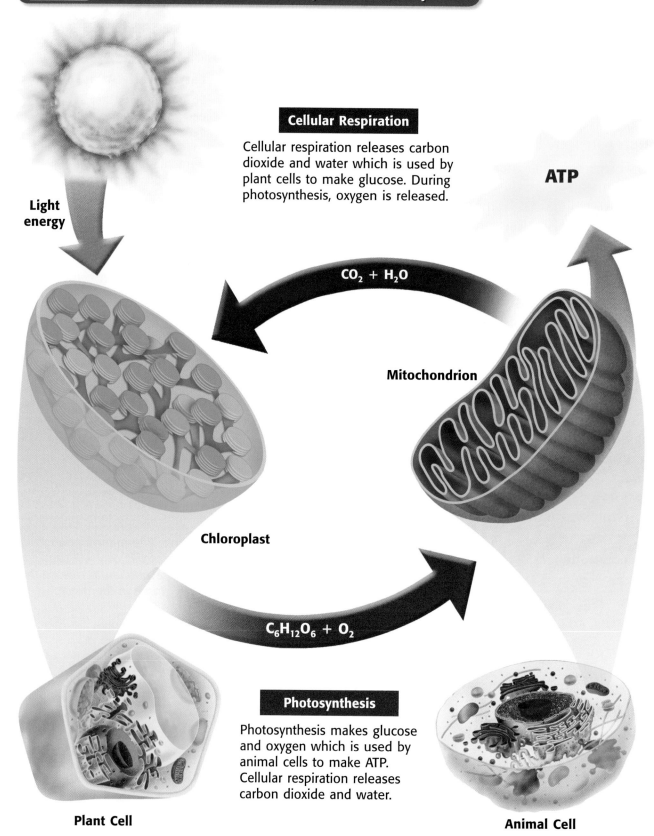

Light energy

Cellular Respiration

Cellular respiration releases carbon dioxide and water which is used by plant cells to make glucose. During photosynthesis, oxygen is released.

ATP

$CO_2 + H_2O$

Mitochondrion

Chloroplast

$C_6H_{12}O_6 + O_2$

Photosynthesis

Photosynthesis makes glucose and oxygen which is used by animal cells to make ATP. Cellular respiration releases carbon dioxide and water.

Plant Cell

Animal Cell

Connection Between Photosynthesis and Respiration

As shown in **Figure 3,** photosynthesis transforms energy from the sun into glucose. During photosynthesis, cells take in CO_2 and release O_2. During cellular respiration, cells use O_2 to break down glucose and release energy and CO_2. Each process makes the materials that are needed for the other process to occur elsewhere.

Fermentation

Have you ever felt a burning sensation in your leg muscles while you were running? When muscle cells can't get the oxygen needed for cellular respiration, they use the process of fermentation to get energy. One kind of fermentation happens in your muscles and produces lactic acid. The buildup of lactic acid contributes to muscle fatigue and causes a burning sensation. This kind of fermentation also happens in the muscle cells of other animals and in some fungi and bacteria. Another type of fermentation occurs in some types of bacteria and in yeast as described in **Figure 4.**

Figure 4 *Yeast forms carbon dioxide during fermentation. The bubbles of CO_2 gas cause the dough to rise and leave small holes in bread after it is baked.*

✓ **Reading Check** What are two kinds of fermentation?

SECTION Review

Summary

- Most of the energy that fuels life processes comes from the sun.
- The sun's energy is converted into food by the process of photosynthesis.
- Cellular respiration breaks down glucose into water, carbon dioxide, and energy.
- Fermentation is a way that cells get energy from their food without using oxygen.

Using Key Terms

1. In your own words, write a definition for the term *fermentation.*

Understanding Key Ideas

2. O_2 is released during
   a. cellular respiration.
   b. photosynthesis.
   c. breathing.
   d. fermentation.

3. How are photosynthesis and cellular respiration related?

4. How are respiration and fermentation similar? How are they different?

Math Skills

5. Cells of plant A make 120 molecules of glucose an hour. Cells of plant B make half as much glucose as plant A does. How much glucose does plant B make every minute?

Critical Thinking

6. **Analyzing Relationships** Why are plants important to the survival of all other organisms?

7. **Applying Concepts** You have been given the job of restoring life to a barren island. What types of organisms would you put on the island? If you want to have animals on the island, what other organisms must you bring? Explain your answer.

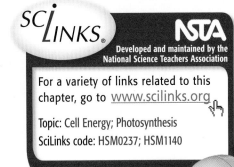

SCiLINKS.

NSTA
Developed and maintained by the
National Science Teachers Association

For a variety of links related to this chapter, go to www.scilinks.org

Topic: Cell Energy; Photosynthesis
SciLinks code: HSM0237; HSM1140

The Cell Cycle

In the time that it takes you to read this sentence, your body will have made millions of new cells! Making new cells allows you to grow and replace cells that have died.

The environment in your stomach is so acidic that the cells lining your stomach must be replaced every few days. Other cells are replaced less often, but your body is constantly making new cells.

The Life of a Cell

As you grow, you pass through different stages in life. Your cells also pass through different stages in their life cycle. The life cycle of a cell is called the **cell cycle.**

The cell cycle begins when the cell is formed and ends when the cell divides and forms new cells. Before a cell divides, it must make a copy of its deoxyribonucleic acid (DNA). DNA is the hereditary material that controls all cell activities, including the making of new cells. The DNA of a cell is organized into structures called **chromosomes.** Copying chromosomes ensures that each new cell will be an exact copy of its parent cell. How does a cell make more cells? It depends on whether the cell is prokaryotic (with no nucleus) or eukaryotic (with a nucleus).

Making More Prokaryotic Cells

Prokaryotic cells are less complex than eukaryotic cells are. Bacteria, which are prokaryotes, have ribosomes and a single, circular DNA molecule but don't have membrane-enclosed organelles. Cell division in bacteria is called *binary fission,* which means "splitting into two parts." Binary fission results in two cells that each contain one copy of the circle of DNA. A few of the bacteria in **Figure 1** are undergoing binary fission.

cell cycle the life cycle of a cell

chromosome in a eukaryotic cell, one of the structures in the nucleus that are made up of DNA and protein; in a prokaryotic cell, the main ring of DNA

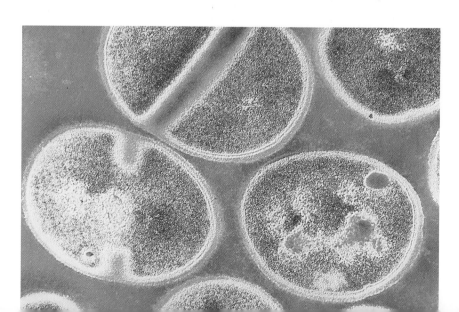

Figure 1 *Bacteria reproduce by binary fission.*

Eukaryotic Cells and Their DNA

Eukaryotic cells are more complex than prokaryotic cells are. The chromosomes of eukaryotic cells contain more DNA than those of prokaryotic cells do. Different kinds of eukaryotes have different numbers of chromosomes. More-complex eukaryotes do not necessarily have more chromosomes than simpler eukaryotes do. For example, fruit flies have 8 chromosomes, potatoes have 48, and humans have 46. **Figure 2** shows the 46 chromosomes of a human body cell lined up in pairs. These pairs are made up of similar chromosomes known as **homologous chromosomes** (hoh MAHL uh guhs KROH muh SOHMZ).

✓ **Reading Check** Do more-complex organisms always have more chromosomes than simpler organisms do? (*See the Appendix for answers to Reading Checks.*)

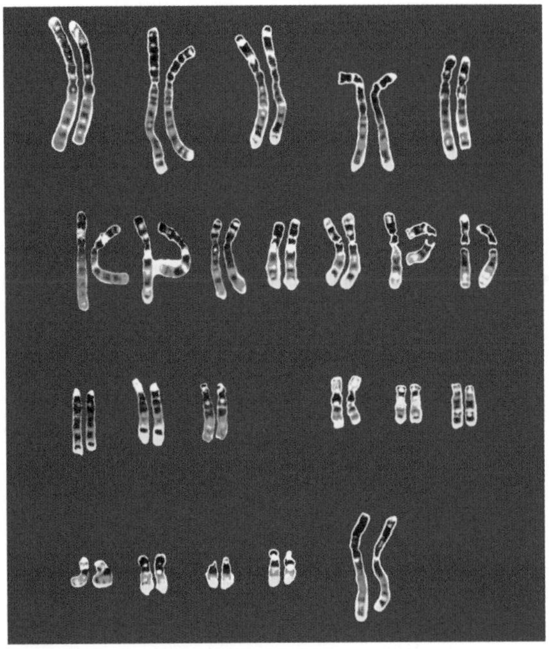

Figure 2 *Human body cells have 46 chromosomes, or 23 pairs of chromosomes.*

Making More Eukaryotic Cells

The eukaryotic cell cycle includes three stages. In the first stage, called *interphase,* the cell grows and copies its organelles and chromosomes. After each chromosome is duplicated, the two copies are called *chromatids.* Chromatids are held together at a region called the *centromere.* The joined chromatids twist and coil and condense into an X shape, as shown in **Figure 3.** After this step, the cell enters the second stage of the cell cycle.

In the second stage, the chromatids separate. The complicated process of chromosome separation is called **mitosis.** Mitosis ensures that each new cell receives a copy of each chromosome. Mitosis is divided into four phases, as shown on the following pages.

In the third stage, the cell splits into two cells. These cells are identical to each other and to the original cell.

homologous chromosomes chromosomes that have the same sequence of genes and the same structure

mitosis in eukaryotic cells, a process of cell division that forms two new nuclei, each of which has the same number of chromosomes

Figure 3 *This duplicated chromosome consists of two chromatids. The chromatids are joined at the centromere.*

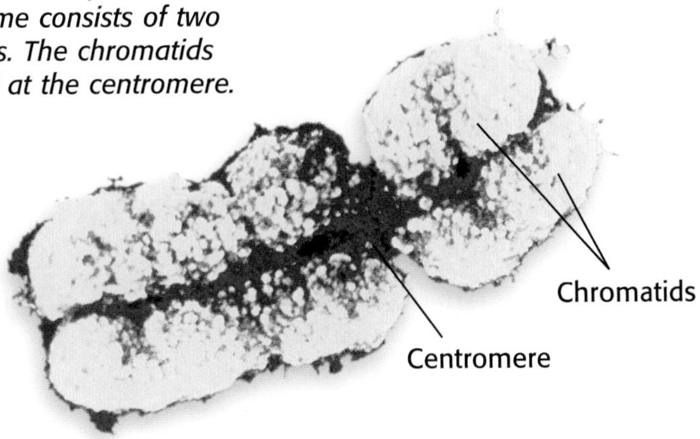

Chromatids

Centromere

CONNECTION TO Language Arts

Picking Apart Vocabulary

Brainstorm what words are similar to the parts of the term *homologous chromosome.* What can you guess about the meaning of the term's root words? Look up the roots of the words, and explain how they help describe the concept.

ACTIVITY

Figure 4 The Cell Cycle

Copying DNA (Interphase)

Before mitosis begins, chromosomes are copied. Each chromosome is then two chromatids.

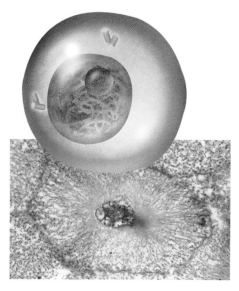

Mitosis Phase 1 (Prophase)

Mitosis begins. The nuclear membrane dissolves. Chromosomes condense into rodlike structures.

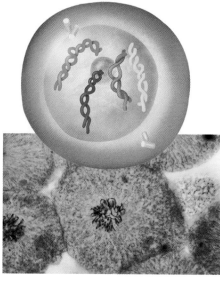

Mitosis Phase 2 (Metaphase)

The chromosomes line up along the equator of the cell. Homologous chromosomes pair up.

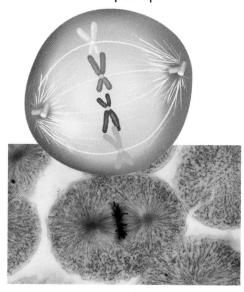

Mitosis and the Cell Cycle

Figure 4 shows the cell cycle and the phases of mitosis in an animal cell. Mitosis has four phases that are shown and described above. This diagram shows only four chromosomes to make it easy to see what's happening inside the cell.

cytokinesis the division of the cytoplasm of a cell

Cytokinesis

In animal cells and other eukaryotes that do not have cell walls, division of the cytoplasm begins at the cell membrane. The cell membrane begins to pinch inward to form a groove, which eventually pinches all the way through the cell, and two daughter cells form. The division of cytoplasm is called **cytokinesis** and is shown at the last step of **Figure 4.**

Eukaryotic cells that have a cell wall, such as the cells of plants, algae, and fungi, reproduce differently. In these cells, a *cell plate* forms in the middle of the cell. The cell plate becomes the new cell membranes that separate the new cells. After the cell splits into two, a new cell wall forms where the cell plate was. The cell plate and a late stage of cytokinesis in a plant cell are shown in **Figure 5.**

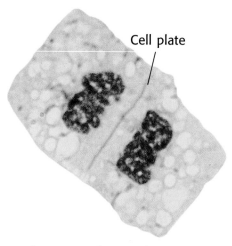

Cell plate

Figure 5 *When a plant cell divides, a cell plate forms and the cell splits into two cells.*

✓ **Reading Check** What is the difference between mitosis in an animal cell and mitosis in a plant cell?

Mitosis Phase 3 (Anaphase)

The chromatids separate and move to opposite sides of the cell.

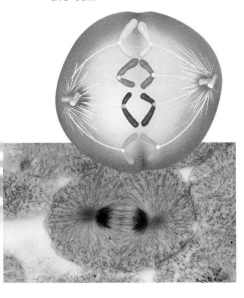

Mitosis Phase 4 (Telophase)

A nuclear membrane forms around each set of chromosomes, and the chromosomes unwind. Mitosis is complete.

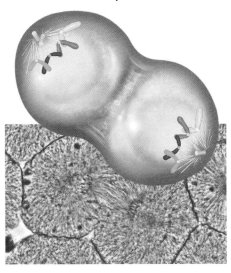

Cytokinesis

In cells that lack a cell wall, the cell pinches in two. In cells that have a cell wall, a cell plate forms between the two new cells.

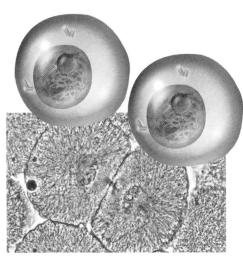

SECTION Review

Summary

- A cell produces more cells by first copying its DNA.
- Eukaryotic cells produce more cells through the four phases of mitosis.
- Mitosis produces two cells that have the same number of chromosomes as the parent cell.
- At the end of mitosis, a cell divides the cytoplasm by cytokinesis.
- In plant cells, a cell plate forms between the two new cells during cytokinesis.

Using Key Terms

1. In your own words, write a definition for each of the following terms: *cell cycle* and *cytokinesis*.

Understanding Key Ideas

2. A eukaryotic cell
   a. has no nucleus.
   b. undergoes binary fission.
   c. has a nucleus.
   d. has a cell wall.

3. Why is it important for chromosomes to be copied before cell division?

4. How are binary fission and mitosis similar? How do they differ?

Math Skills

5. Cell A takes 6 h to complete mitosis. Cell B takes 8 h to complete mitosis. After 24 h, how many more copies of cell A would there be than cell B?

Critical Thinking

6. **Predicting Consequences** What would happen if cytokinesis occurred without mitosis?

7. **Applying Concepts** How does mitosis ensure that a new cell is just like its parent cell?

8. **Making Comparisons** Compare the processes that animal cells and plant cells use to make new cells. How are the processes different?

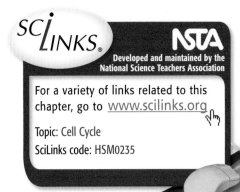

SCILINKS®

NSTA
Developed and maintained by the
National Science Teachers Association

For a variety of links related to this chapter, go to www.scilinks.org

Topic: Cell Cycle
SciLinks code: HSM0235

Inquiry Lab

OBJECTIVES

Examine osmosis in potato cells.

Design a procedure that will give the best results.

MATERIALS

- cups, clear plastic, small
- potato pieces, freshly cut
- potato samples (A, B, and C)
- salt
- water, distilled

SAFETY

The Perfect Taters Mystery

You are the chief food detective at Perfect Taters Food Company. The boss, Mr. Fries, wants you to find a way to keep his potatoes fresh and crisp before they are cooked. His workers have tried several methods, but these methods have not worked. Workers in Group A put the potatoes in very salty water, and something unexpected happened to the potatoes. Workers in Group B put the potatoes in water that did not contain any salt, and something else happened! Workers in Group C didn't put the potatoes in any water, and that didn't work either. Now, you must design an experiment to find out what can be done to make the potatoes stay crisp and fresh.

- Before you plan your experiment, review what you know. You know that potatoes are made of cells. Plant cells contain a large amount of water. Cells have membranes that hold water and other materials inside and keep some things out. Water and other materials must travel across cell membranes to get into and out of the cell.

- Mr. Fries has told you that you can obtain as many samples as you need from the workers in Groups A, B, and C. Your teacher will have these samples ready for you to observe.

- Make a data table like the one below. List your observations in the data table. Make as many observations as you can about the potatoes tested by workers in Groups A, B, and C.

Observations	
Group A	
Group B	
Group C	

Ask a Question

❶ Now that you have made your observations, state Mr. Fries's problem in the form of a question that can be answered by your experiment.

Form a Hypothesis

❷ Form a hypothesis based on your observations and your questions. The hypothesis should be a statement about what causes the potatoes not to be crisp and fresh. Based on your hypothesis, make a prediction about the outcome of your experiment. State your prediction in an if-then format.

Test the Hypothesis

❸ Once you have made a prediction, design your investigation. Check your experimental design with your teacher before you begin. Mr. Fries will give you potato pieces, water, salt, and no more than six containers.

❹ Keep very accurate records. Write your plan and procedure. Make data tables. To be sure your data is accurate, measure all materials carefully and make drawings of the potato pieces before and after the experiment.

Analyze the Results

❶ **Explaining Events** Explain what happened to the potato cells in Groups A, B, and C in your experiment. Include a discussion of the cell membrane and the process of osmosis.

Draw Conclusions

❷ **Analyzing Results** Write a letter to Mr. Fries that explains your experimental method, results, and conclusion. Then, make a recommendation about how he should handle the potatoes so that they will stay fresh and crisp.

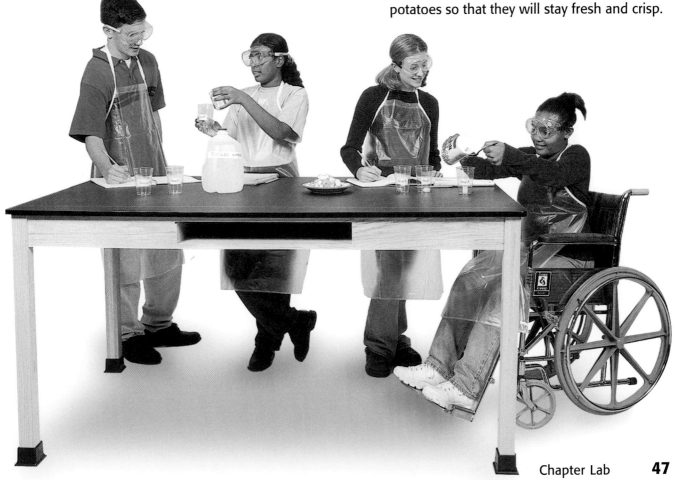

Chapter Review

USING KEY TERMS

1 Use the following terms in the same sentence: *diffusion* and *osmosis*.

2 In your own words, write a definition for each of the following terms: *exocytosis* and *endocytosis*.

Complete each of the following sentences by choosing the correct term from the word bank.

> cellular respiration
> photosynthesis
> fermentation

3 Plants use ___ to make glucose.

4 During ___, oxygen is used to break down food molecules releasing large amounts of energy.

For each pair of terms, explain how the meanings of the terms differ.

5 *cytokinesis* and *mitosis*

6 *active transport* and *passive transport*

7 *cellular respiration* and *fermentation*

UNDERSTANDING KEY IDEAS

Multiple Choice

8 The process in which particles move through a membrane from a region of low concentration to a region of high concentration is

a. diffusion.

b. passive transport.

c. active transport.

d. fermentation.

9 What is the result of mitosis?

a. two identical cells

b. two nuclei

c. chloroplasts

d. two different cells

10 Before the energy in food can be used by a cell, the energy must first be transferred to molecules of

a. proteins.

b. carbohydrates.

c. DNA.

d. ATP.

11 Which of the following cells would form a cell plate during the cell cycle?

a. a human cell

b. a prokaryotic cell

c. a plant cell

d. All of the above

Short Answer

12 Are exocytosis and endocytosis examples of active or passive transport? Explain your answer.

13 Name the cell structures that are needed for photosynthesis and the cell structures that are needed for cellular respiration.

14 Describe the three stages of the cell cycle of a eukaryotic cell.

CRITICAL THINKING

15 **Concept Mapping** Use the following terms to create a concept map: *chromosome duplication, cytokinesis, prokaryote, mitosis, cell cycle, binary fission,* and *eukaryote.*

16 **Making Inferences** Which one of the plants pictured below was given water mixed with salt, and which one was given pure water? Explain how you know, and be sure to use the word *osmosis* in your answer.

17 **Identifying Relationships** Why would your muscle cells need to be supplied with more food when there is a lack of oxygen than when there is plenty of oxygen present?

18 **Applying Concepts** A parent cell has 10 chromosomes.

a. Will the cell go through binary fission or mitosis and cytokinesis to produce new cells?

b. How many chromosomes will each new cell have after the parent cell divides?

INTERPRETING GRAPHICS

The picture below shows a cell. Use the picture below to answer the questions that follow.

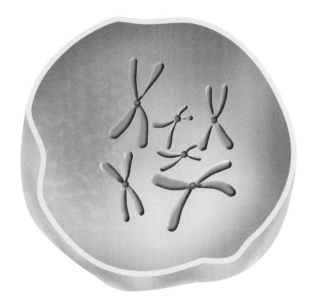

19 Is the cell prokaryotic or eukaryotic?

20 Which stage of the cell cycle is this cell in?

21 How many chromatids are present? How many pairs of homologous chromosomes are present?

22 How many chromosomes will be present in each of the new cells after the cell divides?

Standardized Test Preparation

Read each of the passages below. Then, answer the questions that follow each passage.

Passage 1 Perhaps you have heard that jogging or some other kind of exercise "burns" a lot of Calories. The word *burn* is often used to describe what happens when your cells release stored energy from food. The burning of food in living cells is not the same as the burning of logs in a campfire. When logs burn, the energy stored in wood is released as thermal energy and light in a single reaction. But this kind of reaction is not the kind that happens in cells. Instead, the energy that cells get from food molecules is released at each step of a series of chemical reactions.

1. According to the passage, how do cells release energy from food?
   A in a single reaction
   B as thermal energy and light
   C in a series of reactions
   D by burning

2. Which of the following statements is a fact in the passage?
   F Wood burns better than food does.
   G Both food and wood have stored energy.
   H Food has more stored energy than wood does.
   I When it is burned, wood releases only thermal energy.

3. According to the passage, why might people be confused between what happens in a living cell and what happens in a campfire?
   A The word *burn* may describe both processes.
   B Thermal energy is released during both processes.
   C Wood can be burned and broken down by living cells.
   D Jogging and other exercises use energy.

Passage 2 The word *respiration* means "breathing," but cellular respiration is different from breathing. Breathing supplies your cells with the oxygen that they need for cellular respiration. Breathing also rids your body of carbon dioxide, which is a waste product of cellular respiration. Cellular respiration is the chemical process that releases energy from food. Most organisms obtain energy from food through cellular respiration. During cellular respiration, oxygen is used to break down food (glucose) into CO_2 and H_2O, and energy is released. In humans, most of the energy released is used to maintain body temperature.

1. According to the passage, what is glucose?
   A a type of chemical process
   B a type of waste product
   C a type of organism
   D a type of food

2. According to the passage, how does cellular respiration differ from breathing?
   F Breathing releases carbon dioxide, but cellular respiration releases oxygen.
   G Cellular respiration is a chemical process that uses oxygen to release energy from food, but breathing supplies cells with oxygen.
   H Cellular respiration requires oxygen, but breathing does not.
   I Breathing rids your body of waste products, but cellular respiration stores wastes.

3. According to the passage, how do humans use most of the energy released?
   A to break down food
   B to obtain oxygen
   C to maintain body temperature
   D to get rid of carbon dioxide

The graph below shows the cell cycle. Use this graph to answer the questions that follow.

The Cell Cycle

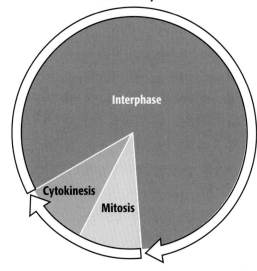

1. Which part of the cell cycle lasts longest?

   A interphase

   B mitosis

   C cytokinesis

   D There is not enough information to determine the answer.

2. Which of the following lists the parts of the cell cycle in the proper order?

   F mitosis, cytokinesis, mitosis

   G interphase, cytokinesis, mitosis

   H interphase, mitosis, interphase

   I mitosis, cytokinesis, interphase

3. Which part of the cell cycle is the briefest?

   A interphase

   B cell division

   C cytokinesis

   D There is not enough information to determine the answer.

4. Why is the cell cycle represented by a circle?

   F The cell cycle is a continuous process that begins again after it finishes.

   G The cell cycle happens only in cells that are round.

   H The cell cycle is a linear process.

   I The cell is in interphase for more than half of the cell cycle.

Read each question below, and choose the best answer.

1. A normal cell spends 90% of its time in interphase. How is 90% expressed as a fraction?

   A 3/4

   B 4/5

   C 85/100

   D 9/10

2. If a cell lived for 3 weeks and 4 days, how many days did it live?

   F 7

   G 11

   H 21

   I 25

3. How is $2 \times 3 \times 3 \times 3 \times 3$ expressed in exponential notation?

   A 3×2^4

   B 2×3^3

   C 3^4

   D 2×3^4

4. Cell A has 3 times as many chromosomes as cell B has. After cell B's chromosomes double during mitosis, cell B has 6 chromosomes. How many chromosomes does cell A have?

   F 3

   G 6

   H 9

   I 18

5. If $x + 2 = 3$, what does $x + 1$ equal?

   A 4

   B 3

   C 2

   D 1

6. If $3x + 2 = 26$, what does $x + 1$ equal?

   F 7

   G 8

   H 9

   I 10

Standardized Test Preparation

Science in Action

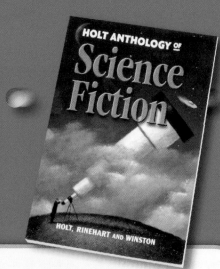

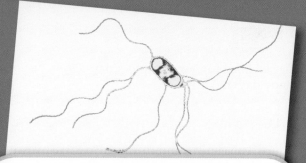

Scientific Discoveries

Electrifying News About Microbes

Your car is out of fuel, and there isn't a service station in sight. This is not a problem! Your car's motor runs on electricity supplied by trillions of microorganisms. Some chemists think that "living" batteries will someday operate everything from watches to entire cities. A group of scientists at King's College in London have demonstrated that microorganisms can convert food into usable electrical energy. The microorganisms convert foods such as table sugar and molasses most efficiently. An efficient microorganisms can convert more than 90% of its food into compounds that will fuel an electric reaction. A less efficient microbe will only convert 50% of its food into these types of compounds.

Math ACTIVITY

An efficient microorganism converts 90% of its food into fuel compounds, and an inefficient microorganism converts only 50%. If the inefficient microorganism makes 60 g of fuel out of a possible 120 g of food, how much fuel would an efficient microorganism make out of the same amount of food?

Science Fiction

"Contagion" by Katherine MacLean

A quarter mile from their spaceship, the *Explorer,* a team of doctors walk carefully along a narrow forest trail. Around them, the forest looks like a forest on Earth in the fall—the leaves are green, copper, purple, and fiery red. But it isn't fall. And the team is not on Earth.

Minos is enough like Earth to be the home of another colony of humans. But Minos might also be home to unknown organisms that could cause severe illness or death among the crew of *Explorer*. These diseases might be enough like diseases on Earth to be contagious, but they might be different enough to be very difficult to treat.

Something large moves among the shadows—it looks like a man. What happens next? Read Katherine's MacLean's "Contagion" in the *Holt Anthology of Science Fiction* to find out.

Language Arts ACTIVITY

WRITING SKILL Write two to three paragraphs that describe what you think might happen next in the story.

Jerry Yakel

Neuroscientist Jerry Yakel credits a sea slug for making him a neuroscientist. In a college class studying neurons, or nerve cells, Yakel got to see firsthand how ions move across the cell membrane of *Aplysia californica,* also known as a sea hare. He says, "I was totally hooked. I knew that I wanted to be a neurophysiologist then and there. I haven't wavered since."

Today, Yakel is a senior investigator for the National Institutes of Environmental Health Sciences, which is part of the U.S. government's National Institutes of Health. "We try to understand how the normal brain works," says Yakel of his team. "Then, when we look at a diseased brain, we train to understand where the deficits are. Eventually, someone will have an idea about a drug that will tweak the system in this or that way."

Yakel studies the ways in which nicotine affects the human brain. "It is one of the most prevalent and potent neurotoxins in the environment," says Yakel. "I'm amazed that it isn't higher on the list of worries for the general public."

Social Studies ACTiViTY

WRITING SKILL Research a famous or historical figure in science. Write a short report that outlines how he or she became interested in science.

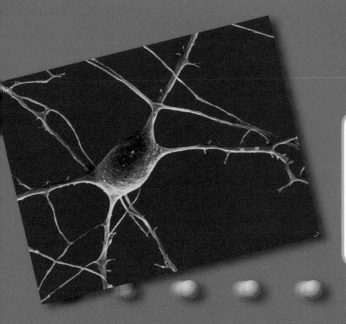

To learn more about these Science in Action topics, visit **go.hrw.com** and type in the keyword **HL5ACTF.**

Current Science

Check out Current Science® articles related to this chapter by visiting go.hrw.com. Just type in the keyword HL5CS04.

3

Heredity

About the PHOTO

The guinea pig in the middle has dark fur, and the other two have light orange fur. The guinea pig on the right has longer hair than the other two. Why do these guinea pigs look different from one another? The length and color of their fur was determined before they were born. These are just two of the many traits determined by genetic information. Genetic information is passed on from parents to their offspring.

PRE-READING ACTIVITY

FOLDNOTES **Key-Term Fold** Before you read the chapter, create the FoldNote entitled "Key-Term Fold" described in the **Study Skills** section of the Appendix. Write a key term from the chapter on each tab of the key-term fold. Under each tab, write the definition of the key term.

START-UP ACTIVITY

Clothing Combos

How do the same parents have children with many different traits?

Procedure

1. Gather **three boxes**. Put **five hats** in the first box, **five gloves** in the second, and **five scarves** in the third.

2. Without looking in the boxes, select one item from each box. Repeat this process, five students at a time, until the entire class has picked "an outfit." Record what outfit each student chooses.

Analysis

1. Were any two outfits exactly alike? Did you see all possible combinations? Explain your answer.

2. Choose a partner. Using your outfits, how many different combinations could you make by giving a third person one hat, one glove, and one scarf? How is this process like parents passing traits to their children?

3. After completing this activity, why do you think parents often have children who look very different from each other?

Mendel and His Peas

Why don't you look like a rhinoceros? The answer to this question seems simple: Neither of your parents is a rhinoceros. But there is more to this answer than meets the eye.

As it turns out, **heredity,** or the passing of traits from parents to offspring, is more complicated than you might think. For example, you might have curly hair, while both of your parents have straight hair. You might have blue eyes even though both of your parents have brown eyes. How does this happen? People have investigated this question for a long time. About 150 years ago, Gregor Mendel performed important experiments. His discoveries helped scientists begin to find some answers to these questions.

✓ **Reading Check** What is heredity? (*See the Appendix for answers to Reading Checks.*)

Who Was Gregor Mendel?

Gregor Mendel, shown in **Figure 1,** was born in 1822 in Heinzendorf, Austria. Mendel grew up on a farm and learned a lot about flowers and fruit trees.

When he was 21 years old, Mendel entered a monastery. The monks taught science and performed many scientific experiments. From there, Mendel was sent to Vienna where he could receive training in teaching. However, Mendel had trouble taking tests. Although he did well in school, he was unable to pass the final exam. He returned to the monastery and put most of his energy into research. Mendel discovered the principles of heredity in the monastery garden.

Unraveling the Mystery

From working with plants, Mendel knew that the patterns of inheritance were not always clear. For example, sometimes a trait that appeared in one generation (parents) was not present in the next generation (offspring). In the generation after that, though, the trait showed up again. Mendel noticed these kinds of patterns in several other living things, too. Mendel wanted to learn more about what caused these patterns.

To keep his investigation simple, Mendel decided to study only one kind of organism. Because he had studied garden pea plants before, they seemed like a good choice.

READING WARM-UP

Objectives

● Explain the relationship between traits and heredity.

● Describe the experiments of Gregor Mendel.

● Explain the difference between dominant and recessive traits.

Terms to Learn

heredity
dominant trait
recessive trait

READING STRATEGY

Brainstorming The key idea of this section is heredity. Brainstorm words and phrases related to heredity.

heredity the passing of genetic traits from parent to offspring

Figure 1 *Gregor Mendel discovered the principles of heredity while studying pea plants.*

Self-Pollinating Peas

In fact, garden peas were a good choice for several reasons. Pea plants grow quickly, and there are many different kinds available. They are also able to self-pollinate. A *self-pollinating plant* has both male and female reproductive structures. So, pollen from one flower can fertilize the ovule of the same flower or the ovule of another flower on the same plant. The flower on the right side of **Figure 2** is self-pollinating.

Why is it important that pea plants can self-pollinate? Because eggs (in an ovule) and sperm (in pollen) from the same plant combine to make a new plant, Mendel was able to grow true-breeding plants. When a *true-breeding plant* self-pollinates, all of its offspring will have the same trait as the parent. For example, a true-breeding plant with purple flowers will always have offspring with purple flowers.

Pea plants can also cross-pollinate. In *cross-pollination*, pollen from one plant fertilizes the ovule of a flower on a different plant. There are several ways that this can happen. Pollen may be carried by insects to a flower on a different plant. Pollen can also be carried by the wind from one flower to another. The left side of **Figure 2** shows these kinds of cross-pollination.

Self-pollination

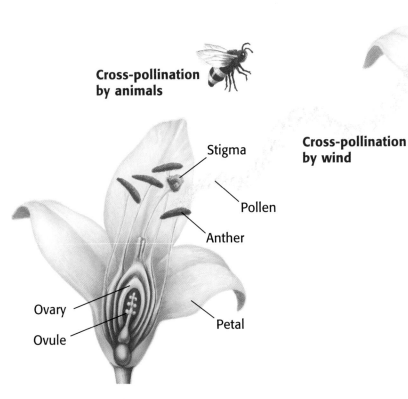

Cross-pollination by animals

Stigma

Cross-pollination by wind

Pollen

Anther

Ovary

Ovule

Petal

Figure 2 *During pollination, pollen from the anthers (male) is transferred to the stigma (female). Fertilization occurs when a sperm from the pollen travels through the stigma and enters the egg in an ovule.*

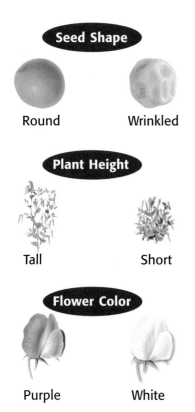

Seed Shape

Round   Wrinkled

Plant Height

Tall   Short

Flower Color

Purple   White

Figure 3 *These are some of the plant characteristics that Mendel studied.*

Characteristics

Mendel studied only one characteristic at a time. A *characteristic* is a feature that has different forms in a population. For example, hair color is a characteristic in humans. The different forms, such as brown or red hair, are called *traits*. Mendel used plants that had different traits for each of the characteristics he studied. For instance, for the characteristic of flower color, he chose plants that had purple flowers and plants that had white flowers. Three of the characteristics Mendel studied are shown in **Figure 3.**

Mix and Match

Mendel was careful to use plants that were true breeding for each of the traits he was studying. By doing so, he would know what to expect if his plants were to self-pollinate. He decided to find out what would happen if he bred, or crossed, two plants that had different traits of a single characteristic. To be sure the plants cross-pollinated, he removed the anthers of one plant so that the plant could not self-pollinate. Then, he used pollen from another plant to fertilize the plant, as shown in **Figure 4.** This step allowed Mendel to select which plants would be crossed to produce offspring.

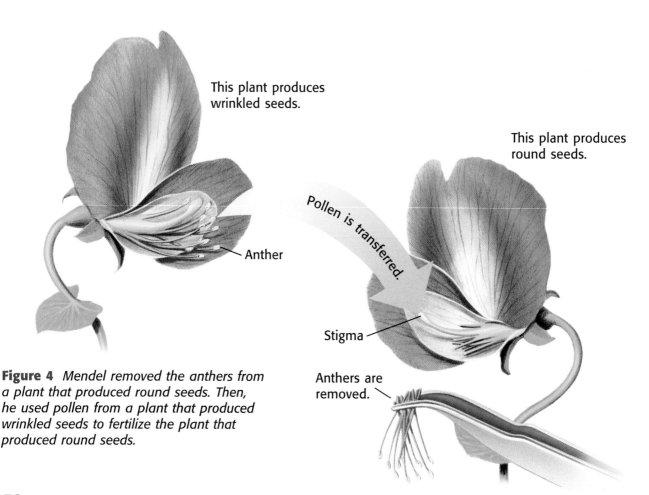

This plant produces wrinkled seeds.

This plant produces round seeds.

Pollen is transferred.

Anther

Stigma

Anthers are removed.

Figure 4 *Mendel removed the anthers from a plant that produced round seeds. Then, he used pollen from a plant that produced wrinkled seeds to fertilize the plant that produced round seeds.*

Mendel's First Experiments

In his first experiments, Mendel crossed pea plants to study seven different characteristics. In each cross, Mendel used plants that were true breeding for different traits for each characteristic. For example, he crossed plants that had purple flowers with plants that had white flowers. This cross is shown in the first part of **Figure 5.** The offspring from such a cross are called *first-generation plants*. All of the first-generation plants in this cross had purple flowers. Are you surprised by the results? What happened to the trait for white flowers?

Mendel got similar results for each cross. One trait was always present in the first generation, and the other trait seemed to disappear. Mendel chose to call the trait that appeared the **dominant trait.** Because the other trait seemed to fade into the background, Mendel called it the **recessive trait.** (To *recede* means "to go away or back off.") To find out what might have happened to the recessive trait, Mendel decided to do another set of experiments.

Mendel's Second Experiments

Mendel allowed the first-generation plants to self-pollinate. **Figure 5** also shows what happened when a first-generation plant with purple flowers was allowed to self-pollinate. As you can see, the recessive trait for white flowers reappeared in the second generation.

Mendel did this same experiment on each of the seven characteristics. In each case, some of the second-generation plants had the recessive trait.

☑ Reading Check Describe Mendel's second set of experiments.

dominant trait the trait observed in the first generation when parents that have different traits are bred

recessive trait a trait that reappears in the second generation after disappearing in the first generation when parents with different traits are bred

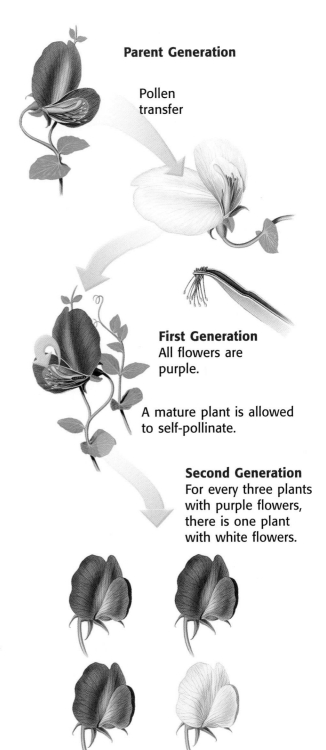

Parent Generation

Pollen transfer

First Generation
All flowers are purple.

A mature plant is allowed to self-pollinate.

Second Generation
For every three plants with purple flowers, there is one plant with white flowers.

Figure 5 *Mendel used the pollen from a plant with purple flowers to fertilize a plant with white flowers. Then, he allowed the offspring to self-pollinate.*

Understanding Ratios

A ratio is a way to compare two numbers. Look at **Table 1.** The ratio of plants with purple flowers to plants with white flowers can be written as 705 to 224 or 705:224. This ratio can be reduced, or simplified, by dividing the first number by the second as follows:

$$\frac{705}{224} = \frac{3.15}{1}$$

which is the same thing as a ratio of 3.15:1.

For every 3 plants with purple flowers, there will be roughly 1 plant with white flowers. Try this problem:

In a box of chocolates, there are 18 nougat-filled chocolates and 6 caramel-filled chocolates. What is the ratio of nougat-filled chocolates to caramel-filled chocolates?

Ratios in Mendel's Experiments

Mendel then decided to count the number of plants with each trait that turned up in the second generation. He hoped that this might help him explain his results. Take a look at Mendel's results, shown in **Table 1.**

As you can see, the recessive trait did not show up as often as the dominant trait. Mendel decided to figure out the ratio of dominant traits to recessive traits. A *ratio* is a relationship between two different numbers that is often expressed as a fraction. Calculate the dominant-to-recessive ratio for each characteristic. (If you need help, look at the Math Practice at left.) Do you notice anything interesting about the ratios? Round to the nearest whole number. Are the ratios all the same, or are they different?

✓ **Reading Check** What is a ratio?

Table 1 Mendel's Results

Characteristic	Dominant traits	Recessive traits	Ratio
Flower color	705 purple	224 white	3.15:1
Seed color	6,002 yellow	2,001 green	?
Seed shape	5,474 round	1,850 wrinkled	?
Pod color	428 green	152 yellow	?
Pod shape	882 smooth	299 bumpy	?
Flower position	651 along stem	207 at tip	?
Plant height	787 tall	277 short	?

Gregor Mendel—Gone but Not Forgotten

Mendel realized that his results could be explained only if each plant had two sets of instructions for each characteristic. Each parent would then donate one set of instructions. In 1865, Mendel published his findings. But good ideas are sometimes overlooked or misunderstood at first. It wasn't until after his death, more than 30 years later, that Mendel's work was widely recognized. Once Mendel's ideas were rediscovered and understood, the door was opened to modern genetics. Genetic research, as shown in **Figure 6,** is one of the fastest changing fields in science today.

Figure 6 *This researcher is continuing the work started by Gregor Mendel more than 100 years ago.*

SECTION Review

Summary

- Heredity is the passing of traits from parents to offspring.
- Gregor Mendel made carefully planned experiments using pea plants that could self-pollinate.
- When parents with different traits are bred, dominant traits are always present in the first generation. Recessive traits are not visible in the first generation but reappear in the second generation.
- Mendel found a 3:1 ratio of dominant-to-recessive traits in the second generation.

Using Key Terms

1. Use each of the following terms in a separate sentence: *heredity, dominant trait,* and *recessive trait.*

Understanding Key Ideas

2. A plant that has both male and female reproductive structures is able to
   a. self-replicate.
   b. self-pollinate.
   c. breed true.
   d. None of the above

3. Explain the difference between self-pollination and cross-pollination.

4. What is the difference between a trait and a characteristic? Give one example of each.

5. Describe Mendel's first set of experiments.

6. Describe Mendel's second set of experiments.

Math Skills

7. In a bag of chocolate candies, there are 21 brown candies and 6 green candies. What is the ratio of brown to green? What is the ratio of green to brown?

Critical Thinking

8. **Predicting Consequences** Gregor Mendel used only true-breeding plants. If he had used plants that were not true breeding, do you think he would have discovered dominant and recessive traits? Explain.

9. **Applying Concepts** In cats, there are two types of ears: normal and curly. A curly-eared cat mated with a normal-eared cat, and all of the kittens had curly ears. Are curly ears a dominant or recessive trait? Explain.

10. **Identifying Relationships** List three other fields of study that use ratios.

Developed and maintained by the
National Science Teachers Association

For a variety of links related to this chapter, go to www.scilinks.org

Topic: Heredity; Dominant and Recessive Traits
SciLinks code: HSM0738; HSM0423

Traits and Inheritance

Mendel calculated the ratio of dominant traits to recessive traits. He found a ratio of 3:1. What did this tell him about how traits are passed from parents to offspring?

READING WARM-UP

Objectives

- Explain how genes and alleles are related to genotype and phenotype.
- Use the information in a Punnett square.
- Explain how probability can be used to predict possible genotypes in offspring.
- Describe three exceptions to Mendel's observations.

Terms to Learn

gene   genotype
allele   probability
phenotype

READING STRATEGY

Paired Summarizing Read this section silently. In pairs, take turns summarizing the material. Stop to discuss ideas that seem confusing.

gene one set of instructions for an inherited trait

allele one of the alternative forms of a gene that governs a characteristic, such as hair color

phenotype an organism's appearance or other detectable characteristic

A Great Idea

Mendel knew from his experiments with pea plants that there must be two sets of instructions for each characteristic. The first-generation plants carried the instructions for both the dominant trait and the recessive trait. Scientists now call these instructions for an inherited trait **genes.** Each parent gives one set of genes to the offspring. The offspring then has two forms of the same gene for every characteristic—one from each parent. The different forms (often dominant and recessive) of a gene are known as **alleles** (uh LEELZ). Dominant alleles are shown with a capital letter. Recessive alleles are shown with a lowercase letter.

Reading Check What is the difference between a gene and an allele? (*See the Appendix for answers to Reading Checks.*)

Phenotype

Genes affect the traits of offspring. An organism's appearance is known as its **phenotype** (FEE noh TIEP). In pea plants, possible phenotypes for the characteristic of flower color would be purple flowers or white flowers. For seed color, yellow and green seeds are the different phenotypes.

Phenotypes of humans are much more complicated than those of peas. Look at **Figure 1** below. The man has an inherited condition called *albinism* (AL buh NIZ uhm). Albinism prevents hair, skin, and eyes from having normal coloring.

Figure 1 *Albinism is an inherited disorder that affects a person's phenotype in many ways.*

Genotype

Both inherited alleles together form an organism's **genotype.** Because the allele for purple flowers (*P*) is dominant, only one *P* allele is needed for the plant to have purple flowers. A plant with two dominant or two recessive alleles is said to be *homozygous* (HOH moh ZIE guhs). A plant that has the genotype *Pp* is said to be *heterozygous* (HET uhr OH ZIE guhs).

Punnett Squares

A Punnett square is used to organize all the possible combinations of offspring from particular parents. The alleles for a true-breeding, purple-flowered plant are written as *PP*. The alleles for a true-breeding, white-flowered plant are written as *pp*. The Punnett square for this cross is shown in **Figure 2.** All of the offspring have the same genotype: *Pp*. The dominant allele, *P*, in each genotype ensures that all of the offspring will be purple-flowered plants. The recessive allele, *p*, may be passed on to the next generation. This Punnett square shows the results of Mendel's first experiments.

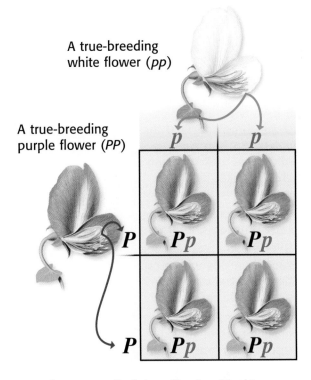

Figure 2 *All of the offspring for this cross have the same genotype—Pp.*

genotype the entire genetic makeup of an organism; also the combination of genes for one or more specific traits

Making a Punnett Square

1. Draw a square, and divide it into four sections.
2. Write the letters that represent alleles from one parent along the top of the box.
3. Write the letters that represent alleles from the other parent along the side of the box.
4. The cross shown at right is between two plants that produce round seeds. The genotype for each is *Rr*. Round seeds are dominant, and wrinkled seeds are recessive. Follow the arrows to see how the inside of the box was filled. The resulting alleles inside the box show all the possible genotypes for the offspring from this cross. What would the phenotypes for these offspring be?

Quick Lab

Taking Your Chances

You have two guinea pigs. Each has brown fur and the genotype *Bb*. You want to predict what their offspring might look like. Try this to find out.

1. Stick a **piece of masking tape** on each side of **two quarters.**

2. Label one side with a capital *B* and the other side with a lowercase *b*.

3. Toss both coins 10 times, making note of your results each time.

4. How many times did you get the *bb* combination?

5. What is the probability that the next toss will result in *bb*?

6. What are the chances that the guinea pigs' offspring will have white fur (with the genotype *bb*)?

Figure 3 *This Punnett square shows the possible results from the cross Pp × Pp.*

A self-pollinating purple flower

Male alleles

Female alleles

	P	p
P	**PP**	**Pp**
p	**pP**	**pp**

More Evidence for Inheritance

In Mendel's second experiments, he allowed the first generation plants to self-pollinate. **Figure 3** shows a self-pollination cross of a plant with the genotype *Pp*. What are the possible genotypes of the offspring?

Notice that one square shows the genotype *Pp*, while another shows *pP*. These are exactly the same genotype. The other possible genotypes of the offspring are *PP* and *pp*. The combinations *PP*, *Pp*, and *pP* have the same phenotype—purple flowers. This is because each contains at least one dominant allele (*P*).

Only one combination, *pp*, produces plants that have white flowers. The ratio of dominant to recessive is 3:1, just as Mendel calculated from his data.

What Are the Chances?

Each parent has two alleles for each gene. When these alleles are different, as in *Pp*, offspring are equally likely to receive either allele. Think of a coin toss. There is a 50% chance you'll get heads and a 50% chance you'll get tails. The chance of receiving one allele or another is as random as a coin toss.

Probability

The mathematical chance that something will happen is known as **probability.** Probability is most often written as a fraction or percentage. If you toss a coin, the probability of tossing tails is 1/2—you will get tails half the time.

probability the likelihood that a possible future event will occur in any given instance of the event

✓ **Reading Check** What is probability?

Probability If you roll a pair of dice, what is the probability that you will roll 2 threes?

Step 1: Count the number of faces on a single die. Put this number in the denominator: 6.

Step 2: Count how many ways you can roll a three with one die. Put this number in the numerator: 1/6.

Step 3: To find the probability that you will throw 2 threes, multiply the probability of throwing the first three by the probability of throwing the second three: $1/6 \times 1/6 = 1/36$.

Now It's Your Turn

If you roll a single die, what is the probability that you will roll an even number?

Calculating Probabilities

To find the probability that you will toss two heads in a row, multiply the probability of tossing the first head (1/2) by the probability of tossing the second head (1/2). The probability of tossing two heads in a row is 1/4.

Genotype Probability

To have white flowers, a pea plant must receive a *p* allele from each parent. Each offspring of a *Pp* × *Pp* cross has a 50% chance of receiving either allele from either parent. So, the probability of inheriting two *p* alleles is $1/2 \times 1/2$, which equals 1/4, or 25%. Traits in pea plants are easy to predict because there are only two choices for each trait, such as purple or white flowers and round or wrinkled seeds. Look at **Figure 4.** Do you see only two distinct choices for fur color?

Figure 4 *These kittens inherited one allele from their mother for each trait.*

CONNECTION TO Chemistry

Round and Wrinkled Round seeds may look better, but wrinkled seeds taste sweeter. The dominant allele for seed shape, *R*, causes sugar to be changed into starch (which is a storage molecule for sugar). This change makes the seed round. Seeds with the genotype *rr* do not make or store this starch. Because the sugar has not been changed into starch, the seed tastes sweeter. If you had a pea plant with round seeds (*Rr*), what would you cross it with to get some offspring with wrinkled seeds? Draw a Punnett square showing your cross.

ACTIVITY

More About Traits

As you may have already discovered, things are often more complicated than they first appear to be. Gregor Mendel uncovered the basic principles of how genes are passed from one generation to the next. But as scientists learned more about heredity, they began to find exceptions to Mendel's principles. A few of these exceptions are explained below.

Incomplete Dominance

Since Mendel's discoveries, researchers have found that sometimes one trait is not completely dominant over another. These traits do not blend together, but each allele has its own degree of influence. This is known as *incomplete dominance.*

One example of incomplete dominance is found in the snapdragon flower. **Figure 5** shows a cross between a true-breeding red snapdragon (R^1R^1) and a true-breeding white snapdragon (R^2R^2). As you can see, all of the possible phenotypes for their offspring are pink because both alleles of the gene have some degree of influence.

Reading Check What is incomplete dominance?

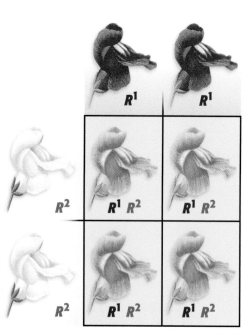

Figure 5 *Cross-breeding two true-breeding snapdragons provides a good example of incomplete dominance.*

One Gene, Many Traits

Sometimes one gene influences more than one trait. An example of this phenomenon is shown by the white tiger in **Figure 6.** The white fur is caused by a single gene, but this gene influences more than just fur color. Do you see anything else unusual about the tiger? If you look closely, you'll see that the tiger has blue eyes. Here, the gene that controls fur color also influences eye color.

Figure 6 *The gene that gave this tiger white fur also influenced its eye color.*

Many Genes, One Trait

Some traits, such as the color of your skin, hair, and eyes, are the result of several genes acting together. Therefore, it's difficult to tell if some traits are the result of a dominant or a recessive gene. Different combinations of alleles result in different eye-color shades, as shown in **Figure 7.**

The Importance of Environment

Genes aren't the only influences on traits. A guinea pig could have the genes for long fur, but its fur could be cut. In the same way, your environment influences how you grow. Your genes may make it possible that you will grow to be tall, but you need a healthy diet to reach your full potential height.

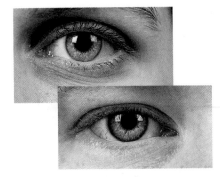

Figure 7 *At least two genes determine human eye color. That's why many shades of a single color are possible.*

SECTION Review

Summary

- Instructions for an inherited trait are called *genes*. For each gene, there are two alleles, one inherited from each parent. Both alleles make up an organism's genotype. Phenotype is an organism's appearance.

- Punnett squares show all possible offspring genotypes.

- Probability can be used to describe possible outcomes in offspring and the likelihood of each outcome.

- Incomplete dominance occurs when one allele is not completely dominant over the other allele.

- Some genes influence more than one trait.

Using Key Terms

1. Use the following terms in the same sentence: *gene* and *allele*.

2. In your own words, write a definition for each of the following terms: *genotype* and *phenotype*.

Understanding Key Ideas

3. Use a Punnett square to determine the possible genotypes of the offspring of a *BB* × *Bb* cross.
   - **a.** all *BB*
   - **b.** *BB, Bb*
   - **c.** *BB, Bb, bb*
   - **d.** all *bb*

4. How are genes and alleles related to genotype and phenotype?

5. Describe three exceptions to Mendel's observations.

Math Skills

6. What is the probability of rolling a five on one die three times in a row?

Critical Thinking

7. **Applying Concepts** The allele for a cleft chin, *C*, is dominant among humans. What are the results of a cross between parents with genotypes *Cc* and *cc*?

Interpreting Graphics

The Punnett square below shows the alleles for fur color in rabbits. Black fur, *B*, is dominant over white fur, *b*.

	?	?
?	Bb	Bb
?	Bb	Bb

8. Given the combinations shown, what are the genotypes of the parents?

9. If black fur had incomplete dominance over white fur, what color would the offspring be?

Developed and maintained by the National Science Teachers Association

For a variety of links related to this chapter, go to www.scilinks.org

Topic: Genotypes; Phenotypes
SciLinks code: HSM0664; HSM1135

Meiosis

Where are genes located, and how do they pass information? Understanding reproduction is the first step to finding the answers.

There are two kinds of reproduction: asexual and sexual. Asexual reproduction results in offspring with genotypes that are exact copies of their parent's genotype. Sexual reproduction produces offspring that share traits with their parents but are not exactly like either parent.

Asexual Reproduction

In *asexual reproduction,* only one parent cell is needed. The structures inside the cell are copied, and then the parent cell divides, making two exact copies. This type of cell reproduction is known as *mitosis.* Most of the cells in your body and most single-celled organisms reproduce in this way.

Sexual Reproduction

In sexual reproduction, two parent cells join together to form offspring that are different from both parents. The parent cells are called *sex cells.* Sex cells are different from ordinary body cells. Human body cells have 46, or 23 pairs of, chromosomes. One set of human chromosomes is shown in **Figure 1.** Chromosomes that carry the same sets of genes are called **homologous** (hoh MAHL uh guhs) **chromosomes.** Imagine a pair of shoes. Each shoe is like a homologous chromosome. The pair represents a homologous pair of chromosomes. But human sex cells are different. They have 23 chromosomes—half the usual number. Each sex cell has only one of the chromosomes from each homologous pair. Sex cells have only one "shoe."

homologous chromosomes chromosomes that have the same sequence of genes and the same structure

meiosis a process in cell division during which the number of chromosomes decreases to half the original number by two divisions of the nucleus, which results in the production of sex cells

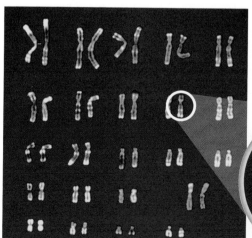
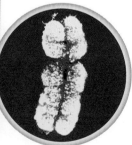

Figure 1 *Human body cells have 23 pairs of chromosomes. One member of a pair of homologous chromosomes is shown below.*

Meiosis

Sex cells are made during meiosis (mie OH sis). **Meiosis** is a copying process that produces cells with half the usual number of chromosomes. Each sex cell receives one-half of each homologous pair. For example, a human egg cell has 23 chromosomes, and a sperm cell has 23 chromosomes. The new cell that forms when an egg cell and a sperm cell join has 46 chromosomes.

✓ **Reading Check** How many chromosomes does a human egg cell have? (*See the Appendix for answers to Reading Checks.*)

Genes and Chromosomes

What does all of this have to do with the location of genes? Not long after Mendel's work was rediscovered, a graduate student named Walter Sutton made an important observation. Sutton was studying sperm cells in grasshoppers. Sutton knew of Mendel's studies, which showed that the egg and sperm must each contribute the same amount of information to the offspring. That was the only way the 3:1 ratio found in the second generation could be explained. Sutton also knew from his own studies that although eggs and sperm were different, they did have something in common: Their chromosomes were located inside a nucleus. Using his observations of meiosis, his understanding of Mendel's work, and some creative thinking, Sutton proposed something very important:

Genes are located on chromosomes!

Understanding meiosis was critical to finding the location of genes. Before you learn about meiosis, review mitosis, shown in **Figure 2.** Meiosis is outlined in **Figure 3** on the next two pages.

CONNECTION TO Language Arts

Greek Roots The word *mitosis* is related to a Greek word that means "threads." Threadlike spindles are visible during mitosis. The word *meiosis* comes from a Greek word that means "to make smaller." How do you think meiosis got its name?

Figure 2 **Mitosis Revisited**

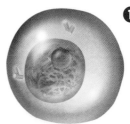

❶ Each chromosome is copied.

❷ The chromosomes thicken and shorten. Each chromosome consists of two identical copies, called *chromatids.*

❸ The nuclear membrane dissolves. The chromatids line up along the equator (center) of the cell.

❹ The chromatids pull apart.

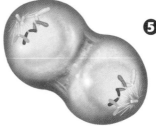

❺ The nuclear membrane forms around the separated chromatids. The chromosomes unwind, and the cell divides.

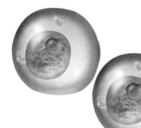

❻ The result is two identical copies of the original cell.

The Steps of Meiosis

During mitosis, chromosomes are copied once, and then the nucleus divides once. During meiosis, chromosomes are copied once, and then the nucleus divides twice. The resulting sperm and eggs have half the number of chromosomes of a normal body cell. **Figure 3** shows all eight steps of meiosis. Read about each step as you look at the figure. Different types of living things have different numbers of chromosomes. In this illustration, only four chromosomes are shown.

Reading Check How many cells are made from one parent cell during meiosis?

Figure 3 Steps of Meiosis

Read about each step as you look at the diagram. Different types of living things have different numbers of chromosomes. In this diagram, only four chromosomes are shown.

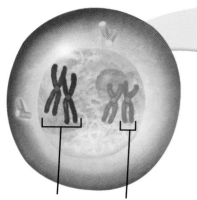

One pair of homologous chromosomes   Two chromatids

1 Before meiosis begins, the chromosomes are in a threadlike form. Each chromosome makes an exact copy of itself, forming two halves called *chromatids*. The chromosomes then thicken and shorten into a form that is visible under a microscope. The nuclear membrane disappears.

2 Each chromosome is now made up of two identical chromatids. Similar chromosomes pair with one another, and the paired homologous chromosomes line up at the equator of the cell.

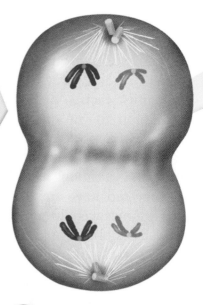

3 The chromosomes separate from their homologous partners and then move to opposite ends of the cell.

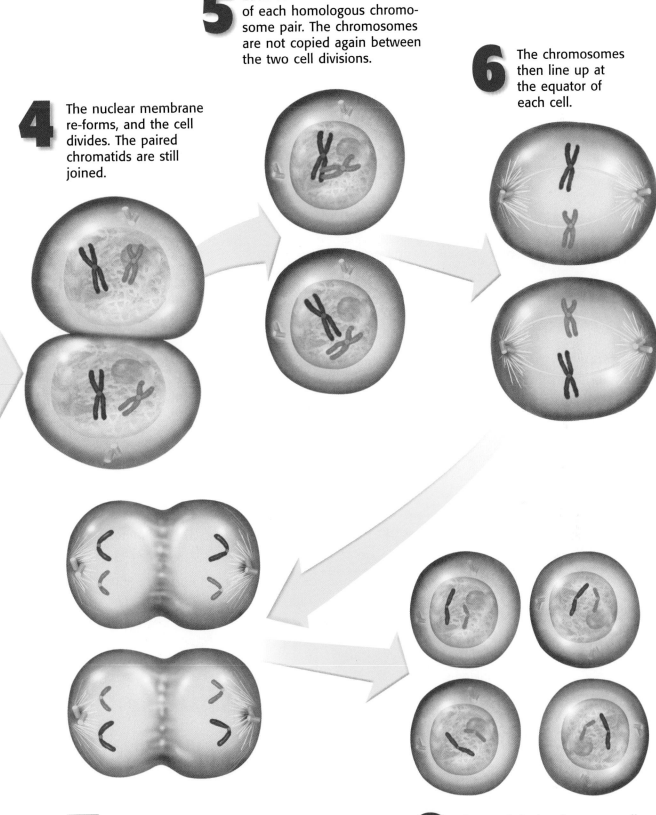

5 Each cell contains one member of each homologous chromosome pair. The chromosomes are not copied again between the two cell divisions.

6 The chromosomes then line up at the equator of each cell.

4 The nuclear membrane re-forms, and the cell divides. The paired chromatids are still joined.

7 The chromatids pull apart and move to opposite ends of the cell. The nuclear membrane forms around the separated chromosomes, and the cells divide.

8 The result is that four new cells have formed from the original single cell. Each new cell has half the number of chromosomes present in the original cell.

Meiosis and Mendel

As Walter Sutton figured out, the steps in meiosis explained Mendel's results. **Figure 4** shows what happens to a pair of homologous chromosomes during meiosis and fertilization. The cross shown is between a plant that is true breeding for round seeds and a plant that is true breeding for wrinkled seeds.

Each fertilized egg in the first generation had one dominant allele and one recessive allele for seed shape. Only one genotype was possible because all sperm formed by the male parent during meiosis had the wrinkled-seed allele, and all of the female parent's eggs had the round-seed allele. Meiosis also helped explain other inherited characteristics.

Figure 4 **Meiosis and Dominance**

Male Parent In the plant-cell nucleus below, each homologous chromosome has an allele for seed shape, and each allele carries the same instructions: to make wrinkled seeds.

Female Parent In the plant-cell nucleus below, each homologous chromosome has an allele for seed shape, and each allele carries the same instructions: to make round seeds.

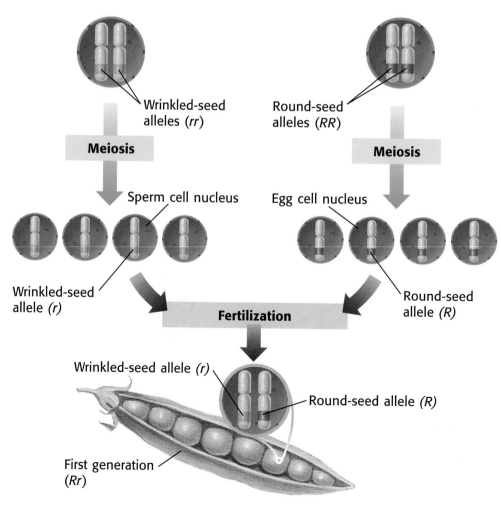

a Following **meiosis,** each sperm cell has a recessive allele for wrinkled seeds, and each egg cell has a dominant allele for round seeds.

b **Fertilization** of any egg by any sperm results in the same genotype (*Rr*) and the same phenotype (round). This result is exactly what Mendel found in his studies.

Wrinkled-seed alleles (*rr*)

Round-seed alleles (*RR*)

Meiosis

Meiosis

Sperm cell nucleus

Egg cell nucleus

Wrinkled-seed allele (*r*)

Round-seed allele (*R*)

Fertilization

Wrinkled-seed allele (*r*)

Round-seed allele (*R*)

First generation (*Rr*)

Sex Chromosomes

Information contained on chromosomes determines many of our traits. **Sex chromosomes** carry genes that determine sex. In humans, females have two X chromosomes. But human males have one X chromosome and one Y chromosome.

During meiosis, one of each of the chromosome pairs ends up in a sex cell. Females have two X chromosomes in each body cell. When meiosis produces the egg cells, each egg gets one X chromosome. Males have both an X chromosome and a Y chromosome in each body cell. Meiosis produces sperm with either an X or a Y chromosome. An egg fertilized by a sperm with an X chromosome will produce a female. If the sperm contains a Y chromosome, the offspring will be male, as shown in **Figure 5.**

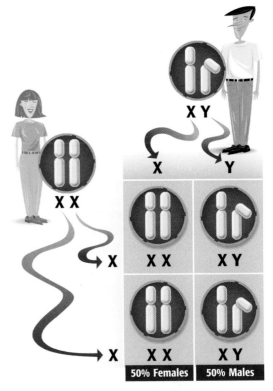

Figure 5 *Egg and sperm combine to form either the XX or XY combination.*

Sex-Linked Disorders

The Y chromosome does not carry all of the genes of an X chromosome. Females have two X chromosomes, so they carry two copies of each gene found on the X chromosome. This makes a backup gene available if one becomes damaged. Males have only one copy of each gene on their one X chromosome. The genes for certain disorders, such as colorblindness, are carried on the X chromosome. These disorders are called *sex-linked disorders*. Because the gene for such disorders is recessive, men are more likely to have sex-linked disorders.

People who are colorblind can have trouble distinguishing between shades of red and green. To help the colorblind, some cities have added shapes to their street lights, as shown in **Figure 6.** Hemophilia (HEE moh FIL ee uh) is another sex-linked disorder. Hemophilia prevents blood from clotting, and people with hemophilia bleed for a long time after small cuts. Hemophilia can be fatal.

sex chromosome one of the pair of chromosomes that determine the sex of an individual

Figure 6 *This stoplight in Canada is designed to help the colorblind see signals easily. This photograph was taken over a few minutes to show all three shapes.*

Figure 7 Pedigree for a Recessive Disease

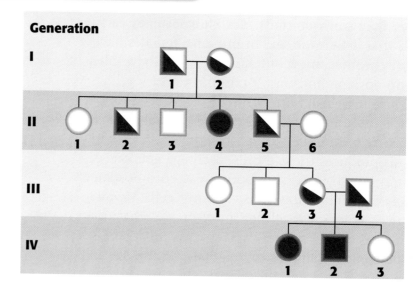

☐ Males ○ Females

Vertical lines connect children to their parents.

■ or ● A solid square or circle indicates that the person has a certain trait.

◪ or ◖ A half-filled square or circle indicates that the person is a carrier of the trait.

pedigree a diagram that shows the occurrence of a genetic trait in several generations of a family

Genetic Counseling

Hemophilia and other genetic disorders can be traced through a family tree. If people are worried that they might pass a disease to their children, they may consult a genetic counselor. These counselors often make use of a diagram known as a **pedigree,** which is a tool for tracing a trait through generations of a family. By making a pedigree, a counselor can often predict whether a person is a carrier of a hereditary disease. The pedigree shown in **Figure 7** traces a disease called *cystic fibrosis* (SIS tik FIE broh sis). Cystic fibrosis causes serious lung problems. People with this disease have inherited two recessive alleles. Both parents need to be carriers of the gene for the disease to show up in their children.

Pedigrees can be drawn up to trace any trait through a family tree. You could even draw a pedigree that would show how you inherited your hair color. Many different pedigrees could be drawn for a typical family.

Selective Breeding

For thousands of years, humans have seen the benefits of the careful breeding of animals. In *selective breeding,* organisms with desirable characteristics are mated. You have probably enjoyed the benefits of selective breeding, although you may not have realized it. For example, you have probably eaten an egg from a chicken that was bred to produce a larger number of eggs. Your pet dog might even be a result of selective breeding. Roses, like the one shown in **Figure 8,** have been selectively bred to produce large flowers. Wild roses are much smaller and have fewer petals than roses that you could buy at a nursery.

Figure 8 *Roses have been selectively bred to create large, bright flowers.*

Summary

- In mitosis, chromosomes are copied once, and then the nucleus divides once. In meiosis, chromosomes are copied once, and then the nucleus divides twice.

- The process of meiosis produces sex cells, which have half the number of chromosomes. These two halves combine during reproduction.

- In humans, females have two X chromosomes. So, each egg contains one X chromosome. Males have both an X and a Y chromosome. So, each sperm cell contains either an X or a Y chromosome.

- Sex-linked disorders occur in males more often than in females. Colorblindness and hemophilia are examples of sex-linked disorders.

- A pedigree is a diagram used to trace a trait through many generations of a family.

Using Key Terms

1. Use each of the following terms in the same sentence: *meiosis* and *sex chromosomes*.

In each of the following sentences, replace the incorrect term with the correct term from the word bank.

    pedigree   homologous chromosomes

    meiosis   mitosis

2. During fertilization, chromosomes are copied, and then the nucleus divides twice.

3. A Punnett square is used to show how inherited traits move through a family.

4. During meiosis, sex cells line up in the middle of the cell.

Understanding Key Ideas

5. Genes are found on
   a. chromosomes.
   b. proteins.
   c. alleles.
   d. sex cells.

6. If there are 14 chromosomes in pea plant cells, how many chromosomes are present in a sex cell of a pea plant?

7. Draw the eight steps of meiosis. Label one chromosome, and show its position in each step.

Interpreting Graphics

Use this pedigree to answer the question below.

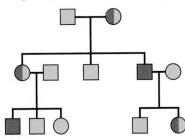

8. Is this disorder sex linked? Explain your reasoning.

Critical Thinking

9. **Identifying Relationships** Put the following in order of smallest to largest: chromosome, gene, and cell.

10. **Applying Concepts** A pea plant has purple flowers. What alleles for flower color could the sex cells carry?

Developed and maintained by the
National Science Teachers Association

For a variety of links related to this chapter, go to www.scilinks.org

Topic: Meiosis; Genetic Diseases, Screening, Counseling

SciLinks code: HSM0935; HSM0651

Model-Making Lab

Bug Builders, Inc.

Imagine that you are a designer for a toy company that makes toy alien bugs. The president of Bug Builders, Inc., wants new versions of the wildly popular Space Bugs, but he wants to use the bug parts that are already in the warehouse. It's your job to come up with a new bug design. You have studied how traits are passed from one generation to another. You will use this knowledge to come up with new combinations of traits and assemble the bug parts in new ways. Model A and Model B, shown below, will act as the "parent" bugs.

OBJECTIVES

Build models to further your understanding of inheritance.

Examine the traits of a population of offspring.

MATERIALS

- allele sacks (14) (supplied by your teacher)
- gumdrops, green and black (feet)
- map pins (eyes)
- marshmallows, large (head and body segments)
- pipe cleaners (tails)
- pushpins, green and blue (noses)
- scissors
- toothpicks, red and green (antennae)

SAFETY

Ask a Question

1 If there are two forms of each of the seven traits, then how many possible combinations are there?

Form a Hypothesis

2 Write a hypothesis that is a possible answer to the question above. Explain your reasoning.

Test the Hypothesis

3 Your teacher will display 14 allele sacks. The sacks will contain slips of paper with capital or lowercase letters on them. Take one piece of paper from each sack. (Remember: Capital letters represent dominant alleles, and lowercase letters represent recessive alleles.) One allele is from "Mom," and one allele is from "Dad." After you have recorded the alleles you have drawn, place the slips of paper back into the sack.

Model A ("Mom")
- red antennae
- 3 body segments
- curly tail
- 2 pairs of legs
- green nose
- black feet
- 3 eyes

Model B ("Dad")
- green antennae
- 2 body segments
- straight tail
- 3 pairs of legs
- blue nose
- green feet
- 2 eyes

Bug Family Traits				
Trait	Model A "Mom" allele	Model B "Dad" allele	New model "Baby" genotype	New model "Baby" phenotype
Antennae color				
Number of body segments				
Tail shape				
Number of leg pairs				
Nose color				
Foot color				
Number of eyes				

DO NOT WRITE IN BOOK

4 Create a table like the one above. Fill in the first two columns with the alleles that you selected from the sacks. Next, fill in the third column with the genotype of the new model ("Baby").

5 Use the information below to fill in the last column of the table.

Genotypes and Phenotypes	
RR or Rr—red antennae	rr—green antennae
SS or Ss—3 body segments	ss—2 body segments
CC or Cc—curly tail	cc—straight tail
LL or Ll—3 pairs of legs	ll—2 pairs of legs
BB or Bb—blue nose	bb—green nose
GG or Gg—green feet	gg—black feet
EE or Ee—2 eyes	ee—3 eyes

6 Now that you have filled out your table, you are ready to pick the parts you need to assemble your bug. (Toothpicks can be used to hold the head and body segments together and as legs to attach the feet to the body.)

Analyze the Results

1 **Organizing Data** Take a poll of the traits of the offspring. What are the ratios for each trait?

2 **Examining Data** Do any of the new models look exactly like the parents? Explain.

Draw Conclusions

3 **Interpreting Information** What are the possible genotypes of the parent bugs?

4 **Making Predictions** How many different genotypes are possible in the offspring?

Applying Your Data

Find a mate for your "Baby" bug. What are the possible genotypes and phenotypes of the offspring from this match?

Chapter Review

USING KEY TERMS

Complete each of the following sentences by choosing the correct term from the word bank.

sex cells	genotype
sex chromosomes	alleles
phenotype	meiosis

1 Sperm and eggs are known as _____.

2 The _____ is the expression of a trait and is determined by the combination of alleles called the _____.

3 _____ produces cells with half the normal number of chromosomes.

4 Different versions of the same genes are called _____.

UNDERSTANDING KEY IDEAS

Multiple Choice

5 Genes carry information that determines
  a. alleles.
  b. ribosomes.
  c. chromosomes.
  d. traits.

6 The process that produces sex cells is
  a. mitosis.
  b. photosynthesis.
  c. meiosis.
  d. probability.

7 The passing of traits from parents to offspring is called
  a. probability.
  b. heredity.
  c. recessive.
  d. meiosis.

8 If you cross a white flower with the genotype *pp* with a purple flower with the genotype *PP*, the possible genotypes in the offspring are
  a. *PP* and *pp*.
  b. all *Pp*.
  c. all *PP*.
  d. all *pp*.

9 For the cross in item 8, what would the phenotypes be?
  a. all white
  b. 3 purple and 1 white
  c. all purple
  d. half white, half purple

10 In meiosis,
  a. chromosomes are copied twice.
  b. the nucleus divides once.
  c. four cells are produced from a single cell.
  d. two cells are produced from a single cell.

11 When one trait is not completely dominant over another, it is called
  a. recessive.
  b. incomplete dominance.
  c. environmental factors.
  d. uncertain dominance.

Short Answer

12 Which sex chromosomes do females have? Which do males have?

13 In one or two sentences, define the term *recessive trait* in your own words.

14 How are sex cells different from other body cells?

15 What is a sex-linked disorder? Give one example of a sex-linked disorder that is found in humans.

CRITICAL THINKING

16 **Concept Mapping** Use the following terms to create a concept map: *meiosis, eggs, cell division, X chromosome, mitosis, Y chromosome, sperm,* and *sex cells.*

17 **Identifying Relationships** If you were a carrier of one allele for a certain recessive disorder, how could genetic counseling help you prepare for the future?

18 **Applying Concepts** If a child has blue eyes and both her parents have brown eyes, what does that tell you about the allele for blue eyes? Explain.

19 **Applying Concepts** What is the genotype of a pea plant that is true-breeding for purple flowers?

INTERPRETING GRAPHICS

Use the Punnett square below to answer the questions that follow.

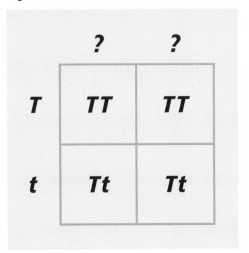

20 What is the unknown genotype?

21 If *T* represents the allele for tall pea plants and *t* represents the allele for short pea plants, what is the phenotype of each parent and of the offspring?

22 If each of the offspring were allowed to self-fertilize, what are the possible genotypes in the next generation?

23 What is the probability of each genotype in item 22?

Standardized Test Preparation

Read the passages below. Then, answer the questions that follow each passage.

Passage 1 The different versions of a gene are called *alleles*. When two different alleles occur together, one is often expressed while the other has no obvious effect on the organism's appearance. The expressed form of the trait is dominant. The trait that was not expressed when the dominant form of the trait was present is called *recessive*. Imagine a plant that has both purple and white alleles for flower color. If the plant blooms purple, then purple is the dominant form of the trait. Therefore, white is the recessive form.

1. According to the passage, which of the following statements is true?

   A All alleles are expressed all of the time.

   B All traits for flower color are dominant.

   C When two alleles are present, the expressed form of the trait is dominant.

   D A recessive form of a trait is always expressed.

2. According to the passage, a trait that is not expressed when the dominant form is present is called

   F recessive.

   G an allele.

   H heredity.

   I a gene.

3. According to the passage, which allele for flower color is dominant?

   A white

   B pink

   C purple

   D yellow

Passage 2 Sickle cell anemia is a recessive genetic disorder. People inherit this disorder only when they inherit the disease-causing recessive allele from both parents. The disease causes the body to make red blood cells that bend into a sickle (or crescent moon) shape. The sickle-shaped red blood cells break apart easily. Therefore, the blood of a person with sickle cell anemia carries less oxygen. Sickle-shaped blood cells also tend to get stuck in blood vessels. When a blood vessel is blocked, the blood supply to organs can be cut off. But the sickle-shaped blood cells can also protect a person from malaria. Malaria is a disease caused by an organism that invades red blood cells.

1. According to the passage, sickle cell anemia is a

   A recessive genetic disorder.

   B dominant genetic disorder.

   C disease caused by an organism that invades red blood cells.

   D disease also called *malaria*.

2. According to the passage, sickle cell anemia can help protect a person from

   F blocked blood vessels.

   G genetic disorders.

   H malaria.

   I low oxygen levels.

3. Which of the following is a fact in the passage?

   A When blood vessels are blocked, vital organs lose their blood supply.

   B When blood vessels are blocked, it causes the red blood cells to bend into sickle shapes.

   C The blood of a person with sickle cell anemia carries more oxygen.

   D Healthy red blood cells never get stuck in blood vessels.

The Punnett square below shows a cross between two flowering plants. Use this Punnett square to answer the questions that follow.

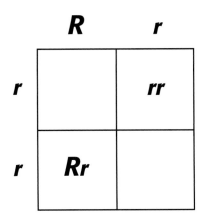

1. What is the genotype of the offspring represented in the upper left-hand box of the Punnett square?

   A *RR*

   B *Rr*

   C *rr*

   D *rrr*

2. What is the genotype of the offspring represented in the lower right-hand box of the Punnett square?

   F *RR*

   G *Rr*

   H *rr*

   I *rrr*

3. What is the ratio of *Rr* (purple-flowered plants) to *rr* (white-flowered plants) in the offspring?

   A 1:3

   B 2:2

   C 3:1

   D 4:0

Read each question below, and choose the best answer.

1. What is another way to write $4 \times 4 \times 4$?

   A 4^2

   B 4^3

   C 3^3

   D 3^4

2. Jane was making a design on top of her desk with pennies. She put 4 pennies in the first row, 7 pennies in the second row, and 13 pennies in the third row. If Jane continues this pattern, how many pennies will she put in the sixth row?

   F 25

   G 49

   H 97

   I 193

3. In which of the following lists are the numbers in order from smallest to greatest?

   A 0.012, 0.120, 0.123, 1.012

   B 1.012, 0.123, 0.120, 0.012

   C 0.123, 0.120, 0.012, 1.012

   D 0.123, 1.012, 0.120, 0.012

4. In which of the following lists are the numbers in order from smallest to greatest?

   F $-12.0, -15.5, 2.2, 4.0$

   G $-15.5, -12.0, 2.2, 4.0$

   H $-12.0, -15.5, 4.0, 2.2$

   I $2.2, 4.0, -12.0, -15.5$

5. Which of the following is equal to -11?

   A $7 + 4$

   B $-4 + 7$

   C $-7 + 4$

   D $-7 + -4$

6. Catherine earned $75 for working 8.5 h. How much did she earn per hour?

   F $10.12

   G $9.75

   H $8.82

   I $8.01

Standardized Test Preparation

Science in Action

This is a normal fruit fly under a scanning electron microscope.

This fruit fly has legs growing where its antennae should be.

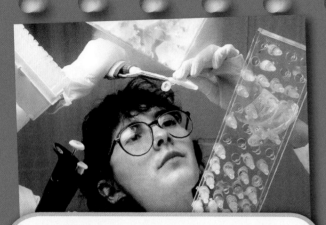

Science, Technology, and Society

Mapping the Human Genome

In 2003, scientists finished one of the most ambitious research projects ever. Researchers with the Human Genome Project (HGP) mapped the human body's complete set of genetic instructions, which is called the *genome*. You might be wondering whose genome the scientists are decoding. Actually, it doesn't matter—only 1% of each person's genetic material is unique. The researchers' goals are to identify how tiny differences in that 1% make each of us who we are and to begin to understand how some differences can cause disease. Scientists are already using the map to think of new ways to treat genetic diseases, such as asthma, diabetes, and kidney disease.

Weird Science

Lab Rats with Wings

Drosophila melanogaster (droh SAHF i luh muh LAN uh GAS tuhr) is the scientific name for the fruit fly. This tiny insect has played a big role in helping scientists understand many illnesses. Because fruit flies reproduce every 2 weeks, scientists can alter a fruit fly gene and see the results of the experiment very quickly. Another important reason for using these "lab rats with wings" is that their genetic code is simple and well understood. Fruit flies have 12,000 genes, but humans have more than 30,000. Scientists use fruit flies to find out about diseases like cancer, Alzheimer's, and muscular dystrophy.

Language Arts ACTiViTY

WRITING SKILL The mythical creature called the *Chimera* (kie MIR uh) was said to be part lion, part goat, and part serpent. According to legend, the Chimera terrorized people for years until it was killed by a brave hero. The word *chimera* now refers to any organism that has parts from many organisms. Write a short story about the Chimera that describes what it looks like and how it came to be.

Social Studies ACTiViTY

WRITING SKILL Research DNA fingerprinting. Write a short report describing how DNA fingerprinting has affected the way criminals are caught.

Stacey Wong

Genetic Counselor If your family had a history of a particular disease, what would you do? Would you eat healthier foods, get more exercise, or visit your doctor regularly? All of those are good ideas, but Stacey Wong went a step farther. Her family's history of cancer helped her decide to become a genetic counselor. "Genetic counselors are usually part of a team of health professionals," she says, which can include physicians, nurses, dieticians, social workers, laboratory personnel, and others. "If a diagnosis is made by the geneticist," says Wong, "then I provide genetic counseling." When a patient visits a genetic counselor, the counselor asks many questions and builds a family medical history. Although counseling involves discussing what it means to have a genetic condition, Wong says "the most important part is to get to know the patient or family we are working with, listen to their concerns, gain an understanding of their values, help them to make decisions, and be their advocate."

Math ACTiViTY

The probability of inheriting genetic disease *A* is 1/10,000. The probability of inheriting genetic disease *B* is also 1/10,000. What is the probability that one person would inherit both genetic diseases *A* and *B*?

To learn more about these Science in Action topics, visit **go.hrw.com** and type in the keyword **HL5HERF**.

Current Science

Check out Current Science® articles related to this chapter by visiting **go.hrw.com**. Just type in the keyword **HL5CS05**.

Genes and DNA

About the PHOTO

These adult mice have no hair—not because their hair was shaved off but because these mice do not grow hair. In cells of these mice, the genes that normally cause hair to grow are not working. The genes were "turned off" by scientists who have learned to control the function of some genes. Scientists changed the genes of these mice to research medical problems such as cancer.

PRE-READING ACTIVITY

Graphic Organizer

Concept Map Before you read the chapter, create the graphic organizer entitled "Concept Map" described in the **Study Skills** section of the Appendix. As you read the chapter, fill in the concept map with details about DNA.

START-UP ACTIVITY

Fingerprint Your Friends

One way to identify people is by taking their finger-prints. Does it really work? Are everyone's fingerprints unique? Try this activity to find out.

Procedure

1. Rub the tip of a **pencil** back and forth across a **piece of tracing paper.** Make a large, dark mark.

2. Rub the tip of one of your fingers on the pencil mark. Then place a small **piece of transparent tape** over the darkened area on your finger.

3. Remove the tape, and stick it on **a piece of white paper.** Repeat steps 1–3 for the rest of your fingers.

4. Look at the fingerprints with a **magnifying lens.** What patterns do you see? Is the pattern the same on every finger?

Analysis

1. Compare your fingerprints with those of your classmates. Do any two people in your class have the same prints? Try to explain your findings.

SECTION 1

What Does DNA Look Like?

For many years, the structure of a DNA molecule was a puzzle to scientists. In the 1950s, two scientists deduced the structure while experimenting with chemical models. They later won a Nobel Prize for helping solve this puzzle!

READING WARM-UP

Objectives

- List three important events that led to understanding the structure of DNA.
- Describe the basic structure of a DNA molecule.
- Explain how DNA molecules can be copied.

Terms to Learn

DNA
nucleotide

READING STRATEGY

Prediction Guide Before reading this section, write the title of each heading in this section. Next, under each heading, write what you think you will learn.

Inherited characteristics are determined by genes, and genes are passed from one generation to the next. Genes are parts of chromosomes, which are structures in the nucleus of most cells. Chromosomes are made of protein and DNA. **DNA** stands for ***d**eoxyribo**n**ucleic **a**cid* (dee AHKS ee RIE boh noo KLEE ik AS id). DNA is the genetic material—the material that determines inherited characteristics. But what does DNA look like?

The Pieces of the Puzzle

Scientists knew that the material that makes up genes must be able to do two things. First, it must be able to give instructions for building and maintaining cells. Second, it must be able to be copied each time a cell divides, so that each cell contains identical genes. Scientists thought that these things could be done only by complex molecules, such as proteins. They were surprised to learn how much the DNA molecule could do.

Nucleotides: The Subunits of DNA

DNA is made of subunits called nucleotides. A **nucleotide** consists of a sugar, a phosphate, and a base. The nucleotides are identical except for the base. The four bases are *adenine, thymine, guanine,* and *cytosine.* Each base has a different shape. Scientists often refer to a base by the first letter of the base, *A, T, G,* and *C.* **Figure 1** shows models of the four nucleotides.

DNA **d**eoxyribo**n**ucleic **a**cid, a molecule that is present in all living cells and that contains the information that determines the traits that a living thing inherits and needs to live

nucleotide in a nucleic-acid chain, a subunit that consists of a sugar, a phosphate, and a nitrogenous base

Figure 1 **The Four Nucleotides of DNA**

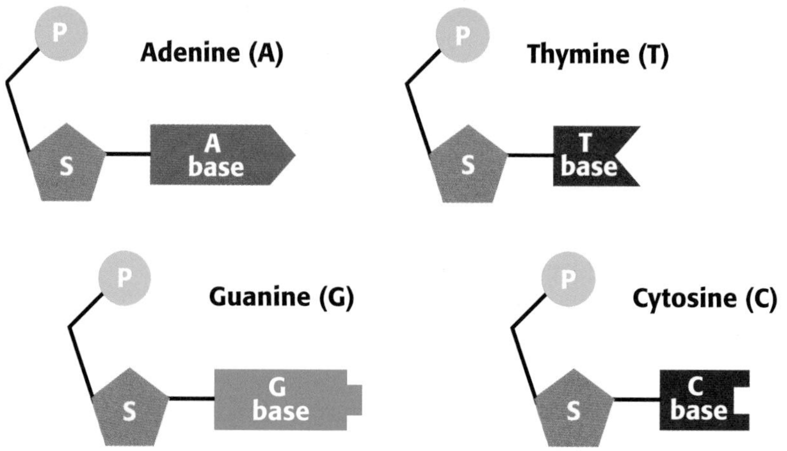

Chargaff's Rules

In the 1950s, a biochemist named Erwin Chargaff found that the amount of adenine in DNA always equals the amount of thymine. And he found that the amount of guanine always equals the amount of cytosine. His findings are known as *Chargaff's rules*. At the time of his discovery, no one knew the importance of these findings. But Chargaff's rules later helped scientists understand the structure of DNA.

Reading Check Summarize Chargaff's rules. (*See the Appendix for answers to Reading Checks.*)

Franklin's Discovery

More clues about the structure of DNA came from scientists in Britain. There, chemist Rosalind Franklin, shown in **Figure 2,** was able to make images of DNA molecules. She used a process known as *X-ray diffraction* to make these images. In this process, X rays are aimed at the DNA molecule. When an X ray hits a part of the molecule, the ray bounces off. The pattern made by the bouncing rays is captured on film. Franklin's images suggested that DNA has a spiral shape.

Watson and Crick's Model

At about the same time, two other scientists were also trying to solve the mystery of DNA's structure. They were James Watson and Francis Crick, shown in **Figure 3.** After seeing Franklin's X-ray images, Watson and Crick concluded that DNA must look like a long, twisted ladder. They were then able to build a model of DNA by using simple materials from their laboratory. Their model perfectly fit with both Chargaff's and Franklin's findings. The model eventually helped explain how DNA is copied and how it functions in the cell.

CONNECTION TO Chemistry

WRITING SKILL **Linus Pauling** Many scientists contributed to the discovery of DNA's structure. In fact, some scientists competed to be the first to make the discovery. One of these competitors was a chemist named Linus Pauling. Research and write a paragraph about how Pauling's work helped Watson and Crick.

Figure 2 *Rosalind Franklin used X-ray diffraction to make images of DNA that helped reveal the structure of DNA.*

Figure 3 *This photo shows James Watson (left) and Francis Crick (right) with their model of DNA.*

DNA's Double Structure

The shape of DNA is shown in **Figure 4.** As you can see, a strand of DNA looks like a twisted ladder. This shape is known as a *double helix* (DUB uhl HEE LIKS). The two sides of the ladder are made of alternating sugar parts and phosphate parts. The rungs of the ladder are made of a pair of bases. Adenine on one side of a rung always pairs with thymine on the other side. Guanine always pairs with cytosine.

Notice how the double helix structure matches Chargaff's observations. When Chargaff separated the parts of a sample of DNA, he found that the matching bases were always present in equal amounts. To model how the bases pair, Watson and Crick tried to match Chargaff's observations. They also used information from chemists about the size and shape of each of the nucleotides. As it turned out, the width of the DNA ladder matches the combined width of the matching bases. Only the correct pairs of bases fit within the ladder's width.

Making Copies of DNA

The pairing of bases allows the cell to *replicate*, or make copies of, DNA. Each base always bonds with only one other base. Thus, pairs of bases are *complementary* to each other, and both sides of a DNA molecule are complementary. For example, the sequence CGAC will bond to the sequence GTCG.

Making a Model of DNA

1. Gather assorted simple materials that you could use to build a basic model of DNA. You might use **clay, string, toothpicks, paper, tape, plastic foam,** or **pieces of food.**

2. Work with a partner or a small team to build your model. Use your book and other resources to check the details of your model.

3. Show your model to your classmates. Give your classmates feedback about the scientific aspects of their models.

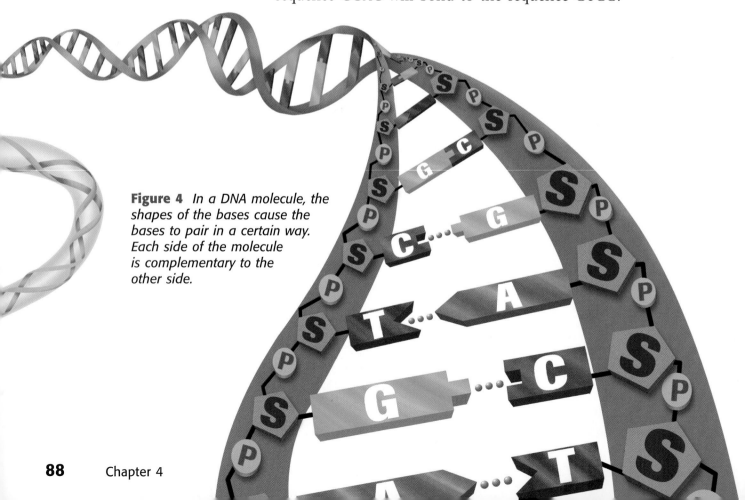

Figure 4 *In a DNA molecule, the shapes of the bases cause the bases to pair in a certain way. Each side of the molecule is complementary to the other side.*

How Copies Are Made

During replication, as shown in **Figure 5,** a DNA molecule is split down the middle, where the bases meet. The bases on each side of the molecule are used as a pattern for a new strand. As the bases on the original molecule are exposed, complementary nucleotides are added to each side of the ladder. Two DNA molecules are formed. Half of each of the molecules is old DNA, and half is new DNA.

When Copies Are Made

DNA is copied every time a cell divides. Each new cell gets a complete copy of all the DNA. The job of unwinding, copying, and re-winding the DNA is done by proteins within the cell. So, DNA is usually found with several kinds of proteins. Other proteins help with the process of carrying out the instructions written in the code of the DNA.

✓ **Reading Check** How often is DNA copied?

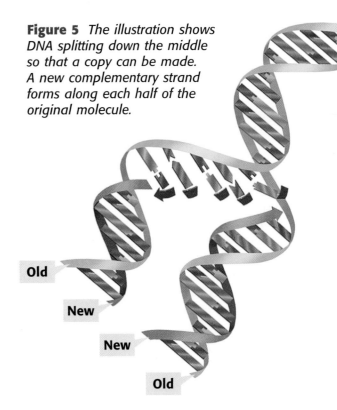

Figure 5 *The illustration shows DNA splitting down the middle so that a copy can be made. A new complementary strand forms along each half of the original molecule.*

Old

New

New

Old

SECTION Review

Summary

- DNA is the material that makes up genes. It carries coded information that is copied in each new cell.

- The DNA molecule looks like a twisted ladder. The two halves are long strings of nucleotides. The rungs are complementary pairs of bases.

- Because each base has a complementary base, DNA can be replicated accurately.

Using Key Terms

1. Use the term *DNA* in a sentence.

2. In your own words, write a definition for the term *nucleotide*.

Understanding Key Ideas

3. List three important events that led to understanding the structure of DNA.

4. Which of the following is NOT part of a nucleotide?
   a. base
   b. sugar
   c. fat
   d. phosphate

Math Skills

5. If a sample of DNA contained 20% cytosine, what percentage of guanine would be in this sample? What percentage of adenine would be in the sample? Explain.

Critical Thinking

6. **Making Inferences** Explain what is meant by the statement "DNA unites all organisms."

7. **Applying Concepts** What would the complementary strand of DNA be for the sequence of bases below?

   C T T A G G C T T A C C A

8. **Analyzing Processes** How are copies of DNA made? Draw a picture as part of your answer.

Developed and maintained by the National Science Teachers Association

For a variety of links related to this chapter, go to www.scilinks.org

Topic: DNA; Genes and Traits
SciLinks code: HSM0418; HSM0647

How DNA Works

Almost every cell in your body contains 1.5 m of DNA. How does all of the DNA fit in a cell? And how does the DNA hold a code that affects your traits?

DNA is found in the cells of all organisms, including bacteria, mosquitoes, and humans. Each organism has a unique set of DNA. But DNA functions the same way in all organisms.

Unraveling DNA

DNA is often wound around proteins, coiled into strands, and then bundled up even more. In a cell that lacks a nucleus, each strand of DNA forms a loose loop within the cell. In a cell that has a nucleus, the strands of DNA and proteins are bundled into chromosomes, as shown in **Figure 1.**

The structure of DNA allows DNA to hold information. The order of the bases on one side of the molecule is a code that carries information. A *gene* consists of a string of nucleotides that give the cell information about how to make a specific trait. There is an enormous amount of DNA, so there can be a large variety of genes. Humans have at least 30,000 genes.

✔ **Reading Check** What makes up a gene? (*See the Appendix for answers to Reading Checks.*)

Figure 1 Unraveling DNA

ⓐ A typical skin cell has a diameter of about 0.0025 cm. The DNA in the nucleus of each cell codes for proteins that determine traits such as skin color.

ⓑ The DNA in the nucleus is part of a material called *chromatin*. Long strands of chromatin are usually bundled loosely within the nucleus.

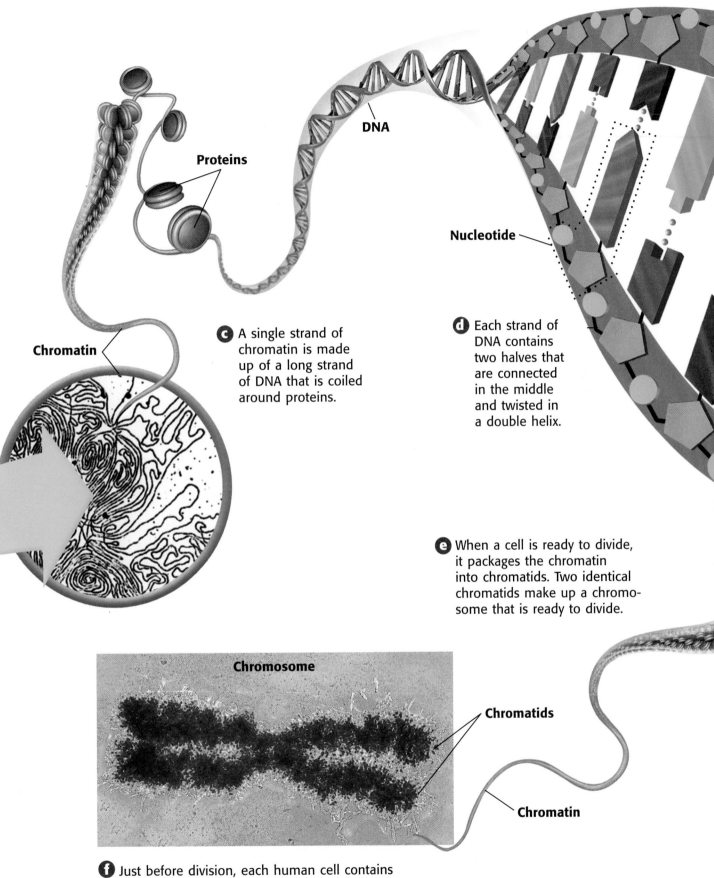

DNA

Proteins

Nucleotide

Chromatin

c A single strand of chromatin is made up of a long strand of DNA that is coiled around proteins.

d Each strand of DNA contains two halves that are connected in the middle and twisted in a double helix.

e When a cell is ready to divide, it packages the chromatin into chromatids. Two identical chromatids make up a chromosome that is ready to divide.

Chromosome

Chromatids

Chromatin

f Just before division, each human cell contains 46 chromosomes. These chromosomes contain two identical copies of all of the cell's genetic material.

INTERNET ACTIVITY

For another activity related to this chapter, go to **go.hrw.com** and type in the keyword **HL5DNAW.**

Genes and Proteins

The DNA code is read like a book—from one end to the other and in one direction. The bases form the alphabet of the code. Groups of three bases are the codes for specific amino acids. For example, the three bases CCA form the code for the amino acid proline. The bases AGC form the code for the amino acid serine. A long string of amino acids forms a protein. Thus, each gene is usually a set of instructions for making a protein.

Proteins and Traits

How are proteins related to traits? Proteins are found throughout cells and cause most of the differences that you can see among organisms. Proteins act as chemical triggers and messengers for many of the processes within cells. Proteins help determine how tall you grow, what colors you can see, and whether your hair is curly or straight. Proteins exist in an almost limitless variety. A single organism may have thousands of genes that code for thousands of proteins.

Help from RNA

Another type of molecule that helps make proteins is called **RNA,** or *ribonucleic acid* (RIE boh noo KLEE ik AS id). RNA is so similar to DNA that RNA can serve as a temporary copy of a DNA sequence. Several forms of RNA help in the process of changing the DNA code into proteins, as shown in **Figure 2.**

RNA ribonucleic acid, a molecule that is present in all living cells and that plays a role in protein production

Figure 2 *Proteins are built in the cytoplasm by using RNA copies of a segment of DNA. The order of the bases on the RNA determines the order of amino acids that are assembled at the ribosome.*

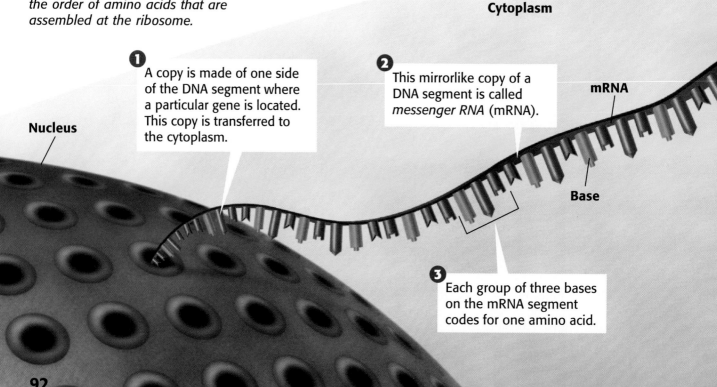

Cytoplasm

1 A copy is made of one side of the DNA segment where a particular gene is located. This copy is transferred to the cytoplasm.

2 This mirrorlike copy of a DNA segment is called *messenger RNA* (mRNA).

mRNA

Nucleus

Base

3 Each group of three bases on the mRNA segment codes for one amino acid.

The Making of a Protein

The first step in making a protein is to copy one side of the segment of DNA containing a gene. A mirrorlike copy of the DNA segment is made out of RNA. This copy of the DNA segment is called *messenger RNA* (mRNA). It moves out of the nucleus and into the cytoplasm of the cell.

In the cytoplasm, the messenger RNA is fed through a protein assembly line. The "factory" that runs this assembly line is known as a ribosome. A **ribosome** is a cell organelle composed of RNA and protein. The messenger RNA is fed through the ribosome three bases at a time. Then, molecules of *transfer RNA* (tRNA) translate the RNA message. Each transfer RNA molecule picks up a specific amino acid from the cytoplasm. Inside the ribosome, bases on the transfer RNA match up with bases on the messenger RNA like pieces of a puzzle. The transfer RNA molecules then release their amino acids. The amino acids become linked in a growing chain. As the entire segment of messenger RNA passes through the ribosome, the growing chain of amino acids folds up into a new protein molecule.

✓ Reading Check What do the transfer RNA molecules transfer?

Code Combinations

A given sequence of three bases codes for one amino acid. For example, AGT is one possible sequence. How many different sequences of the four DNA base types are possible? (Hint: Make a list.)

ribosome a cell organelle composed of RNA and protein; the site of protein synthesis

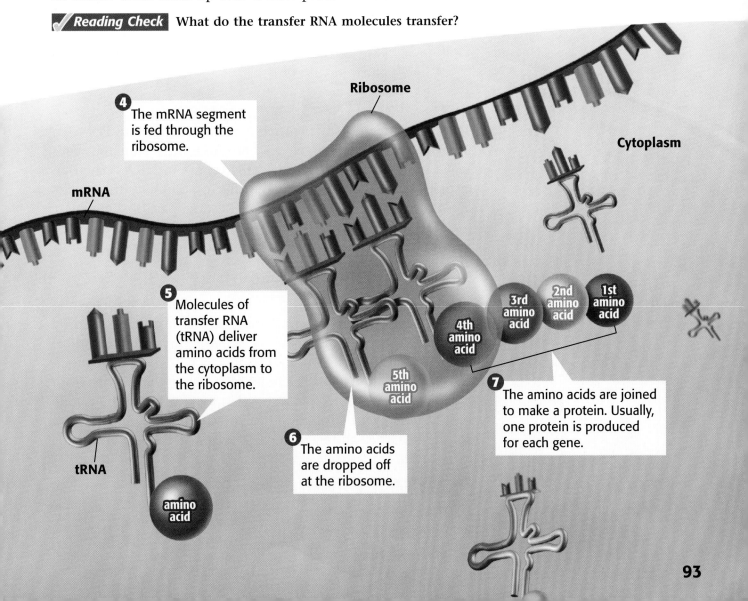

Ribosome

4 The mRNA segment is fed through the ribosome.

Cytoplasm

mRNA

5 Molecules of transfer RNA (tRNA) deliver amino acids from the cytoplasm to the ribosome.

3rd amino acid

2nd amino acid

1st amino acid

4th amino acid

5th amino acid

7 The amino acids are joined to make a protein. Usually, one protein is produced for each gene.

6 The amino acids are dropped off at the ribosome.

tRNA

amino acid

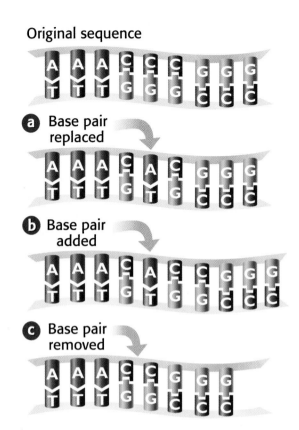

Original sequence

ⓐ Base pair replaced

ⓑ Base pair added

ⓒ Base pair removed

Figure 3 *The original base sequence on the top has been changed to illustrate (a) a substitution, (b) an insertion, and (c) a deletion.*

mutation a change in the nucleotide-base sequence of a gene or DNA molecule

Changes in Genes

Imagine that you have been invited to ride on a new roller coaster at the state fair. Before you climb into the front car, you are told that some of the metal parts on the coaster have been replaced by parts made of a different substance. Would you still want to ride this roller coaster? Perhaps a strong metal was used as a substitute. Or perhaps a material that is not strong enough was used. Imagine what would happen if cardboard were used instead of metal!

Mutations

Substitutions like the ones in the roller coaster can accidentally happen in DNA. Changes in the number, type, or order of bases on a piece of DNA are known as **mutations.** Sometimes, a base is left out. This kind of change is known as a *deletion.* Or an extra base might be added. This kind of change is known as an *insertion.* The most common change happens when the wrong base is used. This kind of change is known as a *substitution.* **Figure 3** illustrates these three types of mutations.

Do Mutations Matter?

There are three possible consequences to changes in DNA: an improved trait, no change, or a harmful trait. Fortunately, cells make some proteins that can detect errors in DNA. When an error is found, it is usually fixed. But occasionally the repairs are not accurate, and the mistakes become part of the genetic message. If the mutation occurs in the sex cells, the changed gene can be passed from one generation to the next.

How Do Mutations Happen?

Mutations happen regularly because of random errors when DNA is copied. In addition, damage to DNA can be caused by abnormal things that happen to cells. Any physical or chemical agent that can cause a mutation in DNA is called a *mutagen.* Examples of mutagens include high-energy radiation from X rays and ultraviolet radiation. Ultraviolet radiation is one type of energy in sunlight. It is responsible for suntans and sunburns. Other mutagens include asbestos and the chemicals in cigarette smoke.

✓ Reading Check What is a mutagen?

An Example of a Substitution

A mutation, such as a substitution, can be harmful because it may cause a gene to produce the wrong protein. Consider the DNA sequence GAA. When copied as mRNA, this sequence gives the instructions to place the amino acid glutamic acid into the growing protein. If a mistake happens and the original DNA sequence is changed to GTA, the sequence will code for the amino acid valine instead.

This simple change in an amino acid can cause the disease *sickle cell anemia.* Sickle cell anemia affects red blood cells. When valine is substituted for glutamic acid in a blood protein, as shown in **Figure 4,** the red blood cells are changed into a sickle shape.

The sickle cells are not as good at carrying oxygen as normal red blood cells are. Sickle cells are also likely to get stuck in blood vessels and cause painful and dangerous clots.

✓ *Reading Check* What causes sickle cell anemia?

SCHOOL to HOME

An Error in the Message

The sentence below is the result of an error similar to a DNA mutation. The original sentence was made up of three-letter words, but an error was made in this copy. Explain the idea of mutations to your parent. Then, work together to find the mutation, and write the sentence correctly.

THE IGB ADC ATA TET HEB IGR EDR AT.

ACTIVITY

Figure 4 How Sickle Cell Anemia Results from a Mutation

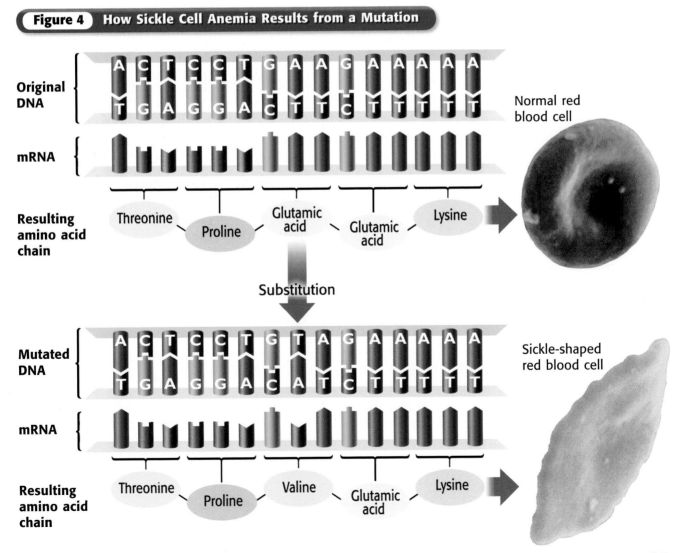

Original DNA

mRNA

Resulting amino acid chain: Threonine — Proline — Glutamic acid — Glutamic acid — Lysine

Normal red blood cell

Substitution

Mutated DNA

mRNA

Resulting amino acid chain: Threonine — Proline — Valine — Glutamic acid — Lysine

Sickle-shaped red blood cell

Uses of Genetic Knowledge

In the years since Watson and Crick made their model, scientists have learned a lot about genetics. This knowledge is often used in ways that benefit humans. But some uses of genetic knowledge also cause ethical and scientific debates.

Genetic Engineering

Scientists can manipulate individual genes within organisms. This kind of manipulation is called *genetic engineering.* In some cases, genes may be transferred from one type of organism to another. An example of a genetically engineered plant is shown in **Figure 5.** Scientists added a gene from fireflies to this plant. The gene produces a protein that causes the plant to glow.

Scientists may use genetic engineering to create new products, such as drugs, foods, or fabrics. For example, bacteria may be used to make the proteins found in spider's silk. Or cows may be used to produce human proteins. In some cases, this practice could produce a protein that is needed by a person who has a genetic disease. However, some scientists worry about the dangers of creating genetically engineered organisms.

Figure 5 *This genetically engineered tobacco plant contains firefly genes.*

Genetic Identification

Your DNA is unique, so it can be used like a fingerprint to identify you. *DNA fingerprinting* identifies the unique patterns in an individual's DNA. DNA samples are now used as evidence in crimes, as shown in **Figure 6.** Similarities between people's DNA can reveal other information, too. For example, DNA can be used to identify family relations or hereditary diseases.

Identical twins have truly identical DNA. Scientists are now able to create something like a twin, called a clone. A *clone* is a new organism that has an exact copy of another organism's genes. Clones of several types of organisms, including some mammals, have been developed by scientists. However, the possibility of cloning humans is still being debated among both scientists and politicians.

Reading Check What is a clone?

Figure 6 *This scientist is gathering dead skin cells from a crime scene. DNA from the cells could be used as evidence of a criminal's identity.*

CONNECTION TO Social Studies

Genetic Property Could you sell your DNA code? Using current laws and technology, someone could sell genetic information like authors sell books. It is also possible to file a patent to establish ownership of the information used to make a product. Thus, a patent can be filed for a unique sequence of DNA or for new genetic engineering technology. Conduct research to find an existing patent on a genetic sequence or genetic engineering technology.

Summary

- A gene is a set of instructions for assembling a protein. DNA is the molecular carrier of these genetic instructions.
- Every organism has DNA in its cells. Humans have 1.5 m of DNA in each cell. This DNA makes up over 30,000 genes.
- Within a gene, each group of three bases codes for one amino acid. A sequence of amino acids is linked to make a protein.
- Proteins are fundamental to the function of cells and the expression of traits.
- Proteins are assembled within the cytoplasm through a multi-step process that is assisted by several forms of RNA.
- Genes can become mutated when the order of the bases is changed. Three main types of mutations are possible: insertion, deletion, and substitution.
- Genetic knowledge has many practical uses. Some applications of genetic knowledge are controversial.

Using Key Terms

1. Use each of the following terms in the same sentence: *ribosome* and *RNA*.

2. In your own words, write a definition for the term *mutation*.

Understanding Key Ideas

3. Explain the relationship between genes and proteins.

4. List three possible types of mutations.

5. Which type of mutation causes sickle cell anemia?
   a. substitution   c. deletion
   b. insertion   d. mutagen

Math Skills

6. A set of 23 chromosomes in a human cell contains 3.2 billion pairs of DNA bases in sequence. On average, about how many pairs of bases are in each chromosome?

Critical Thinking

7. **Applying Concepts** In which cell type might a mutation be passed from generation to generation? Explain.

8. **Making Comparisons** How is genetic engineering different from natural reproduction?

Interpreting Graphics

The illustration below shows a sequence of bases on one strand of a DNA molecule. Use the illustration below to answer the questions that follow.

9. How many amino acids are coded for by the sequence on one side (A) of this DNA strand?

10. What is the order of bases on the complementary side of the strand (B), from left to right?

11. If a G were inserted as the first base on the top side (A), what would the order of bases be on the complementary side (B)?

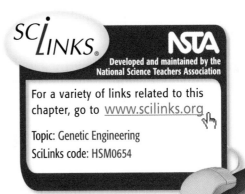

SCILINKS®

Developed and maintained by the National Science Teachers Association

For a variety of links related to this chapter, go to www.scilinks.org

Topic: Genetic Engineering
SciLinks code: HSM0654

Model-Making Lab

Base-Pair Basics

You have learned that DNA is shaped something like a twisted ladder. The side rails of the ladder are made of sugar parts and phosphate parts. The two side rails are connected to each other by parts called *bases*. The bases join in pairs to form the rungs of the ladder. Within DNA, each base can pair with only one other base. Each of these pairs is called a *base pair*. When DNA replicates, enzymes separate the base pairs, which breaks the rungs of the ladder in half. Then, each half of the DNA ladder can be used as a template for building a new half. In this activity, you will construct a paper model of DNA and use it to model the replication process.

Procedure

1. Trace the models of nucleotides below onto white paper. Label the pieces "A" (**a**denine), "T" (**t**hymine), "C" (**c**ytosine), and "G" (**g**uanine). Draw the pieces again on colored paper. Use a different color for each type of base. Draw the pieces as large as you want, and draw as many of the white pieces and as many of the colored pieces as time will allow.

2. Carefully cut out all of the pieces.

3. Put all of the colored pieces in the classroom into a large paper bag. Spread all of the white pieces in the classroom onto a large table.

4. Remove nine colored pieces from the bag. Arrange the colored pieces in any order in a straight column so that the letters *A, T, C,* and *G* are right side up. Be sure to fit the sugar notches to the phosphate tabs. Draw this arrangement.

5. Find the white bases that correctly pair with the nine colored bases. Remember the base-pairing rules, and pair the bases according to those rules.

6. Pair the pieces by fitting tabs to notches. The letters on the white pieces should be upside down. You now have a model of a double-stranded piece of DNA. The strand contains nine pairs of complementary nucleotides. Draw your model.

Nucleotides

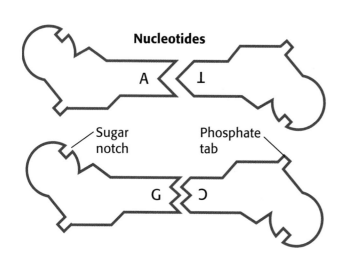

Sugar notch

Phosphate tab

Analyze the Results

1 **Identifying Patterns** Now, separate the two halves of your DNA strand along the middle of the base pair rungs of the ladder. Keep the side rails together by keeping the sugar notches fitted to the phosphate tabs. Draw this arrangement.

2 **Recognizing Patterns** Look at the drawing made in the previous step. Along each strand in the drawing, write the letters of the bases that complement the bases in that strand.

3 **Examining Data** Find all of the bases that you need to complete replication. Find white pieces to pair with the bases on the left, and find colored pieces to pair with the bases on the right. Be sure that the tabs and notches fit and the sides are straight. You have now replicated your model of DNA. Are the two models identical? Draw your results.

Draw Conclusions

4 **Interpreting Information** State the correct base-pairing rules. How do these rules make DNA replication possible?

5 **Evaluating Models** What happens when you attempt to pair thymine with guanine? Do they fit together? Are the sides straight? Do all of the tabs and notches fit? Explain.

Applying Your Data

Construct a 3-D model of a DNA molecule that shows DNA's twisted-ladder structure. Use your imagination and creativity to select materials. You may want to use licorice, gum balls, and toothpicks or pipe cleaners and paper clips.

1. Display your model in your classroom.

2. Take a vote to decide which models are the most accurate and the most creative.

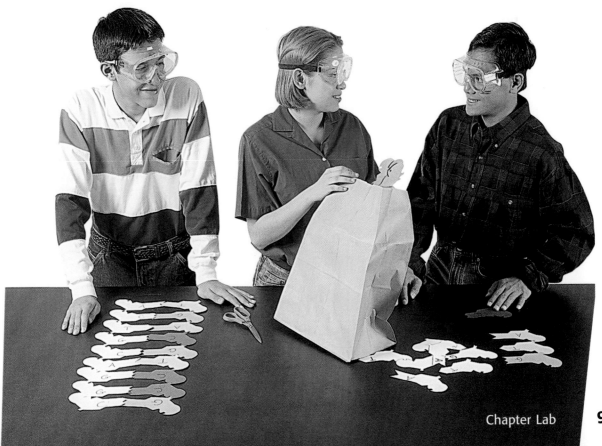

Chapter Review

USING KEY TERMS

1 Use the following terms in the same sentence: *mutation* and *mutagen*.

The statements below are false. For each statement, replace the underlined term to make a true statement.

2 The information in DNA is coded in the order of <u>amino acids</u> along one side of the DNA molecule.

3 The "factory" that assembles proteins based on the DNA code is called a <u>gene</u>.

UNDERSTANDING KEY IDEAS

Multiple Choice

4 James Watson and Francis Crick

  a. took X-ray pictures of DNA.

  b. discovered that genes are in chromosomes.

  c. bred pea plants to study heredity.

  d. made models to figure out DNA's shape.

5 In a DNA molecule, which of the following bases pair together?

  a. adenine and cytosine

  b. thymine and adenine

  c. thymine and guanine

  d. cytosine and thymine

6 A gene can be all of the following EXCEPT

  a. a set of instructions for a trait.

  b. a complete chromosome.

  c. instructions for making a protein.

  d. a portion of a strand of DNA.

7 Which of the following statements about DNA is NOT true?

  a. DNA is found in all organisms.

  b. DNA is made up of five subunits.

  c. DNA has a structure like a twisted ladder.

  d. Mistakes can be made when DNA is copied.

8 Within the cell, where are proteins assembled?

  a. the cytoplasm

  b. the nucleus

  c. the amino acids

  d. the chromosomes

9 Changes in the type or order of the bases in DNA are called

  a. nucleotides.

  b. mutations.

  c. RNA.

  d. genes.

Short Answer

10 What would be the complementary strand of DNA for the following sequence of bases?

C T T A G G C T T A C C A

11 If the DNA sequence TGAGCCATGA is changed to TGAGCACATGA, what kind of mutation has occurred?

12 Explain how the DNA in genes relates to the traits of an organism.

13 Why is DNA frequently found associated with proteins inside of cells?

14 What is the difference between DNA and RNA?

15 How does breeding differ from genetic engineering?

CRITICAL THINKING

16 Concept Mapping Use the following terms to create a concept map: *bases, adenine, thymine, nucleotides, guanine, DNA,* and *cytosine.*

17 Analyzing Processes Draw and label a picture that explains how DNA is copied.

18 Analyzing Processes Draw and label a picture that explains how proteins are made.

19 Applying Concepts The following DNA sequence codes for how many amino acids?

T C A G C C A C C T A T G G A

20 Making Inferences Why does the government make laws about the use of chemicals that are known to be mutagens?

INTERPRETING GRAPHICS

The illustration below shows the process of replication of a DNA strand. Use this illustration to answer the questions that follow.

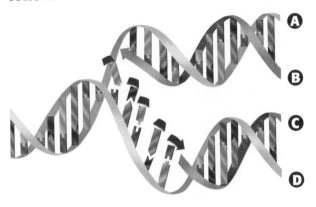

21 Which strands are part of the original molecule?

a. A and B

b. A and C

c. A and D

d. None of the above

22 Which strands are new?

a. A and B

b. B and C

c. C and D

d. None of the above

23 Which strands are complementary?

a. A and C

b. B and C

c. All of the strands

d. None of the strands

Standardized Test Preparation

Read each of the passages below. Then, answer the questions that follow each passage.

Passage 1 The tension in the courtroom was so thick that you could cut it with a knife. The prosecuting attorney presented this evidence: "DNA analysis indicates that blood found on the defendant's shoes matches the blood of the victim. The odds of this match happening by chance are 1 in 20 million." The jury members were stunned by these figures. Can there be any doubt that the defendant is guilty?

DNA is increasingly used as evidence in court cases. Traditional fingerprinting has been used for more than 100 years, and it has been an extremely important identification tool. Recently, DNA fingerprinting, also called *DNA profiling,* has started to replace traditional techniques. DNA profiling has been used to clear thousands of wrongly accused or convicted individuals. However, there is some controversy over whether DNA evidence should be used to prove a suspect's guilt.

1. What does the first sentence in this passage describe?
   A the air pollution in a particular place
   B the feeling that a person might experience during an event
   C the motion of an object
   D the reason that a person was probably guilty of a crime

2. Which of the following best describes the main idea of the second paragraph of this passage?
   F A defendant was proven guilty by DNA analysis.
   G Court battles involving DNA fingerprinting are very exciting.
   H The technique of DNA profiling is increasingly used in court cases.
   I The technique of DNA profiling is controversial.

Passage 2 Most of the biochemicals found in living things are proteins. In fact, other than water, proteins are the most abundant molecules in your cells. Proteins have many functions, including regulating chemical activities, transporting and storing materials, and providing structural support.

Every protein is composed of small "building blocks" called *amino acids*. Amino acids are molecules that are composed of carbon, hydrogen, oxygen, and nitrogen atoms. Some amino acids also include sulfur atoms. Amino acids chemically bond to form proteins of many shapes and sizes.

The function of a protein depends on the shape of the bonded amino acids. If even a single amino acid is missing or out of place, the protein may not function correctly or may not function. Foods such as meat, fish, cheese, and beans contain proteins, which are broken down into amino acids as the foods are digested. Your body can then use these amino acids to make new proteins.

1. In the passage, what does *biochemical* mean?
   A a chemical found in nonliving things
   B a chemical found in living things
   C a pair of chemicals
   D a protein

2. According to the passage, which of the following statements is true?
   F Amino acids contain carbon dioxide.
   G Amino acids contain proteins.
   H Proteins are made of living things.
   I Proteins are made of amino acids.

The diagram below shows an original sequence of DNA and three possible mutations. Use the diagram to answer the questions that follow.

Original sequence

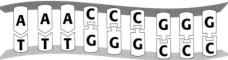

Mutation A

Mutation B

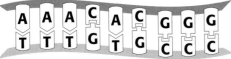

Mutation C

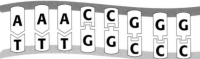

1. In which mutation was an original base pair replaced?
   A Mutation A
   B Mutation B
   C Mutation C
   D There is not enough information to determine the answer.

2. In which mutation was a new base pair added?
   F Mutation A
   G Mutation B
   H Mutation C
   I There is not enough information to determine the answer.

3. In which mutation was an original base pair removed?
   A Mutation A
   B Mutation B
   C Mutation C
   D There is not enough information to determine the answer.

Read each question below, and choose the best answer.

1. Mary was making a design on top of her desk with marbles. She put 3 marbles in the first row, 7 marbles in the second row, 15 marbles in the third row, and 31 marbles in the fourth row. If Mary continues this pattern, how many marbles will she put in the seventh row?
   A 46
   B 63
   C 127
   D 255

2. Bobby walked 3 1/2 km on Saturday, 2 1/3 km on Sunday, and 1 km on Monday. How many kilometers did Bobby walk on those 3 days?
   F 5 1/6
   G 5 5/6
   H 6 1/6
   I 6 5/6

3. Marie bought a new aquarium for her goldfish. The aquarium is 60 cm long, 20 cm wide, and 30 cm high. Which equation could be used to find the volume of water needed to fill the aquarium to 25 cm deep?

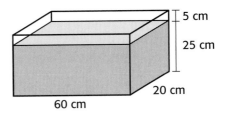

   A $V = 30 \times 60 \times 20$
   B $V = 25 \times 60 \times 20$
   C $V = 30 \times 60 \times 20 - 5$
   D $V = 30 \times 60 \times 25$

4. How is the product of $6 \times 6 \times 6 \times 4 \times 4 \times 4$ expressed in scientific notation?
   F $6^4 \times 3^6$
   G $6^3 \times 4^3$
   H $3^6 \times 3^4$
   I 24^6

Science in Action

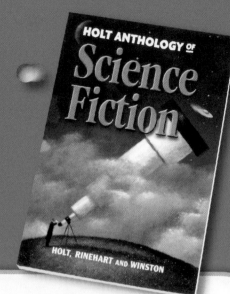

Scientific Debate

Supersquash or Frankenfruit?

Some food that you buy may have been developed in a new way. Food producers may use genetic engineering to make food crops easier to grow or sell, more nutritious, or resistant to pests and disease. More than half of the packaged foods sold in the United States are likely to contain ingredients from genetically modified organisms.

The U.S. government has stated that research shows that these foods are safe. But some scientists are concerned that genes introduced into crop plants could cause new environmental or health problems. For example, people who are allergic to peanuts might also be allergic to tomato plants that contain peanut genes.

Science Fiction

"Moby James" by Patricia A. McKillip

Rob Trask and his family live on a space station. Rob thinks that his real brother was sent back to Earth. The person who claims to be his brother, James, is really either some sort of mutated plant or a mutant pair of dirty sweat socks.

Now, Rob has another problem—his class is reading Herman Melville's novel *Moby Dick*. As he reads the novel, Rob becomes convinced that his brother is a great white mutant whale—Moby James. To see how Rob solves his problems, read "Moby James" in the *Holt Anthology of Science Fiction*.

Language Arts ACTiViTy

WRITING SKILL Read "Moby James" by Patricia A. McKillip. Then, write your own short science-fiction story about a mutant organism. Be sure to incorporate some science into your science fiction.

Math ACTiViTy

Write a survey about genetically altered foods. Ask your teacher to approve your questions. Ask at least 15 people to answer your survey. Create graphs to summarize your results.

Lydia Villa-Komaroff

Genetic Researcher When Lydia Villa-Komaroff was young, science represented "a kind of refuge" for her. She grew up in a very large family that lived in a very small house. "I always wanted to find things out. I was one of those kids who took things apart."

In college, Villa-Komaroff became very interested in the process of embryonic development—how a simple egg grows into a complex animal. This interest led her to study genes and the way that genes code for proteins. For example, insulin is a protein that is normally produced by the human body. Often, people who suffer from diabetes lack the insulin gene, so their bodies can't make insulin. These people may need to inject insulin into their blood as a drug treatment.

Before the research by Villa-Komaroff's team was done, insulin was difficult to produce. Villa-Komaroff's team isolated the human gene that codes for insulin. Then, the scientists inserted the normal human insulin gene into the DNA of bacteria. This inserted gene caused the bacteria to produce insulin. This technique was a new and more efficient way to produce insulin. Now, most of the insulin used for diabetes treatment is made in this way. Many genetic researchers dream of making breakthroughs like the one that Villa-Komaroff made in her work with insulin.

Social Studies ACTIVITY

WRITING SKILL Do some research about several women, such as Marie Curie, Barbara McClintock, or Maxine Frank Singer, who have done important scientific research. Write a short biography about one of these women.

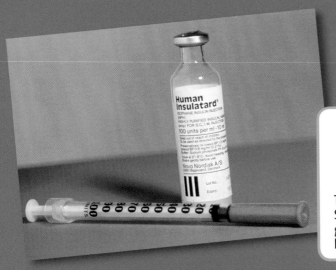

To learn more about these Science in Action topics, visit go.hrw.com and type in the keyword **HL5DNAF.**

Current Science

Check out Current Science® articles related to this chapter by visiting go.hrw.com. Just type in the keyword **HL5CS06.**

The Evolution of Living Things

About the PHOTO

What happened to this fish's face? This flounder wasn't born this way, but it did develop naturally. When young, a flounder looks and swims as most fish do. But as it becomes an adult, one of its eyes moves to the other side of its head, and the flounder begins to swim sideways. An adult flounder is adapted to swim and hide along the sandy bottom of coastal areas.

PRE-READING ACTIVITY

Graphic Organizer

Concept Map Before you read the chapter, create the graphic organizer entitled "Concept Map" described in the **Study Skills** section of the Appendix. As you read the chapter, fill in the concept map with details about evolution and natural selection.

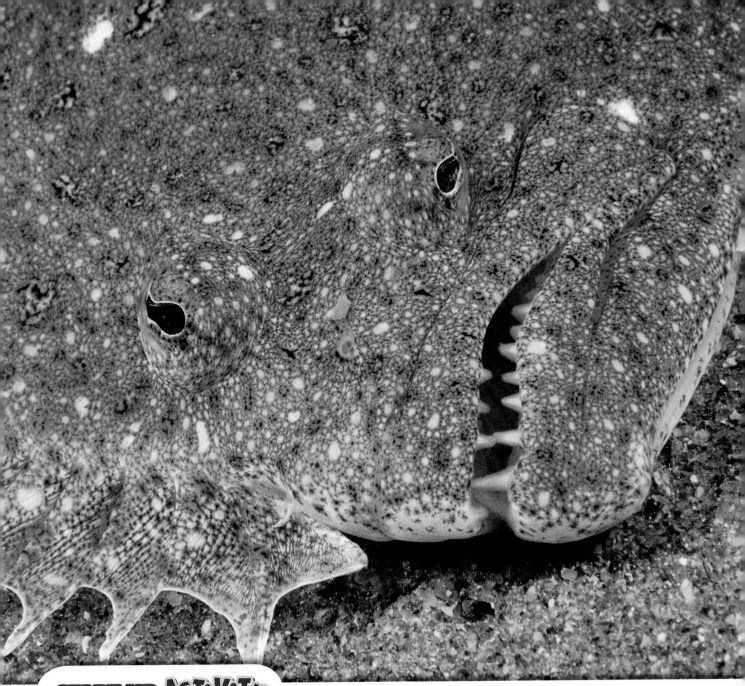

START-UP ACTIVITY

Out of Sight, Out of Mind

In this activity, you will see how traits can affect the success of an organism in a particular environment.

Procedure

1. Count out **25 colored marshmallows** and **25 white marshmallows.**

2. Ask your partner to look away while you spread the marshmallows out on a **white cloth.** Do not make a pattern with the marshmallows. Now, ask your partner to turn around and pick the first marshmallow that he or she sees.

3. Repeat step 2 ten times.

Analysis

1. How many white marshmallows did your partner pick? How many colored marshmallows did he or she pick?

2. What did the marshmallows and the cloth represent in your investigation? What effect did the color of the cloth have?

3. When an organism blends into its environment, the organism is *camouflaged*. How does this activity model camouflaged organisms in the wild? What are some weaknesses of this model?

Change over Time

If someone asked you to describe a frog, you might say that a frog has long hind legs, has bulging eyes, and croaks. But what color skin would you say that a frog has?

Once you start to think about frogs, you realize that frogs differ in many ways. These differences set one kind of frog apart from another. The frogs in **Figures 1, 2,** and **3** look different from each other, yet they may live in the same areas.

Differences Among Organisms

As you can see, each frog has a different characteristic that might help the frog survive. A characteristic that helps an organism survive and reproduce in its environment is called an **adaptation.** Adaptations may be physical, such as a long neck or striped fur. Or adaptations may be behaviors that help an organism find food, protect itself, or reproduce.

Living things that have the same characteristics may be members of the same species. A **species** is a group of organisms that can mate with one another to produce fertile offspring. For example, all strawberry poison arrow frogs are members of the same species and can mate with each other to produce more strawberry poison arrow frogs. Groups of individuals of the same species living in the same place make up a *population.*

✔ **Reading Check** How can you tell that organisms are members of the same species? (*See the Appendix for answers to Reading Checks.*)

Figure 2 The bright coloring of the strawberry poison arrow frog warns predators that the frog is poisonous.

▼ **Figure 1** The red-eyed tree frog hides among a tree's leaves during the day and comes out at night.

Figure 3 The smoky ▶ jungle frog blends into the forest floor.

Do Species Change over Time?

In a single square mile of rain forest, there may be dozens of species of frogs. Across the Earth, there are millions of different species of organisms. The species that live on Earth today range from single-celled bacteria, which lack cell nuclei, to multicellular fungi, plants, and animals. Have these species always existed on Earth?

Scientists think that Earth has changed a great deal during its history, and that living things have changed, too. Scientists estimate that the planet is 4.6 billion years old. Since life first appeared on Earth, many species have died out, and many new species have appeared. **Figure 4** shows some of the species that have existed during Earth's history.

Scientists observe that species have changed over time. They also observe that the inherited characteristics in populations change over time. Scientists think that as populations change over time, new species form. Thus, newer species descend from older species. The process in which populations gradually change over time is called **evolution.** Scientists continue to develop theories to explain exactly how evolution happens.

adaptation a characteristic that improves an individual's ability to survive and reproduce in a particular environment

species a group of organisms that are closely related and can mate to produce fertile offspring

evolution the process in which inherited characteristics within a population change over generations such that new species sometimes arise

Figure 4 *This diagram shows some of the many kinds of organisms that have lived on Earth since the planet formed 4.6 billion years ago.*

Figure 5 *The fossil on the left is of a trilobite, an ancient aquatic animal. The fossils on the right are of seed ferns.*

Evidence of Changes over Time

Evidence that evolution has happened is buried within Earth. Earth's crust is arranged in layers. These layers are made up of different kinds of rock and soil stacked on top of each other. These layers form when *sediments*, particles of sand, dust, or soil, are carried by wind and water and are deposited in an orderly fashion. Older layers are deposited before newer layers and are buried deeper within Earth.

Fossils

Sometimes, the remains or imprints of once-living organisms are found in the layers of rock. These remains are called **fossils.** Examples of fossils are shown in **Figure 5.** Fossils can be complete organisms, parts of organisms, or just a set of footprints. Fossils usually form when a dead organism is covered by a layer of sediment. Over time, more sediment settles on top of the organism. Minerals in the sediment may seep into the organism and gradually replace the organism with stone. If the organism rots away completely after being covered, it may leave an imprint of itself in the rock.

fossil the remains or physical evidence of an organism preserved by geological processes

fossil record a historical sequence of life indicated by fossils found in layers of the Earth's crust

The Fossil Record

By studying fossils, scientists have made a timeline of life that is known as the **fossil record.** The fossil record organizes fossils by their estimated ages and physical similarities. Fossils found in newer layers of Earth's crust tend to be similar to present-day organisms. This similarity indicates that the fossilized organisms were close relatives of present-day organisms. Fossils from older layers are less similar to present-day organisms than fossils from newer layers are. The older fossils are of earlier life-forms, which may not exist anymore.

✓ Reading Check How does the fossil record organize fossils?

Evidence of Ancestry

The fossil record provides evidence about the order in which species have existed. Scientists observe that all living organisms have characteristics in common and inherit characteristics in similar ways. So, scientists think that all living species descended from common ancestors. Evidence of common ancestors can be found in fossils and in living organisms.

Drawing Connections

Scientists examine the fossil record to figure out the relationships between extinct and living organisms. They draw models, such as the one shown in **Figure 6,** that illustrate their hypotheses. The short horizontal line at the top left in the diagram represents a species that lived in the past. Each branch in the diagram represents a group of organisms that descended from that species.

As shown in **Figure 6,** scientists think that whales and some types of hoofed mammals have a common ancestor. This ancestor was probably a mammal that lived on land between 50 million and 70 million years ago. During this time period, the dinosaurs died out and a variety of mammals appeared in the fossil record. The first ocean-dwelling mammals appeared about 50 million years ago. Scientists think that all mammal species alive today evolved from common ancestors.

Scientists have named and described hundreds of thousands of living and ancient species. Scientists use information about these species to sketch out a "tree of life" that includes all known organisms. But scientists know that their information is incomplete. For example, parts of Earth's history lack a fossil record. In fact, fossils are rare because specific conditions are necessary for fossils to form.

CONNECTION TO Geology

Sedimentary Rock Fossils are most often found in sedimentary rock. *Sedimentary rock* usually forms when rock is broken into sediment by wind, water, and other means. The wind and water move the sediment around and deposit it. Over time, layers of sediment pile up. Lower layers are compressed and changed into rock. Find out if your area has any sedimentary rocks that contain fossils. Mark the location of such rocks on a copy of a local map. **ACTIVITY**

Figure 6 *This diagram is a model of the proposed relationships between ancient and modern mammals that have characteristics similar to whales.*

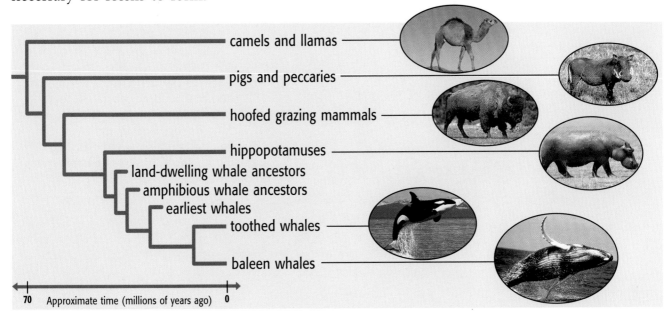

- camels and llamas
- pigs and peccaries
- hoofed grazing mammals
- hippopotamuses
- land-dwelling whale ancestors
- amphibious whale ancestors
- earliest whales
- toothed whales
- baleen whales

70   Approximate time (millions of years ago)   0

Examining Organisms

Examining an organism carefully can give scientists clues about its ancestors. For example, whales seem similar to fish. But unlike fish, whales breathe air, give birth to live young, and produce milk. These traits show that whales are *mammals*. Thus, scientists think that whales evolved from ancient mammals.

Case Study: Evolution of the Whale

Scientists think that the ancient ancestor of whales was probably a mammal that lived on land and that could run on four legs. A more recent ancestor was probably a mammal that spent time both on land and in water. Comparisons of modern whales and a large number of fossils have supported this hypothesis. **Figure 7** illustrates some of this evidence.

✓ **Reading Check** What kind of organism do scientists think was an ancient ancestor of whales?

Figure 7 Evidence of Whale Evolution

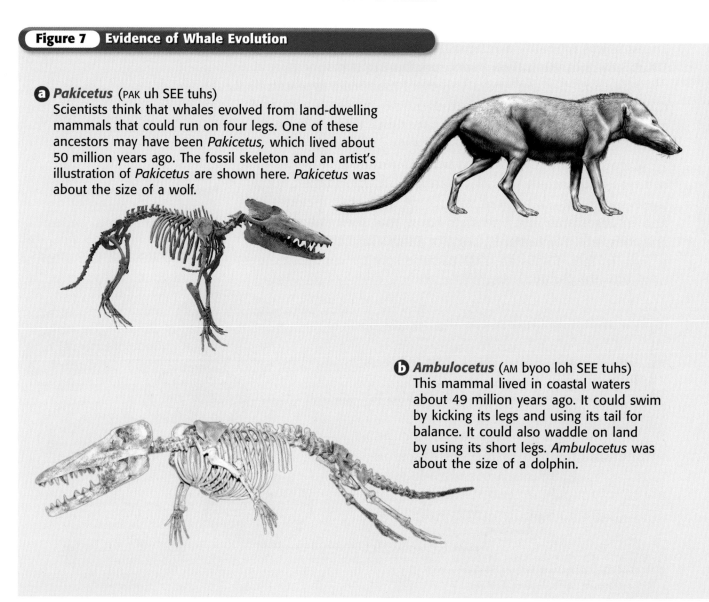

ⓐ *Pakicetus* (PAK uh SEE tuhs)
Scientists think that whales evolved from land-dwelling mammals that could run on four legs. One of these ancestors may have been *Pakicetus,* which lived about 50 million years ago. The fossil skeleton and an artist's illustration of *Pakicetus* are shown here. *Pakicetus* was about the size of a wolf.

ⓑ *Ambulocetus* (AM byoo loh SEE tuhs)
This mammal lived in coastal waters about 49 million years ago. It could swim by kicking its legs and using its tail for balance. It could also waddle on land by using its short legs. *Ambulocetus* was about the size of a dolphin.

Walking Whales

The organisms in **Figure 7** form a sequence between ancient four-legged mammals and modern whales. Several pieces of evidence indicate that these species are related by ancestry. Each species shared some traits with an earlier species. However, some species had new traits that were shared with later species. Yet, each species had traits that allowed it to survive in a particular time and place in Earth's history.

Further evidence can be found inside the bodies of living whales. For example, although modern whales do not have hind limbs, inside their bodies are tiny hip bones, as shown in **Figure 7.** Scientists think that these hip bones were inherited from the whales' four-legged ancestors. Scientists often look at this kind of evidence when they want to determine the relationships between organisms.

The Weight of Whales

Whales are the largest animals ever known on Earth. One reason whales can grow so large is that they live in water, which supports their weight in a way that their bones could not. The blue whale—the largest type of whale in existence—is about 24 m long and has a mass of about 99,800 kg. Convert these measurements into feet and pounds, and round to whole numbers.

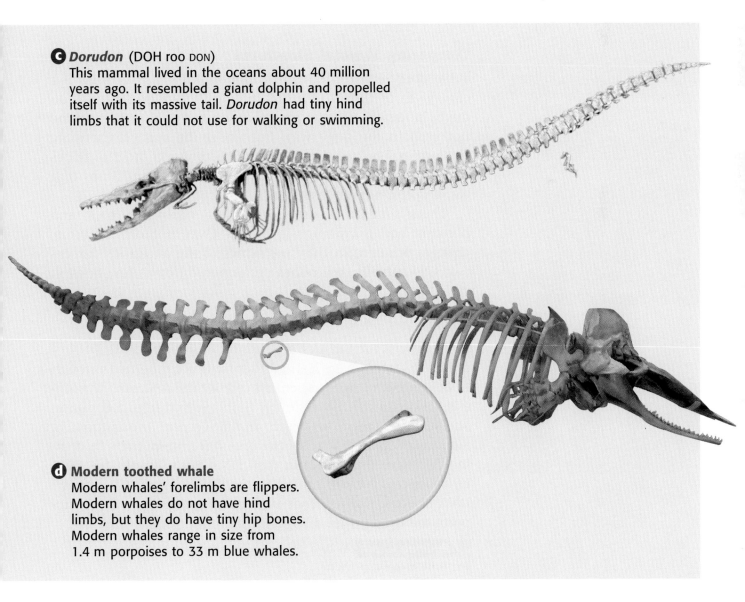

ᴳ Dorudon (DOH roo DON)
This mammal lived in the oceans about 40 million years ago. It resembled a giant dolphin and propelled itself with its massive tail. *Dorudon* had tiny hind limbs that it could not use for walking or swimming.

ᵈ Modern toothed whale
Modern whales' forelimbs are flippers. Modern whales do not have hind limbs, but they do have tiny hip bones. Modern whales range in size from 1.4 m porpoises to 33 m blue whales.

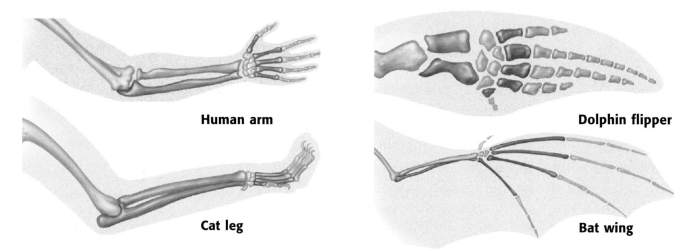

Human arm

Dolphin flipper

Cat leg

Bat wing

Figure 8 The bones in the front limbs of these animals are similar. Similar bones are shown in the same color. These limbs are different sizes in life.

Comparing Organisms

Evidence that groups of organisms have common ancestry can be found by comparing the groups' DNA. Because every organism inherits DNA, every organism inherits the traits determined by DNA. Organisms contain evidence that populations and species undergo changes in traits and DNA over time.

Comparing Skeletal Structures

What does your arm have in common with the front leg of a cat, the front flipper of a dolphin, or the wing of a bat? You might notice that these structures do not look alike and are not used in the same way. But under the surface, there are similarities. Look at **Figure 8.** The structure and order of bones of a human arm are similar to those of the front limbs of a cat, a dolphin, and a bat.

These similarities suggest that cats, dolphins, bats, and humans had a common ancestor. Over millions of years, changes occurred in the limb bones of the ancestor's descendants. Eventually, the bones performed different functions in each type of animal.

Comparing DNA

Interestingly, the DNA of a house cat is similar to the DNA of a tiger. Scientists have learned that traits are inherited through DNA's genetic code. So, scientists can test the following hypothesis: If species that have similar traits evolved from a common ancestor, the species will have similar genetic information. In fact, scientists find that species that have many traits in common do have similarities in their DNA. For example, the DNA of house cats is more similar to the DNA of tigers than to the DNA of dogs. The fact that all existing species have DNA supports the theory that all species share a common ancestor.

✓ Reading Check If two species have similar DNA, what hypothesis is supported?

Summary

- Evolution is the process in which inherited characteristics within a population change over generations, sometimes giving rise to new species. Scientists continue to develop theories to explain how evolution happens.

- Evidence that organisms evolve can be found by comparing living organisms to each other and to the fossil record. Such comparisons provide evidence of common ancestry.

- Scientists think that modern whales evolved from an ancient, land-dwelling mammal ancestor. Fossil organisms that support this hypothesis have been found.

- Evidence of common ancestry among living organisms is provided by comparing DNA and inherited traits. Species that have a common ancestor will have traits and DNA that are more similar to each other than to those of distantly related species.

Using Key Terms

Complete each of the following sentences by choosing the correct term from the word bank.

adaptation   species
fossil   evolution

1. Members of the same ___ can mate with one another to produce offspring.

2. A(n) ___ helps an organism survive.

3. When populations change over time, ___ has occurred.

Understanding Key Ideas

4. A human's arm, a cat's front leg, a dolphin's front flipper, and a bat's wing

   a. have similar kinds of bones.

   b. are used in similar ways.

   c. are very similar to insect wings and jellyfish tentacles.

   d. have nothing in common.

5. How does the fossil record show that species have changed over time?

6. What evidence do fossils provide about the ancestors of whales?

Critical Thinking

7. **Making Comparisons** Other than the examples provided in the text, how are whales different from fishes?

8. **Forming Hypotheses** Is a person's DNA likely to be more similar to the DNA of his or her biological parents or to the DNA of one of his or her cousins? Explain your answer.

Interpreting Graphics

9. The photograph below shows the layers of sedimentary rock exposed during the construction of a road. Imagine that a species that lived 200 million years ago is found in layer **b**. Would the species' ancestor, which lived 250 million years ago, most likely be found in layer **a** or in layer **c**? Explain your answer.

How Does Evolution Happen?

Imagine that you are a scientist in the 1800s. Fossils of some very strange animals have been found. And some familiar fossils have been found where you would least expect them. How did seashells end up on the tops of mountains?

In the 1800s, geologists began to realize that the Earth is much older than anyone had previously thought. Evidence showed that gradual processes had changed the Earth's surface over millions of years. Some scientists saw evidence of evolution in the fossil record. However, no one had been able to explain *how* evolution happens—until Charles Darwin.

Charles Darwin

In 1831, 21-year-old Charles Darwin, shown in **Figure 1,** graduated from college. Like many young people just out of college, Darwin didn't know what he wanted to do with his life. His father wanted him to become a doctor, but seeing blood made Darwin sick. Although he eventually earned a degree in theology, Darwin was most interested in the study of plants and animals.

So, Darwin signed on for a five-year voyage around the world. He served as the *naturalist*—a scientist who studies nature—on the British ship the HMS *Beagle,* similar to the ship in **Figure 2.** During the trip, Darwin made observations that helped him form a theory about how evolution happens.

Figure 1 *Charles Darwin* ▶ *wanted to understand the natural world.*

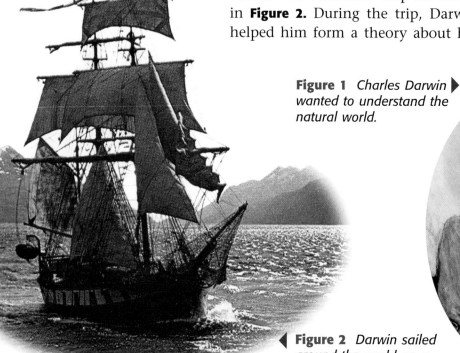

◀ **Figure 2** *Darwin sailed around the world on a ship similar to this one.*

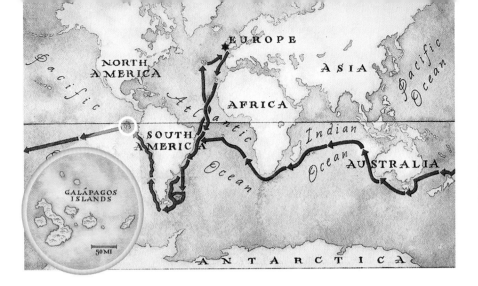

Figure 3 *The course of the HMS* Beagle *is shown by the red line. The journey began and ended in England.*

Darwin's Excellent Adventure

The *Beagle*'s journey is charted in **Figure 3.** Along the way, Darwin collected thousands of plant and animal samples. He kept careful notes of his observations. One interesting place that the ship visited was the Galápagos Islands. These islands are found 965 km (600 mi) west of Ecuador, a country in South America.

✔ **Reading Check** Where are the Galápagos Islands? (*See the Appendix for answers to Reading Checks.*)

Darwin's Finches

Darwin noticed that the animals and plants on the Galápagos Islands were a lot like those in Ecuador. However, they were not exactly the same. The finches of the Galápagos Islands, for example, were a little different from the finches in Ecuador. And the finches on each island differed from the finches on the other islands. As **Figure 4** shows, the beak of each finch is adapted to the way the bird usually gets food.

Figure 4 Some Finches of the Galápagos Islands

The **large ground finch** has a wide, strong beak that it uses to crack open big, hard seeds. This beak works like a nutcracker.

The **cactus finch** has a tough beak that it uses for eating cactus parts and insects. This beak works like a pair of needle-nose pliers.

The **warbler finch** has a small, narrow beak that it uses to catch small insects. This beak works like a pair of tweezers.

Darwin's Thinking

After returning to England, Darwin puzzled over the animals of the Galápagos Islands. He tried to explain why the animals seemed so similar to each other yet had so many different adaptations. For example, Darwin hypothesized that the island finches were descended from South American finches. The first finches on the islands may have been blown from South America by a storm. Over many generations, the finches may have adapted to different ways of life on the islands.

During the course of his travels, Darwin came up with many new ideas. Before sharing these ideas, he spent several years analyzing his evidence. He also gathered ideas from many other people.

Ideas About Breeding

In Darwin's time, farmers and breeders had produced many kinds of farm animals and plants. These plants and animals had traits that were desired by the farmers and breeders. **Traits** are specific characteristics that can be passed from parent to offspring through genes. The process in which humans select which plants or animals to reproduce based on certain desired traits is called **selective breeding.** Most pets, such as the dogs in **Figure 5,** have been bred for various desired traits.

You can see the results of selective breeding in many kinds of organisms. For example, people have bred horses that are particularly fast or strong. And farmers have bred crops that produce large fruit or that grow in specific climates.

trait a genetically determined characteristic

selective breeding the human practice of breeding animals or plants that have certain desired characteristics

Figure 5 *Over the past 12,000 years, dogs have been selectively bred to produce more than 150 breeds.*

Population Growth Versus Food Supply

1. Get an **egg carton** and a **bag of rice.** Use a **marker** to label one row of the carton "Food supply." Then, label the second row "Human population."

2. In the row labeled "Food supply," place one grain of rice in the first cup. Place two grains of rice in the second cup, and place three grains of rice in the third cup. In each subsequent cup, place one more grain than you placed in the previous cup. Imagine that each grain represents enough food for one person's lifetime.

3. In the row labeled "Human population," place one grain of rice in the first cup. Place two grains of rice in the second cup, and place four grains in the third cup. In each subsequent cup, place twice as many grains as you placed in the previous cup. This rice represents people.

4. How many units of food are in the sixth cup? How many "people" are in the sixth cup? If this pattern continued, what would happen?

5. Describe how the patterns in the food supply and in the human population differ. Explain how the patterns relate to Malthus's hypothesis.

Ideas About Population

During Darwin's time, Thomas Malthus wrote a famous book entitled *An Essay on the Principle of Population.* Malthus noted that humans have the potential to reproduce rapidly. He warned that food supplies could not support unlimited population growth. **Figure 6** illustrates this relationship. However, Malthus pointed out that human populations are limited by choices that humans make or by problems such as starvation and disease.

After reading Malthus's work, Darwin realized that any species can produce many offspring. He also knew that the populations of all species are limited by starvation, disease, competition, and predation. Only a limited number of individuals survive to reproduce. Thus, there is something special about the survivors. Darwin reasoned that the offspring of the survivors inherit traits that help the offspring survive in their environment.

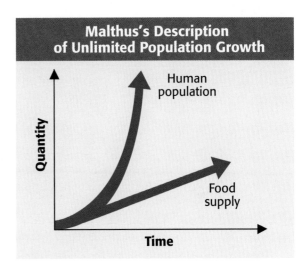

Figure 6 *Malthus thought that the human population could increase more quickly than the food supply, with the result that there would not be enough food for everyone.*

Ideas About Earth's History

Darwin had begun to think that species could evolve over time. But most geologists at the time did not think that Earth was old enough to allow for slow changes. Darwin learned new ideas from *Principles of Geology,* a book by Charles Lyell. This book presented evidence that Earth had formed by natural processes over a long period of time. It became clear to Darwin that Earth was much older than anyone had imagined.

Reading Check What did Darwin learn from Charles Lyell?

Darwin's Theory of Natural Selection

After he returned from his voyage on the HMS *Beagle*, Darwin privately struggled with his ideas for about 20 years. Then, in 1858, Darwin received a letter from a fellow naturalist named Alfred Russel Wallace. Wallace had arrived at the same ideas about evolution that Darwin had. Darwin grew more and more motivated to present his ideas. In 1859, Darwin published a famous book called *On the Origin of Species by Means of Natural Selection.* In his book, Darwin proposed the theory that evolution happens through a process that he called **natural selection.** This process, explained in **Figure 7,** has four parts.

natural selection the process by which individuals that are better adapted to their environment survive and reproduce more successfully than less well adapted individuals do; a theory to explain the mechanism of evolution

☑ **Reading Check** What is the title of Darwin's famous book?

Figure 7 **Four Parts of Natural Selection**

❶ **Overproduction** A tarantula's egg sac may hold 500–1,000 eggs. Some of the eggs will survive and develop into adult spiders. Some will not.

❷ **Inherited Variation** Every individual has its own combination of traits. Each tarantula is similar to, but not identical to, its parents.

❸ **Struggle to Survive** Some tarantulas may be caught by predators, such as this wasp. Other tarantulas may starve or get a disease. Only some of the tarantulas will survive to adulthood.

❹ **Successful Reproduction** The tarantulas that are best adapted to their environment are likely to have many offspring that survive.

Genetics and Evolution

Darwin lacked evidence for parts of his theory. For example, he knew that organisms inherit traits, but not *how* they inherit traits. He knew that there is great variation among organisms, but not *how* that variation occurs. Today, scientists have found most of the evidence that Darwin lacked. They know that variation happens as a result of differences in genes. Changes in genes may happen whenever organisms produce offspring. Some genes make an organism more likely to survive to reproduce. The process called *selection* happens when only organisms that carry these genes can survive to reproduce. New fossil discoveries and new information about genes add to scientists' understanding of natural selection and evolution.

SECTION Review

Summary

- Darwin explained that evolution occurs through natural selection. His theory has four parts:

  1. Each species produces more offspring than will survive to reproduce.

  2. Individuals within a population have slightly different traits.

  3. Individuals within a population compete with each other for limited resources.

  4. Individuals that are better equipped to live in an environment are more likely to survive to reproduce.

- Modern genetics helps explain the theory of natural selection.

Using Key Terms

1. In your own words, write a definition for the term *trait*.

2. Use the following terms in the same sentence: *selective breeding* and *natural selection*.

Understanding Key Ideas

3. Modern scientific explanations of evolution

   a. have replaced Darwin's theory.

   b. rely on genetics instead of natural selection.

   c. fail to explain how traits are inherited.

   d. combine the principles of natural selection and genetic inheritance.

4. Describe the observations that Darwin made about the species on the Galápagos Islands.

5. Summarize the ideas that Darwin developed from books by Malthus and Lyell.

6. Describe the four parts of Darwin's theory of evolution by natural selection.

7. What knowledge did Darwin lack that modern scientists now use to explain evolution?

Math Skills

8. In a sample of 80 beetles, 50 beetles had 4 spots each, and the rest had 6 spots each. What was the average number of spots per beetle?

Critical Thinking

9. **Making Comparisons** In selective breeding, humans influence the course of evolution. What determines the course of evolution in natural selection?

10. **Predicting Consequences** Suppose that an island in the Pacific Ocean was just formed by a volcano. Over the next million years, how might species evolve on this island?

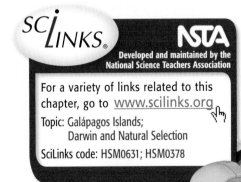

SCiLINKS®

NSTA
Developed and maintained by the
National Science Teachers Association

For a variety of links related to this chapter, go to www.scilinks.org
Topic: Galápagos Islands;
Darwin and Natural Selection
SciLinks code: HSM0631; HSM0378

Natural Selection in Action

Have you ever had to take an antibiotic? Antibiotics are supposed to kill bacteria. But sometimes, bacteria are not killed by the medicine. Do you know why?

READING WARM-UP

Objectives

● Give three examples of natural selection in action.

● Outline the process of speciation.

Terms to Learn

generation time
speciation

READING STRATEGY

Prediction Guide Before reading this section, write the title of each heading in this section. Next, under each heading, write what you think you will learn.

A population of bacteria might develop an adaptation through natural selection. Most bacteria are killed by the chemicals in antibiotics. But in some cases, a few bacteria are naturally *resistant* to the chemicals, so they are not killed. These survivors are then able to pass this adaptation to their offspring. This situation is an example of how natural selection works.

Changes in Populations

The theory of natural selection explains how a population changes in response to its environment. If natural selection is always taking place, a population will tend to be well adapted to its environment. But not all individuals are the same. The individuals that are likely to survive and reproduce are those that are best adapted at the time.

Adaptation to Hunting

Changes in populations are sometimes observed when a new force affects the survival of individuals. In Uganda, scientists think that hunting is affecting the elephant population. In 1930, about 99% of the male elephants in one area had tusks. Only 1% of the elephants were born without tusks. Today, as few as 85% of the male elephants in that area have tusks. What happened?

A male African elephant that has tusks is shown in **Figure 1.** The ivory of an elephant's tusks is very valuable. People hunt the elephants for their tusks. As a result, fewer of the elephants that have tusks survive to reproduce, and more of the tuskless elephants survive. When the tuskless elephants reproduce, they pass the tuskless trait to their offspring.

Figure 1 *The ivory tusks of African elephants are very valuable. Some elephants are born without tusks.*

Figure 2 Natural Selection of Insecticide Resistance

❶ An insecticide will kill most insects, but a few may survive. These survivors have genes that make them resistant to the insecticide.

❷ The survivors then reproduce, passing the insecticide-resistance genes to their offspring.

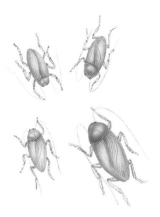

❸ In time, the replacement population of insects is made up mostly of individuals that have the insecticide-resistance genes.

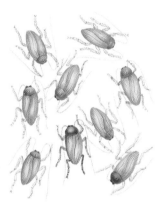

❹ When the same kind of insecticide is used on the insects, only a few are killed because most of them are resistant to that insecticide.

Insecticide Resistance

People have always wanted to control the insect populations around their homes and farms. Many insecticides are used to kill insects. But some chemicals that used to work well do not work as well anymore. Some individual insects within the population are resistant to certain insecticides. **Figure 2** shows how a population of insects might become resistant to common insecticides.

More than 500 kinds of insects are now resistant to certain insecticides. Insects can quickly develop resistance because they often produce many offspring and have short generation times. **Generation time** is the average time between one generation of offspring and the next.

generation time the period between the birth of one generation and the birth of the next generation

✔ *Reading Check* Why do insects quickly develop resistance to insecticides? (*See the Appendix for answers to Reading Checks.*)

Competition for Mates

In the process of evolution, survival is simply not enough. Natural selection is at work when individuals reproduce. In organisms that reproduce sexually, finding a mate is part of the struggle to reproduce. Many species have so much competition for mates that interesting adaptations result. For example, the females of many bird species prefer to mate with males that have certain types of colorful feathers.

Forming a New Species

Sometimes, drastic changes that can form a new species take place. In the animal kingdom, a *species* is a group of organisms that can mate with each other to produce fertile offspring. A new species may form after a group becomes separated from the original population. This group forms a new population. Over time, the two populations adapt to their different environments. Eventually, the populations can become so different that they can't mate anymore. Each population may then be considered a new species. The formation of a new species as a result of evolution is called **speciation** (SPEE shee AY shuhn). **Figure 3** shows how new species of Galápagos finches may have formed. Speciation may happen in other ways as well.

speciation the formation of new species as a result of evolution

Separation

Speciation often begins when a part of a population becomes separated from the rest. The process of separation can happen in several ways. For example, a newly formed canyon, mountain range, or lake can divide the members of a population.

✓ **Reading Check** How can parts of a population become separated?

Figure 3 **The Evolution of Galápagos Finch Species**

❶ Some finches left the mainland and reached one of the islands (separation).

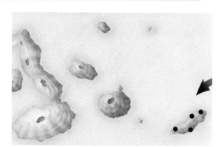

❷ The finches reproduced and adapted to the environment (adaptation).

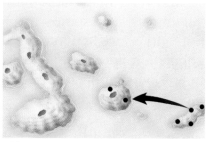

❸ Some finches flew to a second island (separation).

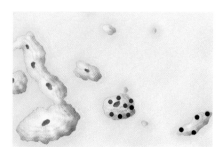

❹ The finches reproduced and adapted to the different environment (adaptation).

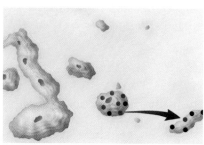

❺ Some finches flew back to the first island but could no longer interbreed with the finches there (division).

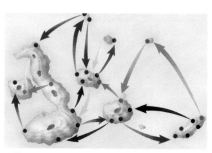

❻ This process may have occurred over and over again as the finches flew to the other islands.

Adaptation

Populations constantly undergo natural selection. After two groups have separated, natural selection may act on each group in different ways. Over many generations, the separated groups may evolve different sets of traits. If the environmental conditions for each group differ, the adaptations in the groups will also differ.

Division

Over many generations, two separated groups of a population may become very different. Even if a geographical barrier is removed, the groups may not be able to interbreed anymore. At this point, the two groups are no longer the same species.

Figure 4 shows another way that populations may stop interbreeding. Leopard frogs and pickerel frogs probably had the same ancestor species. Then, at some point, some of these frogs began to mate at different times during the year.

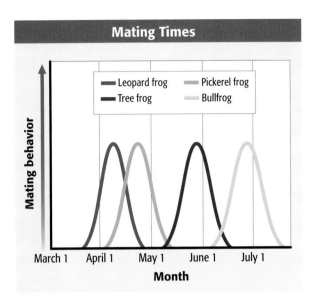

Mating Times

Leopard frog　Pickerel frog
Tree frog　Bullfrog

Mating behavior (y-axis)

March 1　April 1　May 1　June 1　July 1

Month

Figure 4 *The leopard frog and the pickerel frog are similar species. However, leopard frogs do not search for mates at the same time of year that pickerel frogs do.*

SECTION Review

Summary

- Natural selection explains how populations adapt to changes in their environment. A variety of examples of such adaptations can be found.

- Natural selection also explains how one species may evolve into another. Speciation occurs as populations undergo separation, adaptation, and division.

Using Key Terms

1. In your own words, write a definition for the term *speciation*.

Understanding Key Ideas

2. Two populations have evolved into two species when
   a. the populations are separated.
   b. the populations look different.
   c. the populations can no longer interbreed.
   d. the populations adapt.

3. Explain why the number of tuskless elephants in Uganda may be increasing.

Math Skills

4. A female cockroach can produce 80 offspring at a time. If half of the offspring produced by a certain female are female and each female produces 80 offspring, how many cockroaches are there in the third generation?

Critical Thinking

5. **Forming Hypotheses** Most kinds of cactus have leaves that grow in the form of spines. The stems or trunks become thick, juicy pads or barrels. Explain how these cactus parts might have evolved.

6. **Making Comparisons** Suggest an organism other than an insect that might evolve an adaptation to human activities.

Inquiry Lab

Survival of the Chocolates

Imagine a world populated with candy, and hold that delicious thought in your head for just a moment. Try to apply the idea of natural selection to a population of candy-coated chocolates. According to the theory of natural selection, individuals who have favorable adaptations are more likely to survive. In the "species" of candy-coated chocolates you will study in this experiment, the characteristics of individual chocolates may help them "survive." For example, shell strength (the strength of the candy coating) could be an adaptive advantage. Plan an experiment to find out which characteristics of the chocolates are favorable "adaptations."

OBJECTIVES

Form a hypothesis about the fate of the candy-coated chocolates.

Predict what will happen to the candy-coated chocolates.

Design and conduct an experiment to test your hypothesis.

MATERIALS

- chocolates, candy-coated, small, in a variety of colors (about 100)
- items to be determined by the students and approved by the teacher

SAFETY

Ask a Question

1 What might "survival" mean for a candy-coated chocolate? What are some ways you can test which chocolates are the "strongest" or "most fit" for their environment? Also, write down any other questions that you could ask about the "survival" of the chocolates.

Form a Hypothesis

2 Form a hypothesis, and make a prediction. For example, if you chose to study candy color, your prediction might be similar to this: If the ___ colored shell is the strongest, then fewer of the chocolates with this color of shell will ___ when ___.

Test the Hypothesis

3 Design a procedure to determine which type of candy-coated chocolate is most likely to survive. In your plan, be sure to include materials and tools you may need to complete this procedure.

4 Check your experimental design with your teacher before you begin. Your teacher will supply the candy and assist you in gathering materials and tools.

5 Record your results in a data table. Be sure to organize your data in a clear and understandable way.

Analyze the Results

1 **Describing Events** Write a report that describes your experiment. Be sure to include tables and graphs of the data you collected.

Draw Conclusions

2 **Evaluating Data** In your report, explain how your data either support or do not support your hypothesis. Include possible errors and ways to improve your procedure.

Applying Your Data

Can you think of another characteristic of the chocolates that can be tested to determine which type is best adapted to survive? Explain your idea, and describe how you might test it.

Chapter Review

USING KEY TERMS

Complete each of the following sentences by choosing the correct term from the word bank.

adaptation
evolution
generation time
species
speciation
fossil record
selective breeding
natural selection

1 When a single population evolves into two populations that cannot interbreed anymore, ___ has occurred.

2 Darwin's theory of ___ explained the process by which organisms become well-adapted to their environment.

3 A group of organisms that can mate with each other to produce offspring is known as a(n) ___.

4 The ___ provides information about organisms that have lived in the past.

5 In ___, humans select organisms with desirable traits that will be passed from one generation to another.

6 A(n) ___ helps an organism survive better in its environment.

7 Populations of insects and bacteria can evolve quickly because they usually have a short ___.

UNDERSTANDING KEY IDEAS

Multiple Choice

8 Fossils are commonly found in
  a. sedimentary rock.
  b. all kinds of rock.
  c. granite.
  d. loose sand.

9 The fact that all organisms have DNA as their genetic material is evidence that
  a. all organisms undergo natural selection.
  b. all organisms may have descended from a common ancestor.
  c. selective breeding takes place every day.
  d. genetic resistance rarely occurs.

10 Charles Darwin puzzled over differences in the ___ of the different species of Galápagos finches.
  a. webbed feet
  b. beaks
  c. bone structure of the wings
  d. eye color

11 Darwin observed variations among individuals within a population, but he did not realize that these variations were caused by
  a. interbreeding.
  b. differences in food.
  c. differences in genes.
  d. selective breeding.

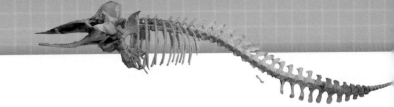

Short Answer

12 Identify two ways that organisms can be compared to provide evidence of evolution from a common ancestor.

13 Describe evidence that supports the hypothesis that whales evolved from land-dwelling mammals.

14 Why are some animals more likely to survive to adulthood than other animals are?

15 Explain how genetics is related to evolution.

16 Outline an example of the process of speciation.

CRITICAL THINKING

17 Concept Mapping Use the following terms to create a concept map: *struggle to survive, theory, genetic variation, Darwin, overpopulation, natural selection,* and *successful reproduction.*

18 Making Inferences How could natural selection affect the songs that birds sing?

19 Forming Hypotheses In Australia, many animals look like mammals from other parts of the world. But most of the mammals in Australia are marsupials, which carry their young in pouches after birth. Few kinds of marsupials are found anywhere else in the world. What is a possible explanation for the presence of so many of these unique mammals in Australia?

20 Analyzing Relationships Geologists have evidence that the continents were once a single giant continent. This giant landform eventually split apart, and the individual continents moved to their current positions. What role might this drifting of continents have played in evolution?

INTERPRETING GRAPHICS

The graphs below show information about the infants that are born and the infants that have died in a population. The weight of each infant was measured at birth. Use the graphs to answer the questions that follow.

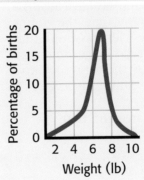

Infant Births by Birth Weight

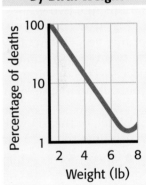

Infant Deaths by Birth Weight

21 What is the most common birth weight?

22 At which birth weight is an infant most likely to survive?

23 How do the principles of natural selection help explain why there are more deaths among babies whose birth weights are low than among babies whose birth weights are average?

Standardized Test Preparation

Read each of the passages below. Then, answer the questions that follow each passage.

Passage 1 When the Grand Canyon was forming, a single population of tassel-eared squirrels may have been separated into two groups. Today, descendants of the two groups live on opposite sides of the canyon. The two groups share many characteristics, but they do not look the same. For example, both groups have tasseled ears, but each group has a unique fur color pattern. An important difference between the groups is that the Abert squirrels live on the south rim of the canyon, and the Kaibab squirrels live on the north rim.

The environments on the two sides of the Grand Canyon are different. The north rim is about 370 m higher than the south rim. Almost twice as much precipitation falls on the north rim than on the south rim every year. Over many generations, the two groups of squirrels have adapted to their new environments. Over time, the groups became very different. Many scientists think that the two types of squirrels are no longer the same species. The development of these two squirrel groups is an example of speciation in progress.

1. Which of the following statements **best** describes the main idea of this passage?
   A Speciation is evident in two groups of squirrels in the Grand Canyon area.
   B Two groups of squirrels in the Grand Canyon area are closely related.
   C Two species can form from one species. This process is called *speciation*.
   D There are two groups of squirrels because the Grand Canyon has two sides.

2. Which of the following statements about the two types of squirrels is true?
   F They look the same.
   G They live in similar environments.
   H They have tasseled ears.
   I They can interbreed with each other.

Passage 2 You know from experience that individuals in a <u>population</u> are not exactly the same. If you look around the room, you will see a lot of differences among your classmates. You may have even noticed that no two dogs or two cats are exactly the same. No two individuals have exactly the same adaptations. For example, one cat may be better at catching mice, and another is better at running away from dogs. Observations such as these form the basis of the theory of natural selection. Because adaptations help organisms survive to reproduce, the individuals that are better adapted to their environment are more likely to pass their traits to future generations.

1. In the passage, what does *population* mean?
   A a school
   B some cats and dogs
   C a group of the same type of organism
   D a group of individuals that are the same

2. In this passage, which of the following are given as examples of adaptations?
   F differences among classmates
   G differences among cats
   H differences between cats and dogs
   I differences among environments

3. Which of the following statements about the individuals in a population that survive to reproduce is true?
   A They have the same adaptations.
   B They are likely to pass on adaptations to the next generation.
   C They form the basis of the theory of natural selection.
   D They are always better hunters.

The graph below shows average beak sizes of a group of finches on one island over several years. Use the graph to answer the questions that follow.

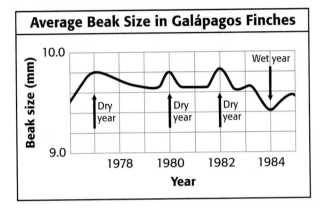

Average Beak Size in Galápagos Finches

1. In which of the years studied was average beak size the largest?

   A 1977

   B 1980

   C 1982

   D 1984

2. If beak size in this group of birds is linked to the amount of rainfall, what can you infer about the year 1976 on this island?

   F The year 1976 was drier than 1977.

   G The year 1976 was drier than 1980.

   H The year 1976 was wetter than 1977.

   I The year 1976 was wetter than 1984.

3. During which year(s) was rainfall probably the lowest on the island?

   A 1978, 1980, and 1982

   B 1977, 1980, 1982, and 1984

   C 1982

   D 1984

4. Which of the following statements **best** summarizes this data?

   F Average beak size stayed about the same except during wet years.

   G Average beak size decreased during dry years and increased during wet years.

   H Average beak size increased during dry years and decreased during wet years.

   I Average beak size changed randomly.

Read each question below, and choose the best answer.

Average Beak Measurements of Birds of the Colores Islands			
Island	Average beak length (mm)	Average beak width (mm)	Number of unique species
Verde	9.7	6.5	5
Azul	8.9	8.7	15
Rosa	5.2	8.0	10

1. What is the ratio of the number of species on Verde Island to the total number of species on all three of the Colores Islands?

   A 1:2

   B 1:5

   C 1:6

   D 5:15

2. What percentage of all bird species on the Colores Islands are on Rosa Island?

   F approximately 15%

   G approximately 30%

   H approximately 50%

   I approximately 80%

3. On which of the islands is the ratio of average beak length to average beak width closest to 1:1?

   A Verde Island

   B Azul Island

   C Rosa Island

   D There is not enough information to determine the answer.

4. On which island does the bird with the smallest beak length live?

   F Verde Island

   G Azul Island

   H Rosa Island

   I There is not enough information to determine the answer.

Science in Action

Science, Technology, and Society

Seed Banks

All over the world, scientists are making deposits in a special kind of bank. These banks are not for money, but for seeds. Why should seeds be saved? Saving seeds saves plants that may someday save human lives. These plants could provide food or medicine in the future. Throughout human history, many medicines have been developed from plants. And scientists keep searching for new chemicals among the incredible variety of plants in the world. But time is running out. Many plant species are becoming extinct before they have even been studied.

Math ACTIVITY

Many drugs were originally developed from plants. Suppose that 100 plants are used for medicines this year, but 5% of plant species become extinct each year. How many of the medicinal plants would be left after 1 year? after 10 years? Round your answers to whole numbers.

Science Fiction

"The Anatomy Lesson" by Scott Sanders

Do you know the feeling you get when you have an important test? A medical student faces a similar situation in this story. The student needs to learn the bones of the human body for an anatomy exam the next day. The student goes to the anatomy library to study. The librarian lets him check out a box of bones that are supposed to be from a human skeleton. But something is wrong. There are too many bones. They are the wrong shape. They don't fit together correctly. Somebody must be playing a joke! Find out what's going on and why the student and the librarian will never be the same after "The Anatomy Lesson." You can read it in the *Holt Anthology of Science Fiction*.

Language Arts ACTIVITY

WRITING SKILL Before you read this story, predict what you think will happen. Write a paragraph that "gives away" the ending that you predict. After you have read the story, listen to some of the predictions made by your classmates. Discuss your opinions about the possible endings.

Raymond Pierotti

Canine Evolution Raymond Pierotti thinks that it's natural that he became an evolutionary biologist. He grew up exploring the desert around his home in New Mexico. He was fascinated by the abundant wildlife surviving in the bleak landscape. "One of my earliest memories is getting coyotes to sing with me from my backyard," he says.

Pierotti now studies the evolutionary relationships between wolves, coyotes, and domestic dogs. Some of his ideas come from the traditions of the Comanches. According to the Comanche creation story, humans came from wolves. Although Pierotti doesn't believe that humans evolved from wolves, he sees the creation story as a suggestion that humans and wolves have evolved together. "Wolves are very similar to humans in many ways," says Pierotti. "They live in family groups and hunt together. It is possible that wolves actually taught humans how to hunt in packs, and there are ancient stories of wolves and humans hunting together and sharing the food. I think it was this relationship that inspired the Comanche creation stories."

Social Studies ACTiViTY

WRITING SKILL Research a story of creation that comes from a Greek, Roman, or Native American civilization. Write a paragraph summarizing the myth, and share it with a classmate.

To learn more about these Science in Action topics, visit **go.hrw.com** and type in the keyword **HL5EVOF**.

Current Science

Check out Current Science® articles related to this chapter by visiting go.hrw.com. Just type in the keyword **HL5CS07**.

The History of Life on Earth

About the PHOTO

What is 23,000 years old and 9 ft tall? The partial remains of the woolly mammoth in this picture! The mammoth was found in the frozen ground in Siberia in 1999. Scientists think that several types of woolly mammoths roamed the northern hemisphere until about 4,000 years ago.

PRE-READING ACTIVITY

FOLDNOTES **Layered Book** Before you read the chapter, create the Foldnote entitled "Layered Book" described in the **Study Skills** section of the Appendix. Label the tabs of the layered book with "Precambrian time," "Paleozoic era," "Mesozoic era," and "Cenozoic era." As you read the chapter, write information you learn about each category under the appropriate tab.

START-UP ACTIVITY

Making a Fossil

In this activity, you will make a model of a fossil.

Procedure

1. Get a **paper plate,** some **modeling clay,** and a **leaf** or a **shell** from your teacher.

2. Flatten some of the modeling clay on the paper plate. Push the leaf or shell into the clay. Be sure that your leaf or shell has made a mark in the clay. Remove the leaf or shell carefully.

3. Ask your teacher to cover the clay with **plaster of Paris.** Allow the plaster to dry overnight.

4. Carefully remove the paper plate and the clay from the plaster the next day.

Analysis

1. Consider the following objects—a clam, a seed, a jellyfish, a crab, a leaf, and a mushroom. Which of the objects do you think would make good fossils? Explain your answers.

2. In nature, fossils form only under certain conditions. For example, fossils may form when a dead organism is covered by tiny bits of sand or dirt for a long period of time. The presence of oxygen can prevent fossils from forming. Considering these facts, what are some limitations of your model of how a fossil is formed?

Evidence of the Past

In 1995, scientist Paul Sereno found a dinosaur skull that was 1.5 m long in the Sahara, a desert in Africa. The dinosaur may have been the largest land predator that has ever existed!

Scientists such as Paul Sereno look for clues to help them reconstruct what happened in the past. These scientists, called *paleontologists* (PAY lee uhn TAHL uh jists), use fossils to reconstruct the history of life before humans existed. Fossils show us that life on Earth has changed a great deal. They also provide us clues about how those changes happened.

Fossils

Fossils are traces or imprints of living things—such as animals, plants, bacteria, and fungi—that are preserved in rock. Fossils sometimes form when a dead organism is covered by a layer of sediment. The sediment may later be pressed together to form sedimentary rock. **Figure 1** shows one way that fossils can form in sedimentary rock.

fossil the remains or physical evidence of an organism preserved by geological processes

Figure 1 **One Way Fossils Can Form**

❶ Fossils can form in several ways. The most common way is when an organism dies and becomes buried in sediment.

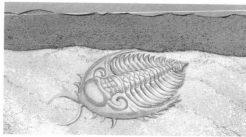

❷ The organism gradually decomposes and leaves a hollow impression, or *mold*, in the sediment.

❸ Over time, the mold fills with sediment, which forms a *cast* of the organism.

Figure 2 Using Half-Lives to Date Fossils

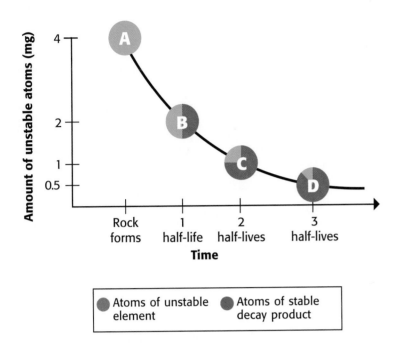

A The unstable atoms in this sample of rock have a half-life of 1.3 billion years. The sample contained 4 mg of unstable atoms when it formed.

B After 1.3 billion years, (one half-life for this type of unstable atom), 2 mg of the unstable atoms have decayed to become stable atoms, and 2 mg of unstable atoms remain.

C After 2.6 billion years (two half-lives for this sample), the rock sample contains 3 mg of stable decay atoms and 1 mg of unstable atoms.

D After three half-lives, only 0.5 mg of unstable atoms remain in the rock sample. This is equal to one-eighth of the original amount.

The Age of Fossils

Sedimentary rock has many layers. The oldest layers are usually on the bottom. The newest layers are usually on the top. The layers can tell a scientist the relative age of fossils. Fossils found in the bottom layers are usually older than the fossils in the top layers. So, scientists can determine whether a fossil is older or younger than other fossils based on its position in sedimentary rock. Estimating the age of rocks and fossils in this way is called **relative dating.**

In addition, scientists can determine the age of a fossil more precisely. **Absolute dating** is a method that measures the age of fossils or rocks in years. In one type of absolute dating, scientists examine atoms. *Atoms* are the particles that make up all matter. Atoms, in turn, are made of smaller particles. Some atoms are unstable and will decay by releasing energy, particles, or both. When an atom decays it becomes a different, and more stable, kind of atom. Each kind of unstable atom decays at its own rate. As shown in **Figure 2,** the time it takes for half of the unstable atoms in a sample to decay is the *half-life* of that type of unstable atom. By measuring the ratio of unstable atoms to stable atoms, scientists can determine the approximate age of a sample of rock.

✓ Reading Check Which type of fossil dating is more precise? *(See the Appendix for answers to Reading Checks.)*

relative dating any method of determining whether an event or object is older or younger than other events or objects

absolute dating any method of measuring the age of an object or event in years

Fractions of Fractions
Find the answer to each of the following problems. Be sure to show your work. You may want to draw pictures.
1. 1/2 × 1/2 × 1/2 × 1/2
2. 1/2 × 1/8
3. 1/4 × 1/4

The Geologic Time Scale

Think about important events that have happened during your lifetime. You usually recall each event in terms of the day, month, or year in which it happened. These divisions of time make it easier to recall when you were born, when you kicked the winning soccer goal, or when you started the fifth grade. Scientists also use a type of calendar to divide the Earth's long history. The span of time from the formation of the Earth to now is very long. Therefore, the calendar is divided into very long units of time.

The calendar scientists use to outline the history of life on Earth is called the **geologic time scale,** shown in **Table 1.** After a fossil is dated, a paleontologist can place the fossil in chronological order with other fossils. This ordering forms a picture of the past that shows how organisms have changed over time.

Divisions in the Geologic Time Scale

Paleontologists have divided the geologic time scale into large blocks of time. Each block may be divided into smaller blocks of time as scientists continue to find more fossil information.

The divisions known as *era*s are characterized by the type of organism that dominated the Earth at the time. For instance, the Mesozoic era—dominated by dinosaurs and other reptiles—is referred to as the *Age of Reptiles.* Eras began with a change in the type of organism that was most dominant.

Paleontologists sometimes adjust and add details to the geologic time scale. For example, the early history of the Earth has been poorly understood. There is little evidence that life existed billions of years ago. So, the earliest part of the geologic time scale is not named as an era. But more evidence of life before the Paleozoic era is being gathered. Scientists have proposed using this evidence to name new eras before the Paleozoic era.

Table 1 Geologic Time Scale

Era	Period	Time*
Cenozoic era		
	Quaternary	2
	Tertiary	65
Mesozoic era		
	Cretaceous	144
	Jurassic	206
	Triassic	248
Paleozoic era		
	Permian	290
	Carboniferous	345
	Devonian	408
	Silurian	439
	Ordovician	495
	Cambrian	543
Precambrian time		
		4,600

*indicates how many millions of years ago the period began

CONNECTION TO Social Studies

A Place in Time Most of the periods of the Paleozoic era were named by geologists for places where rocks from that period are found. Research the name of each period of the Paleozoic era listed in **Table 1.** On a copy of a world map, label the locations related to each name.

ACTiViTY

Figure 3 Scientists think that a meteorite hit Earth about 65 million years ago and caused major climate changes.

Mass Extinctions

Some of the important divisions in the geologic time scale mark times when rapid changes happened on Earth. During these times, many species died out completely, or became **extinct**. When a species is extinct, it does not reappear. At certain points in the Earth's history, a large number of species disappeared from the fossil record. These periods when many species suddenly become extinct are called *mass extinctions*.

Scientists are not sure what caused each of the mass extinctions. Most scientists think that the extinction of the dinosaurs happened because of extreme changes in the climate on Earth. These changes could have resulted from a giant meteorite hitting the Earth, as shown in **Figure 3.** Or, forces within the Earth could have caused many volcanoes and earthquakes.

geologic time scale the standard method used to divide the Earth's long natural history into manageable parts

extinct describes a species that has died out completely

✓ Reading Check What are mass extinctions?

Making a Geologic Timeline

1. Use a **metric ruler** to mark 10 cm sections on a **strip of paper** that is 46 cm long.

2. Label each 10 cm section in order from top to bottom as follows: 1 bya (billion years ago), 2 bya, etc. The timeline begins at 4.6 bya.

3. Divide each 10 cm section into 10 equal subsections. Divide the top 1 cm into 10 subsections. Calculate the number of years that are represented by 1 mm on this scale.

4. On your timeline, label the following events:
   a. Earth forms. (4.6 billion years ago)
   b. First animals appear. (600 million years ago)
   c. Dinosaurs appear. (251 million years ago)
   d. Dinosaurs are extinct. (65 million years ago)
   e. Humans appear. (100,000 years ago)

5. Label other events from the chapter.

6. Describe what most of the timeline looks like.

7. Compare the length of time dinosaurs existed with the length of time humans have existed.

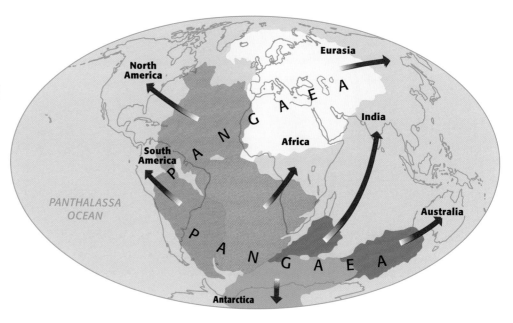

Figure 4 *The continents have been slowly moving throughout the history of Earth. The colored areas show the location of the continents 245 million years ago, and blue outlines show where the continents are today.*

The Changing Earth

Did you know that fossils of tropical plants have been found in Antarctica? Antarctica, now frozen, must have once had a warm climate to support these plants. The fossils provide evidence that Antarctica was once located near the equator!

Pangaea

Have you ever noticed that the continents look like pieces of a puzzle? German scientist Alfred Wegener had a similar thought in the early 1900s. He proposed that long ago the continents formed one landmass surrounded by a gigantic ocean. Wegener called that single landmass *Pangaea* (pan JEE uh), which means "all Earth." **Figure 4** shows how the continents may have formed from Pangaea.

✓ Reading Check What idea did Alfred Wegener propose?

Do the Continents Move?

In the mid-1960s, J. Tuzo Wilson of Canada came up with the idea that the continents were not moving by themselves. Wilson thought that huge pieces of the Earth's crust were pushed around by forces within the planet. Each huge piece of crust is called a *tectonic plate*. Wilson's theory of how these huge pieces of crust move around the Earth is called **plate tectonics.**

According to Wilson, the outer crust of the Earth is broken into seven large, rigid plates and several smaller ones. The continents and oceans ride on top of these plates. The motion of the plates causes the continents to move. For example, the plates that carry South America and Africa are slowly moving apart, as shown in **Figure 5.**

plate tectonics the theory that explains how large pieces of the Earth's outermost layer, called *tectonic plates*, move and change shape

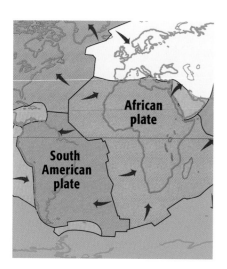

Figure 5 *The continents ride on tectonic plates, outlined here in black. The plates are still moving about 1 to 10 cm per year.*

Adaptation to Slow Changes

When conditions on the Earth change, organisms may become extinct. A rapid change, such as a meteorite impact, may cause a mass extinction. But slow changes, such as moving continents, allow time for adaptation.

Anywhere on Earth, you are able to see living things that are well adapted to the location where they live. Yet in the same location, you may find evidence of organisms that lived there in the past that were very different. For example, the animals currently living in Antarctica are able to survive very cold temperatures. But under the frozen surface of Antarctica are the remains of tropical forests. Conditions on Earth have changed many times in history, and life has changed, too.

CONNECTION TO Geology

Mid-Atlantic Ridge In 1947, scientists examined rock from a ridge that runs down the middle of the Atlantic Ocean, between Africa and the Americas. They found that this rock was much younger than the rock on the continents. Explain what this finding indicates about the tectonic plates.

SECTION Review

Summary

- Fossils are formed most often in sedimentary rock. The age of a fossil can be determined using relative dating and absolute dating.

- The geologic time scale is a timeline that is used by scientists to outline the history of Earth and life on Earth.

- Conditions for life on Earth have changed many times. Rapid changes, such as a meteorite impact, might have caused mass extinctions. But many groups of organisms have adapted to changes such as the movement of tectonic plates.

Using Key Terms

1. Use the following terms in the same sentence: *fossil* and *extinct*.

2. In your own words, write a definition for the term *plate tectonics*.

Understanding Key Ideas

3. Explain how a fossil forms in sedimentary rock.

4. What kind of information does the geologic time scale show?

5. About how many years of Earth's history was Precambrian time?

6. What are two possible causes of mass extinctions?

Math Skills

7. The Earth formed 4.6 billion years ago. Modern humans have existed for about 100,000 years. Simple worms have existed for at least 500 million years. For what fraction of the history of Earth have humans existed? have worms existed?

Critical Thinking

8. **Identifying Relationships** Why are both absolute dating and relative dating used to determine the age of fossils?

9. **Making Inferences** Fossils of *Mesosaurus*, the small aquatic reptile shown below, have been found only in Africa and South America. Using what you know about plate tectonics, how would you explain this finding?

SciLINKS

Developed and maintained by the National Science Teachers Association

For a variety of links related to this chapter, go to www.scilinks.org

Topic: Evidence of the Past
SciLinks code: HSM0545

Eras of the Geologic Time Scale

The walls of the Grand Canyon are layered with different kinds and colors of rocks. The deeper down into the canyon you go, the older the layers of rocks. Try to imagine a time when the bottom layer was the only layer that existed.

Each layer of rock tells a story about what was happening on Earth when that layer was on top. The rocks and fossils in each layer tell the story. Scientists have compared the stories told by fossils and rocks all over the Earth. From these stories, scientists have divided geologic history into four major parts. These divisions are Precambrian time, the Paleozoic era, the Mesozoic era, and the Cenozoic era.

Precambrian Time

The layers at the bottom of the Grand Canyon are from the oldest part of the geologic time scale. **Precambrian time** (pree KAM bree UHN TIEM) is the time from the formation of Earth 4.6 billion years ago to about 543 million years ago. Life on Earth began during this time.

Scientists think that the early Earth was very different than it is today. The atmosphere was made of gases such as water vapor, carbon dioxide, and nitrogen. Also, the early Earth was a place of great turmoil, as illustrated in **Figure 1.** Volcanic eruptions, meteorite impacts, and violent storms were common. Intense radiation from the sun bombarded Earth's surface.

✓ Reading Check **Describe the early Earth.** (*See the Appendix for answers to Reading Checks.*)

READING WARM-UP

Objectives

- Outline the major developments that allowed life to exist on Earth.
- Describe the types of organisms that arose during the four major divisions of the geologic time scale.

Terms to Learn

Precambrian time
Paleozoic era
Mesozoic era
Cenozoic era

READING STRATEGY

Mnemonics As you read this section, create a mnemonic device to help you remember the eras of geologic time.

Precambrian time the period in the geologic time scale from the formation of the Earth to the beginning of the Paleozoic era, from about 4.6 billion to 543 million years ago

Figure 1 *This illustration shows the conditions under which the first life on Earth may have formed.*

How Did Life Begin?

Scientists think that life developed from simple chemicals in the oceans and in the atmosphere. Energy from radiation and storms could have caused these chemicals to react. Some of these reactions formed the complex molecules that made life possible. Eventually, these molecules may have joined to form structures such as cells.

The early atmosphere of the Earth did not contain oxygen gas. The first organisms did not need oxygen to survive. These organisms were *prokaryotes* (proh KAR ee OHTS), or single-celled organisms that lack a nucleus.

Photosynthesis and Oxygen

There is evidence that *cyanobacteria,* a new kind of prokaryotic organism, appeared more than 3 billion years ago. Some cyanobacteria are shown in **Figure 2.** Cyanobacteria use sunlight to produce their own food. Along with doing other things, this process releases oxygen. The first cyanobacteria began to release oxygen gas into the oceans and air.

Eventually, some of the oxygen formed a new layer of gas in the upper atmosphere. This gas, called *ozone,* absorbs harmful radiation from the sun, as shown in **Figure 3.** Before ozone formed, life existed only in the oceans and underground. The new ozone layer reduced the radiation on Earth's surface.

Multicellular Organisms

After about 1 billion years, organisms that were larger and more complex than prokaryotes appeared in the fossil record. These organisms, known as *eukaryotes* (yoo KAR ee OHTS), contain a nucleus and other complex structures in their cells. Eventually, eukaryotic cells may have evolved into organisms that are composed of many cells.

INTERNET ACTIVITY

For another activity related to this chapter, go to **go.hrw.com** and type in the keyword **HL5HISW.**

Figure 2 *Cyanobacteria are the simplest living organisms that use the sun's energy to produce their own food.*

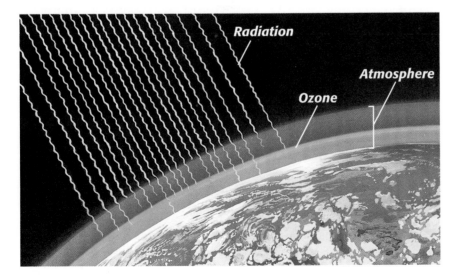

Radiation

Atmosphere

Ozone

Figure 3 *Oxygen in the atmosphere formed a layer of ozone, which helps to absorb harmful radiation from the sun.*

Figure 4 *Organisms that first appeared in the Paleozoic era include reptiles, amphibians, fishes, worms, and ferns.*

Paleozoic era the geologic era that followed Precambrian time and that lasted from 543 million to 248 million years ago

The Paleozoic Era

The **Paleozoic era** (PAY lee OH ZOH ik ER uh) began about 543 million years ago and ended about 248 million years ago. Considering the length of Precambrian time, you can see that the Paleozoic era was relatively recent. Rocks from the Paleozoic era are rich in fossils of animals such as sponges, corals, snails, clams, squids, and trilobites. Fishes, the earliest animals with backbones, appeared during this era, and sharks became abundant. **Figure 4** shows an artist's depiction of life in the Paleozoic era.

The word *Paleozoic* comes from Greek words that mean "ancient life." When scientists first named this era, they thought it held the earliest forms of life. Scientists now think that earlier forms of life existed, but less is known about those life-forms. Before the Paleozoic era, most organisms lived in the oceans and left few fossils.

Life on Land

During the 300 million years of the Paleozoic era, plants, fungi, and air-breathing animals slowly colonized land. By the end of the era, forests of giant ferns, club mosses, horsetails, and conifers covered much of the Earth. All major plant groups except for flowering plants appeared during this era. These plants provided food and shelter for animals.

Fossils indicate that crawling insects were some of the first animals to live on land. They were followed by large salamander-like animals. Near the end of the Paleozoic era, reptiles and winged insects appeared.

The largest mass extinction known took place at the end of the Paleozoic era. By 248 million years ago, as many as 90% of all Paleozoic species had become extinct. The mass extinction wiped out entire groups of marine organisms, such as trilobites. The oceans were completely changed.

CONNECTION TO Oceanography

Prehistoric Marine Organisms Find a variety of pictures and descriptions of marine organisms from the Cambrian period of the Paleozoic era. Choose three organisms that you find interesting. Draw or write a description of each organism. Find out whether scientists think the organism is related to any living group of organisms, and add this information to your description.

The Mesozoic Era

The **Mesozoic era** (MES oh ZOH ik ER uh) began about 248 million years ago and lasted about 183 million years. *Mesozoic* comes from Greek words that mean "middle life." Scientists think that the surviving reptiles evolved into many different species after the Paleozoic era. Therefore, the Mesozoic era is commonly called the *Age of Reptiles*.

Life in the Mesozoic Era

Dinosaurs are the most well known reptiles that evolved during the Mesozoic era. Dinosaurs dominated the Earth for about 150 million years. A great variety of dinosaurs lived on Earth. Some had unique adaptations, such as ducklike bills for feeding or large spines on their bodies for defense. In addition to dinosaurs roaming the land, giant marine lizards swam in the ocean. The first birds also appeared during the Mesozoic era. In fact, scientists think that some of the dinosaurs became the ancestors of birds.

The most important plants during the early part of the Mesozoic era were conifers, which formed large forests. Flowering plants appeared later in the Mesozoic era. Some of the organisms of the Mesozoic era are illustrated in **Figure 5.**

The Extinction of Dinosaurs

At the end of the Mesozoic era, 65 million years ago, dinosaurs and many other animal and plant species became extinct. What happened to the dinosaurs? According to one hypothesis, a large meteorite hit the Earth and generated giant dust clouds and enough heat to cause worldwide fires. The dust and smoke from these fires blocked out much of the sunlight and caused many plants to die out. Without enough plants to eat, the plant-eating dinosaurs died out. And the meat-eating dinosaurs that fed on the plant-eating dinosaurs died. Global temperatures may have dropped for many years. However, some mammals and birds survived.

✓ Reading Check What kind of event happened at the end of both the Paleozoic and Mesozoic eras?

Figure 5 *The Mesozoic era was dominated by dinosaurs. The era ended with the mass extinction of many species.*

Mesozoic era the geologic era that lasted from 248 million to 65 million years ago; also called the *Age of Reptiles*

Figure 6 *Many types of mammals evolved during the Cenozoic era.*

The Cenozoic Era

The **Cenozoic era** (SEN uh ZOH ik ER uh) began about 65 million years ago and continues today. *Cenozoic* comes from Greek words that mean "recent life." Scientists have more information about the Cenozoic era than about any of the previous eras. Fossils from the Cenozoic era formed recently in geologic time, so they are found in rock layers closer to the Earth's surface. The closer the fossils are to the surface, the easier they are to find.

During the Cenozoic era, many kinds of mammals, birds, insects, and flowering plants appeared. Some organisms that appeared in the Cenozoic era are shown in **Figure 6.**

✓ Reading Check What does *Cenozoic* mean?

The Age of Mammals

The Cenozoic era is sometimes called the *Age of Mammals*. Mammals have dominated the Cenozoic era the way reptiles dominated the Mesozoic era. Early Cenozoic mammals were small, forest dwellers. Larger mammals appeared later in the era. Some of these larger mammals had long legs for running, teeth that were specialized for eating different kinds of food, and large brains. Cenozoic mammals have included mastodons, saber-toothed cats, camels, giant ground sloths, and small horses.

Relative Scale It's hard to imagine 4.6 billion years. One way is to use a *relative scale*. For example, we can represent all of Earth's history by using the 12 h shown on a clock. The scale would begin at noon, representing 4.6 billion years ago, and end at midnight, representing the present. Because 12 h represent 4.6 billion years, 1 h represents about 383 million years. (Hint: 4.6 billion ÷ 12 = 383 million) So, what time on the clock represents the beginning of the Paleozoic era, 543 million years ago?

Step 1: Write the ratio.

$$\frac{x}{543{,}000{,}000 \text{ years}} = \frac{1 \text{ h}}{383{,}000{,}000 \text{ years}}$$

Step 2: Solve for x.

$$x = \frac{543{,}000{,}000 \text{ years} \times 1 \text{ h}}{383{,}000{,}000 \text{ years}} = 1.42 \text{ h}$$

Step 3: Convert the answer to the clock scale.

$$1.42 \text{ h} = 1 \text{ h} + (0.42 \times 60 \text{ min/h})$$
$$1.42 \text{ h} = 1 \text{ h } 25 \text{ min}$$

So, the Paleozoic era began 1 h 25 min before midnight, at about 10:35.

Now It's Your Turn

1. Use this method to calculate the relative times at which the Mesozoic and Cenozoic eras began.

The Cenozoic Era Today

We are currently living in the Cenozoic era. Modern humans appeared during this era. The environment and landscapes that we see around us today are part of this era.

However, the climate has changed many times during the Cenozoic era. Earth's history includes some periods called *ice ages,* during which the climate was very cold. During the ice ages, ice sheets and glaciers extended from the Earth's poles. To survive, many organisms migrated toward the equator. Other organisms adapted to the cold or became extinct.

When will the Cenozoic era end? No one knows. In the future, geologists might draw the line at a time when life on Earth again undergoes major changes.

Cenozoic era the most recent geologic era, beginning 65 million years ago; also called the *Age of Mammals*

SECTION Review

Summary

- The Earth is about 4.6 billion years old. Life formed from nonliving matter long ago.

- Precambrian time includes the formation of the Earth and the appearance of simple organisms.

- The first cells did not need oxygen. Later, photosynthetic cells evolved and released oxygen into the atmosphere.

- During the Paleozoic era, animals appeared in the oceans and on land, and plants grew on land.

- Dinosaurs dominated the Earth during the Mesozoic era.

- Mammals have dominated the Cenozoic era. This era continues today.

Using Key Terms

1. Use each of the following terms in a separate sentence: *Precambrian time, Paleozoic era, Mesozoic era,* and *Cenozoic era.*

Understanding Key Ideas

2. Unlike the atmosphere today, the atmosphere 3.5 billion years ago did not contain
   a. carbon dioxide.
   b. nitrogen.
   c. gases.
   d. ozone.

3. How do prokaryotic cells and eukaryotic cells differ?

4. Explain why cyanobacteria were important to the development of life on Earth.

5. Place in chronological order the following events on Earth:
   a. The first cells appeared that could make their own food from sunlight.
   b. The ozone layer formed.
   c. Simple chemicals reacted to form the molecules of life.
   d. Animals appeared.
   e. The first organisms appeared.
   f. Humans appeared.
   g. The Earth formed.

Math Skills

6. Calculate the total number of years that each of the geologic eras lasted, rounding to the nearest 100 million. Then, calculate each of these values as a percentage of the total 4.6 billion years of Earth's history. Round your answer to the units place.

Critical Thinking

7. **Making Inferences** Which chemicals probably made up the first cells on Earth?

8. **Forming Hypotheses** Think of your own hypothesis to explain the disappearance of the dinosaurs. Explain your hypothesis.

SCiLINKS®

NSTA
Developed and maintained by the National Science Teachers Association

For a variety of links related to this chapter, go to www.scilinks.org

Topic: Geologic Time Scale
SciLinks code: HSM0669

Humans and Other Primates

Have you ever heard someone say that humans descended from monkeys or apes? Well, scientists would not exactly say that. The scientific theory is that humans, apes, and monkeys share a common ancestor. This common ancestor probably lived more than 45 million years ago.

Most scientists agree that there is enough evidence to support this theory. Many fossils of organisms have been found that show traits of both humans and apes. Also, comparisons of modern humans and apes support this theory.

Primates

What characteristics make us human? Humans are classified as primates. **Primates** are a group of mammals that includes humans, apes, monkeys, and lemurs. Primates have the characteristics illustrated in **Figure 1.**

The First Primates

The ancestors of primates may have co-existed with the dinosaurs. These ancestors were probably mouselike mammals that were active at night, lived in trees, and ate insects. The first primates did not exist until after the dinosaurs died out. About 45 million years ago, primates that had larger brains appeared. These were the first primates that had traits similar to monkeys, apes, and humans.

Objectives

● Describe two characteristics that all primates share.

● Describe three major groups of hominids.

Terms to Learn

primate
hominid
Homo sapiens

READING STRATEGY

Discussion Read this section silently. Write down questions that you have about this section. Discuss your questions in a small group.

primate a type of mammal characterized by opposable thumbs and binocular vision

---

Figure 1 **Characteristics of Primates**

◀ Both eyes are located at the front of the head, and they provide binocular, or three-dimensional, vision.

Almost all primates, such as ▶ these orangutans, have five flexible fingers—four fingers and an opposable thumb. This thumb enables primates to grip objects. Most primates besides humans also have opposable big toes.

Apes and Chimpanzees

Scientists think that the chimpanzee, a type of ape, is the closest living relative of humans. This theory does not mean humans descended from chimpanzees. It means that humans and chimpanzees share a common ancestor. Sometime between 5 million and 30 million years ago, the ancestors of humans, chimpanzees, and other apes began to evolve along different lines.

Hominids

Humans are in a family separate from other primates. This family, called **hominids,** includes only humans and their human-like ancestors. The main characteristic that separates hominids from other primates is bipedalism. *Bipedalism* means "walking primarily upright on two feet." Evidence of bipedalism can be seen in a primate's skeletal structure. **Figure 2** shows a comparison of the skeletal features of apes and hominids.

hominid a type of primate characterized by bipedalism, relatively long lower limbs, and lack of a tail

✓ **Reading Check** In which family are humans classified? (*See the Appendix for answers to Reading Checks.*)

Figure 2 Comparison of Primate Skeletons

The bones of gorillas (a type of ape) and humans (a type of hominid) have a very similar form, but the human skeleton is adapted for walking upright.

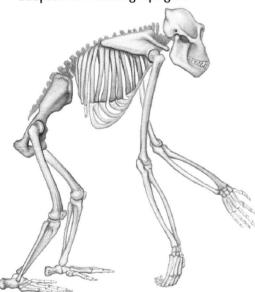

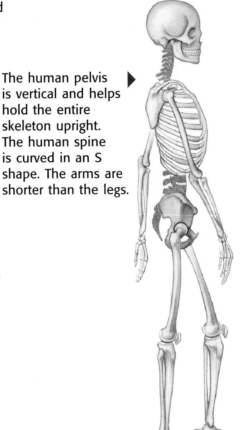

The human pelvis is vertical and helps hold the entire skeleton upright. The human spine is curved in an S shape. The arms are shorter than the legs.

▲ The gorilla pelvis tilts the ape's large rib cage and heavy neck and head forward. The gorilla spine is curved in a C shape. The arms are long to provide balance on the ground.

Figure 3 *This skull was found in the Sahel desert in Chad, Africa. The skull is estimated to be 6 million to 7 million years old.*

Hominids Through Time

Paleontologists are constantly filling in pieces of the hominid family picture. They have found many different fossils of ancient hominids and have named at least 18 types of hominids. However, scientists do not agree on the classification of every fossil. Fossils are classified as hominids when they share some of the characteristics of modern humans. But each type of hominid was unique in terms of size, the way it walked, the shape of its skull, and other characteristics.

The Earliest Hominids

The earliest hominids had traits that were more humanlike than apelike. These traits include the ability to walk upright as well as smaller teeth, flatter faces, and larger brains than earlier primates. The oldest hominid fossils have been found in Africa. So, scientists think hominid evolution began in Africa. **Figure 3** shows a fossil that may be from one of the earliest hominids. It is 6 million to 7 million years old.

✓ Reading Check Where are the earliest hominid fossils found?

Australopithecines

Many early hominids are classified as *australopithecines* (AW struh LOH PITH uh SEENS). Members of this group were similar to apes but were different from apes in several ways. For example, their brains were slightly larger than the brains of apes. Some of them may have used stone tools. They climbed trees but also walked on two legs.

Fossil evidence of australopithecines has been found in several places in Africa. The fossilized footprints in **Figure 4** were probably made by a member of this group over 3 million years ago. Some skeletons of australopithecines have been found near what appear to be simple tools.

Figure 4 *Anthropologist Mary Leakey discovered these 3.6 million year old footprints in Tanzania, Africa.*

A Variety of Early Hominids

Many australopithecines and other types of hominids lived at the same time. Some australopithecines had slender bodies. They had humanlike jaws and teeth but had small, apelike skulls. They probably lived in forests and grasslands and ate a vegetarian diet. Scientists think that some of these types of hominids may have been the ancestors of modern humans.

Some early hominids had large bodies and massive teeth and jaws. They had a unique skull structure and relatively small brains. Most of these types of hominids lived in tropical forests and probably ate tough plant material, such as roots. Scientists do not think that these large-bodied hominids are the ancestors of modern humans.

Global Hominids

About 2.3 million years ago, a new group of hominids appeared. These hominids were similar to the slender australopithecines but were more humanlike. These new hominids had larger and more complex brains, rounder skulls, and flatter faces than early hominids. They showed advanced tool-making abilities and walked upright.

These new hominids were members of the group *Homo,* which includes modern humans. Fossil evidence indicates that several members of the *Homo* group existed at the same time and on several continents. Members of this group were probably scavengers that ate a variety of foods. Some of these hominids may have adapted to climate change by migrating and changing the way they lived.

An early member of this new group was *Homo habilis* (HOH moh HAB uh luhs), which lived about 2 million years ago. In another million years, a hominid called *Homo erectus* (HOH moh i REK tuhs) appeared. This type of hominid could grow as tall as modern humans do. A museum creation of a member of *Homo erectus* is shown in **Figure 5.** No one knows what early hominids looked like. Scientists construct models based on skulls and other evidence.

Figure 5 *Fossils of a hominid known as* Homo erectus *have been found in Africa, Europe, and Asia.*

Recent Hominids

As recently as 30,000 years ago, two types of hominids may have lived in the same areas at the same time. Both had the largest brains of any hominids and made advanced tools, clothing, and art. Scientists think that modern humans may have descended from one of these two types of hominids.

Neanderthals

One recent hominid is known as *Neanderthal* (nee AN duhr TAWL). Neanderthals lived in Europe and western Asia. They may have lived as early as 400,000 years ago. They hunted large animals, made fires, and wore clothing. They also may have cared for the sick and elderly and buried their dead with cultural rituals. About 30,000 years ago, Neanderthals disappeared. No one knows what caused their extinction.

Early and Modern Humans

Modern humans are classified as the species **Homo sapiens** (HOH moh SAY pee UHNZ). The earliest *Homo sapiens* existed in Africa 100,000 to 150,000 years ago. The group probably migrated out of Africa about 40,000 years ago. Compared with Neanderthals, *Homo sapiens* has a smaller and flatter face, and has a skull that is more rounded. Of all known hominids, only *Homo sapiens* still exists.

Homo sapiens seems to be the first to create art. Early humans produced sculptures, carvings, paintings, and clothing such as that shown in **Figure 6.** The preserved villages and burial grounds of early humans show that they had an organized and complex society.

Homo sapiens the species of hominids that includes modern humans and their closest ancestors and that first appeared about 100,000 to 150,000 years ago

Figure 6 *These photos show museum recreations of early* Homo sapiens.

Drawing the Hominid Family Tree

Paleontologists review their hypotheses when they learn something new about a group of organisms and their related fossils. As more hominid fossils are discovered, there are more features to compare. Sometimes, scientists add details to the relationships they see between each group. Sometimes, new groups of hominids are recognized. Human evolution was once thought to be a line of descent from ancient primates to modern humans. But scientists now speak of a "tree" or even a "bush" to describe the evolution of various hominids in the fossil record.

✓ Reading Check What is likely to happen when a new hominid fossil is discovered?

SECTION
Review

Summary

- Humans, apes, and monkeys are primates. Almost all primates have opposable thumbs and binocular vision.

- Hominids, a subgroup of primates, include humans and their humanlike ancestors. The oldest known hominid fossils may be 7 million years old.

- Early hominids included australopithecines and the *Homo* group.

- Early *Homo sapiens* did not differ very much from present-day humans. *Homo sapiens* is the only type of hominid living today.

Using Key Terms

1. Use each of the following words in the same sentence: *primate, hominid,* and *Homo sapiens.*

Understanding Key Ideas

2. The unique characteristics of primates are

   a. bipedalism and thumbs.

   b. opposable thumbs.

   c. opposable thumbs and binocular vision.

   d. opposable toes and thumbs.

3. Describe the major evolutionary developments from early hominids to modern humans.

4. Compare members of the *Homo* group with australopithecines.

Critical Thinking

5. **Forming Hypotheses** Suggest some reasons why Neanderthals might have become extinct.

6. **Making Inferences** Imagine you are a scientist excavating an ancient campsite. What might you infer about the people who used the site if you found the charred bones of large animals and various stone blades among human fossils?

Interpreting Graphics

The figure below shows a possible ancestral relationships between humans and some modern apes. Use this figure to answer the questions that follow.

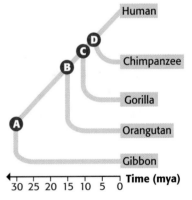

7. Which letter represents the ancestor of all the apes?

8. To which living ape are gorillas most closely related?

Inquiry Lab

Mystery Footprints

Sometimes, scientists find clues preserved in rocks that are evidence of the activities of organisms that lived thousands of years ago. Evidence such as preserved footprints can provide important information about an organism. Imagine that your class has been asked by a group of paleontologists to help study some human footprints. These footprints were found embedded in rocks in an area just outside of town.

OBJECTIVES

Form a hypothesis to explain observations of traces left by other organisms.

Design and **conduct** an experiment to test one of these hypotheses.

Analyze and **communicate** the results in a scientific way.

MATERIALS

- ruler, metric or meterstick
- sand, slightly damp
- large box, at least 1 m² or large enough to contain 3 or 4 footprints

SAFETY

Ask a Question

❶ Your teacher will give you some mystery footprints in sand. Examine the mystery footprints. Brainstorm what you might learn about the people who walked on this patch of sand.

Form a Hypothesis

❷ As a class, formulate several testable hypotheses about the people who left the footprints. Form groups of three people, and choose one hypothesis for your group to investigate.

Test the Hypothesis

❸ Draw a table for recording your data. For example, if you have two sets of mystery footprints, your table might look similar to the one below.

Mystery Footprints		
	Footprint set 1	**Footprint set 2**
Length		
Width		
Depth of toe	DO NOT	
Depth of heel	WRITE IN	
Length of stride	BOOK	

4 With the help of your group, you may first want to analyze your own footprints to help you draw conclusions about the mystery footprints. For example, use a meterstick to measure your stride when you are running. Is your stride different when you are walking? What part of your foot touches the ground first when you are running? When you are running, which part of your footprint is deeper?

5 Make a list of the kind of footprint each different activity produces. For example, you might write, "When I am running, my footprints are deep near the toe area and 110 cm apart."

Analyze the Results

1 **Classifying** Compare the data from your footprints with the data from the mystery footprints. How are the footprints alike? How are they different?

2 **Identifying Patterns** How many people do you think made the mystery footprints? Explain your interpretation.

3 **Analyzing Data** Can you tell if the mystery footprints were made by men, women, children, or a combination? Can you tell if they were standing still, walking, or running? Explain your interpretation.

Draw Conclusions

4 **Drawing Conclusions** Do your data support your hypothesis? Explain.

5 **Evaluating Methods** How could you improve your experiment?

Communicating Your Data

WRITING SKILL Summarize your group's conclusions in a report for the scientists who asked for your help. Begin by stating your hypothesis. Then, summarize the methods you used to study the footprints. Include the comparisons you made between your footprints and the mystery footprints. Add pictures if you wish. State your conclusions. Finally, offer some suggestions about how you could improve your investigation.

Chapter Review

USING KEY TERMS

Complete each of the following sentences by choosing the correct term from the word bank.

Precambrian time   Paleozoic era
Mesozoic era   Cenozoic era

1 During ___, life is thought to have originated from nonliving matter.

2 The Age of Mammals refers to the ___.

3 The Age of Reptiles refers to the ___.

4 Plants colonized land during the ___.

For each pair of terms, explain how the meanings of the terms differ.

5 *relative dating* and *absolute dating*

6 *primates* and *hominids*

UNDERSTANDING KEY IDEAS

Multiple Choice

7 If the half-life of an unstable element is 5,000 years, what percentage of the parent material will be left after 10,000 years?

a. 100%

b. 75%

c. 50%

d. 25%

8 The first cells on Earth appeared in

a. Precambrian time.

b. the Paleozoic era.

c. the Mesozoic era.

d. the Cenozoic era.

9 In which era are we currently living?

a. Precambrian time

b. Paleozoic era

c. Mesozoic era

d. Cenozoic era

10 Scientists think that the closest living relatives of humans are

a. lemurs.

b. monkeys.

c. gorillas.

d. chimpanzees.

Short Answer

11 Describe how plant and animal remains can become fossils.

12 What information do fossils provide about the history of life?

13 List three important steps in the early development of life on Earth.

14 List two important groups of organisms that appeared during each of the three most recent geologic eras.

15 Describe the event that scientists think caused the mass extinction at the end of the Mesozoic era.

16 From which geologic era are fossils most commonly found?

17 Describe two characteristics that are shared by all primates.

18 Which hominid species is alive today?

19 Concept Mapping Use the following terms to create a concept map: *Earth's history, humans, Paleozoic era, dinosaurs, Precambrian time, land plants, Mesozoic era, cyanobacteria,* and *Cenozoic era.*

20 Applying Concepts Can footprints be fossils? Explain your answer.

21 Making Inferences If you find rock layers containing fish fossils in a desert, what can you infer about the history of the desert?

22 Applying Concepts Explain how an environmental change can threaten the survival of a species. Give two examples.

23 Analyzing Ideas Why do scientists think the first cells did not need oxygen to survive?

24 Identifying Relationships How does the extinction that occurred at the end of the Mesozoic era relate to the Age of Mammals?

25 Making Comparisons Make a table listing the similarities and differences between australopithecines, early members of the group *Homo,* and modern members of the species *Homo sapiens.*

The graph below shows data about fossilized teeth that were found within a series of rock layers. Use this graph to answer the questions that follow.

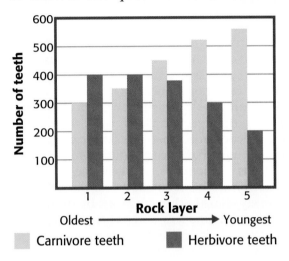

26 Which of the following statements best describes the information presented in the graph?

 a. Over time, the number of carnivores decreased and the number of herbivores increased.
 b. Over time, the number of carnivores increased and the number of herbivores increased.
 c. Over time, the number of carnivores and herbivores remained the same.
 d. Over time, the number of carnivores increased and the number of herbivores decreased.

27 At what point did carnivore teeth begin to outnumber herbivore teeth?

 a. between layer 1 and layer 2
 b. between layer 2 and layer 3
 c. between layer 3 and layer 4
 d. between layer 4 and layer 5

READING

Read each of the passages below. Then, answer the questions that follow each passage. Decide which is the best answer to each question.

Passage 1 In 1995, paleontologist Paul Sereno and his team were working in an unexplored region of Morocco when they made an incredible find—an enormous dinosaur skull! The skull measured about 1.6 m in length, which is about the height of a refrigerator. Given the size of the skull, Sereno concluded that the skeleton of the entire animal must have been about 14 m long—about as big as a school bus, and even larger than *Tyrannosaurus rex*. This 90-million-year-old predator most likely chased other dinosaurs by running on large, powerful hind legs, and its bladelike teeth meant certain death for its prey. Sereno named his new discovery *Carcharodontosaurus saharicus*, which means "shark-toothed reptile from the Sahara."

1. Paul Sereno estimated the total size of this *Carcharodontosaurus* based on

   A the size of *Tyrannosaurus rex*.

   B the fact that it was a predator.

   C the fact that it had bladelike teeth.

   D the fact that its skull was 1.6 m long.

2. Which of the following is evidence that the *Carcharodontosaurus* was a predator?

   F It had bladelike teeth.

   G It had a large skeleton.

   H It was found with the bones of a smaller animal nearby.

   I It is 90 million years old.

3. Which of the following is a fact in the passage?

   A *Carcharodontosaurus* was the largest predator that ever existed.

   B *Carcharodontosaurus* had bladelike teeth.

   C *Carcharodontosaurus* was as large as *Tyrannosaurus rex*.

   D *Carcharodontosaurus* was a shark-like reptile.

Passage 2 In 1912, Alfred Wegener proposed a hypothesis called *continental drift*. At the time, many scientists laughed at his idea. Yet Wegener's idea jolted the very foundations of geology.

Wegener used rock, fossil, and glacial evidence from opposite sides of the Atlantic Ocean to support the idea that continents can "drift." For example, Wegener recognized similar rocks and rock structures in the Appalachian Mountains and the Scottish Highlands, as well as similarities between rock layers in South Africa and Brazil. He thought that these striking similarities could be explained only if these geologic features were once part of the same continent. Wegener proposed that because continents are less dense, they float on top of the denser rock of the ocean floor.

Although continental drift explained many of Wegener's observations, he could not find evidence to explain exactly how continents move. But by the 1960s, this evidence was found and continental drift was well understood. However, Wegener's contributions went unrecognized until years after his death.

1. Which of the following did Wegener use as evidence to support his hypothesis?

   A similarities between nearby rock layers

   B similarities between rock layers in different parts of the world

   C a hypothesis that continents float

   D an explanation of how continents move

2. Which of the following statements is supported by the above passage?

   F A hypothesis is never proven.

   G A new hypothesis may take many years to be accepted by scientists.

   H The hypothesis of continental drift was not supported by evidence.

   I Wegener's hypothesis was proven wrong.

The map below shows the areas where fossils of certain organisms have been found. Use the map below to answer the questions that follow.

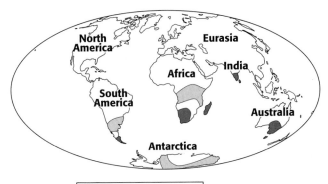

Fossils of *Glossopteris* and *Mesosaurus*

- Glossopteris
- Mesosaurus

1. *Mesosaurus* was a small, aquatic reptile and *Glossopteris* was an ancient plant species. What do these two have in common?

A Their fossils have been found on several continents.

B Their fossils are found in exactly the same places.

C Their fossils have been found only in North America.

D Their fossils have only been found near oceans.

2. Which of the following statements is best supported by these findings?

F All of the continents were once connected to each other.

G South America was once connected to Africa.

H *Glossopteris* is adapted to life at the South Pole.

I *Mesosaurus* could swim.

3. The map provides evidence that the following continents were once connected to each other, with the exception of

A North America.

B Africa.

C Antarctica.

D South America.

Read each question below, and choose the best answer.

1. Four students are sharing a birthday cake. The first student takes half of the cake. The second student take half of what remains of the cake. Then, the third student takes half of what remains of the cake. What fraction of the cake is left for the fourth student?

A 1/2

B 1/4

C 1/8

D 1/16

2. One sixteenth is equal to what percentage?

F 6.25%

G 12.5%

H 25%

I 50%

3. What is one-half of one-fourth?

A 1/2

B 1/4

C 1/8

D 1/16

4. Half-life is the time it takes for one-half of the radioactive atoms in a rock sample to decay, or change into different atoms. Carbon-14 is a radioactive isotope with a half-life of 5,730 years. In a sample that is 11,460 years old, what percentage of carbon-14 from the original sample would remain?

F 100%

G 50%

H 25%

I 12.5%

5. If a sample contains an isotope with a half-life of 10,000 years, how old would the sample be if 1/8 of the original isotope remained in the sample?

A 5,000 years

B 10,000 years

C 20,000 years

D 30,000 years

Standardized Test Preparation

Science in Action

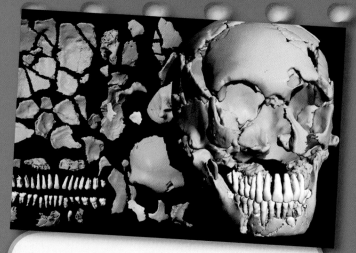

Residents of this neighborhood in Jerusalem, Israel, objected when anthropologists started to dig in the area.

Science, Technology, and Society

Using Computers to Examine Fossils

Paleontologists want to examine fossils without taking apart or damaging the fossils. Fortunately, they can now use a technology called *computerized axial tomography*, or *CAT scanning*, which provides views inside objects without touching the objects. A CAT scan is a series of cross-section pictures of an object. A computer can assemble these "slices" to create a three-dimensional picture of the entire object. Computer graphic programs can also be used to move pictures of fossil pieces around to see how the pieces fit together. The fossil skull above was reconstructed using CAT scans and computers.

Scientific Debate

Who Owns the Past?

Does a piece of land include all the layers below it? If you start digging, you may find evidence of past life. In areas that have been inhabited by human ancestors, you may find artifacts that they left behind. But who has the right to dig up these "leftovers" from the past? And who owns them?

In areas that contain many remains of the past, digging up land often leads to conflicts. Landowners may want to build on their own land. But when remains of ancient human cultures are found, living relatives of those cultures may lay claim to the remains. Paleontologists are often caught in the middle, because they want to study and preserve evidence of past life.

Math ACTIVITY

The average volume of a Neanderthal adult's brain was about 1,400 cm³, while that of an adult gorilla is about 400 cm³. Calculate how much larger a Neanderthal brain was than a gorilla brain. Express your answer as a percentage.

Social Studies ACTIVITY

WRITING SKILL Research an area where there is a debate over what to do with fossils or remains of human ancestors. Write a newspaper article about the issue. Be sure to present all sides of the debate.

The Leakey Family

A Family of Fossil Hunters In some families, a business is passed down from one generation to the next. For the Leakey's, the family business is paleoanthropology (PAY lee OH AN thruh PAWL uh jee)—the study of the origin of humans. The first famous Leakey was Dr. Louis Leakey, who was known for his hominid fossil discoveries in Africa in the 1950s. Louis formed many important hypotheses about human evolution. Louis' wife, Mary, made some of the most-important hominid fossil finds of her day.

Louis and Mary's son, Richard, carried on the family tradition of fossil hunting. He found his first fossil, which was of an extinct pig, when he was six years old. As a young man, he went on safari expeditions in which he collected photographs and specimens of African wildlife. Later, he met and married a zoologist named Meave. The photo at right shows Richard (right), Meave (left), and their daughter Louise (middle) Each of the Leakeys has contributed important finds to the study of ancient hominids.

Language Arts ACTiViTY

WRITING SKILL Visit the library and look for a book by or about the Leakey family and other scientists who have worked with them. Write a short book review to encourage your classmates to read the book.

To learn more about these Science in Action topics, visit **go.hrw.com** and type in the keyword **HL5HISF.**

Current Science

Check out Current Science® articles related to this chapter by visiting go.hrw.com. Just type in the keyword **HL5CS08.**

Classification

About the PHOTO

Look at the katydids, grasshoppers, and mantids in the photo. A scientist is classifying these insects. Every insect has a label describing the insect. These descriptions will be used to help the scientist know if each insect has already been discovered and named. When scientists discover a new insect or other organism, they have to give the organism a name. The name chosen is unique and should help other scientists understand some basic facts about the organism.

PRE-READING ACTIVITY

FOLDNOTES **Booklet** Before you read the chapter, create the FoldNote entitled "Booklet" described in the **Study Skills** section of the Appendix. Label each page of the booklet with a main idea from the chapter. As you read the chapter, write what you learn about each main idea on the appropriate page of the booklet.

START-UP ACTIVITY

Classifying Shoes

In this group activity, each group will develop a system of classification for shoes.

Procedure

1. Gather **10 shoes.** Number pieces of **masking tape** from 1 to 10. Label the sole of each shoe with a numbered piece of tape.

2. Make a list of shoe features. Make a table that has a column for each feature. Complete the table by describing each shoe.

3. Use the data in the table to make a shoe identification key.

4. The key should be a list of steps. Each step should have two contrasting statements about the shoes. The statements will lead you either to the next step or to a specific shoe.

5. If your shoe is not identified in one step, go on to the next step or steps until the shoe is identified.

6. Trade keys with another group. How did the other group's key help you identify the shoes?

Analysis

1. How was listing the shoe features before making the key helpful?

2. Were you able to identify the shoes using another group's key? Explain.

Sorting It All Out

Imagine that you live in a tropical rain forest and must get your own food, shelter, and clothing from the forest. What do you need to know to survive in the forest?

To survive in the rain forest, you need to know which plants are safe to eat and which are not. You need to know which animals you can eat and which might eat you. In other words, you need to study the living things around you and organize them into categories, or classify them. **Classification** is putting things into orderly groups based on similar characteristics.

Why Classify?

For thousands of years, humans have classified living things based on usefulness. The Chácabo people of Bolivia know of 360 types of plants that grow in the forest where they live. Of these 360 plant types, 305 are useful to the Chácabo.

Some biologists, such as those shown in **Figure 1,** classify living and extinct organisms. Scientists classify organisms to help make sense and order of the many kinds of living things in the world. Biologists use a system to classify living things. This system groups organisms according to the characteristics they share. The classification of living things makes it easier for biologists to answer many important questions, such as the following:

- How many known species are there?
- What are the defining characteristics of each species?
- What are the relationships between these species?

Reading Check What are three questions that classifying organisms can help answer? (*See the Appendix for answers to Reading Checks.*)

classification the division of organisms into groups, or classes, based on specific characteristics

Figure 1 *These biologists are sorting rain-forest plant material.*

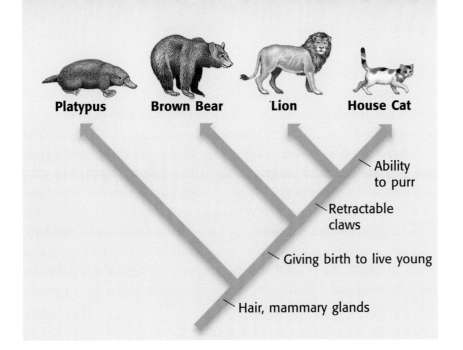

Platypus **Brown Bear** **Lion** **House Cat**

Ability to purr

Retractable claws

Giving birth to live young

Hair, mammary glands

Figure 2 *This branching diagram shows the similarities and differences between four mammals.*

How Do Scientists Classify Organisms?

Before the 1600s, many scientists divided organisms into two groups: plants and animals. But, as more organisms were discovered, some organisms did not fit into either group. In the 1700s, a Swedish scientist named Carolus Linnaeus (KAR uh luhs li NAY uhs) founded modern taxonomy. **Taxonomy** (taks AHN uh mee) is the science of describing, classifying, and naming living things. Linnaeus tried to classify all living things based on their shape and structure. He described a seven-level system of classification, which is still used today.

Classification Today

Taxonomists use the seven-level system to classify living things based on shared characteristics. Scientists also use shared characteristics to hypothesize how closely related living things are. The more characteristics the organisms share, the more closely related the organisms may be. For example, the platypus, brown bear, lion, and house cat are thought to be related because they share many characteristics. These animals have hair and mammary glands, so they are grouped together as mammals. But they can be further classified into more-specific groups.

Branching Diagrams

Look at the branching diagram in **Figure 2.** Several characteristics are listed along the line that points to the right. Each characteristic is shared by the animals to the right of it. All of the animals shown have hair and mammary glands. But only the bear, lion, and house cat give birth to live young. The lion and the house cat have retractable claws, but the other animals do not. Thus, the lion and the house cat are more closely related to each other than to the other animals.

taxonomy the science of describing, naming, and classifying organisms

A Branching Diagram

1. Construct a diagram similar to the one in **Figure 2.**
2. Use a frog, a snake, a kangaroo, and a rabbit in your diagram.
3. Think of one major change that happened before the frog evolved.
4. For the last three organisms, think of a change that happened between one of these organisms and the other two. Write all of these changes in your diagram.

Levels of Classification

Every living thing is classified into one of six kingdoms. Kingdoms are the largest, most general groups. All living things in a kingdom are sorted into several phyla (singular, *phylum*). The members of one phylum are more like each other than they are like members of other phyla. All of the living things in a phylum are further sorted into classes. Each class includes one or more orders. Orders are separated into families. Families are broken into genera (singular, *genus*). And genera are sorted into species. A species is a group of organisms that are closely related and can mate to produce fertile offspring. **Figure 3** shows the classification of a house cat from kingdom Animalia to genus and species, *Felis domesticus*.

Scientific Names

By classifying organisms, biologists are able to give organisms scientific names. A scientific name is always the same for a specific kind of organism no matter how many common names there might be. Before Linnaeus's time, scholars used names that were as long as 12 words to identify species. The names were hard to work with because they were so long. And different scientists named organisms differently, so an organism could have more than one name.

INTERNET ACTIVITY

For another activity related to this chapter, go to **go.hrw.com** and type in the keyword **HL5CLSW**.

Figure 3 *The seven levels of classification are kingdom, phylum, class, order, family, genus, and species.*

Kingdom Animalia	Phylum Chordata	Class Mammalia	Order Carnivora
All animals are in the **kingdom Animalia.**	All animals in the **phylum Chordata** have a hollow nerve cord. Most have a backbone.	Animals in the **class Mammalia** have a backbone. They also nurse their young.	Animals in the **order Carnivora** have a backbone and nurse their young. They also have special teeth for tearing meat.

Two-Part Names

Linnaeus simplified the naming of living things by giving each species a two-part scientific name. For example, the scientific name for the Asian elephant is *Elephas maximus* (EL uh fuhs MAK suh muhs). The first part of the name, *Elephas,* is the genus name. The second part, *maximus,* is the species name. No other species has both this genus name and this species name. Naming rules help scientists communicate clearly about living things.

All genus names begin with a capital letter. All species names begin with a lowercase letter. Usually, both words are underlined or italicized. But if the surrounding text is italicized, the genus and species names are not italicized, as shown in **Figure 4.** These printing styles show a reader which names are genus and species names.

Scientific names, which are usually in Latin or Greek, contain information about an organism. The name of the animal shown in **Figure 4** is *Tyrannosaurus rex. Tyrannosaurus* is a combination of two Greek words and means "tyrant lizard." The word *rex* is Latin for "king." The name tells you that this animal was probably not a passive grass eater! Sometimes, *Tyrannosaurus rex* is referred to as *T. rex.* The species name is not correct without the genus name or its abbreviation.

Figure 4 *You would never call* Tyrannosaurus rex *just* rex!

Reading Check What are the two parts of a scientific name?

Family *Felidae*	Genus *Felis*	Species *Felis domesticus*
Animals in the **family Felidae** are cats. They have a backbone, nurse their young, have special teeth for tearing meat, and have retractable claws.	Animals in the **genus Felis** have traits of other animals in the same family. However, these cats cannot roar; they can only purr.	The **species Felis domesticus** is the common house cat. The house cat shares traits with all of the organisms in the levels above the species level, but it also has unique traits.

Dichotomous Keys

You might someday turn over a rock and find an organism that you don't recognize. How would you identify the organism? Taxonomists have developed special guides to help scientists identify organisms. A **dichotomous key** (die KAHT uh muhs KEE) is an identification aid that uses sequential pairs of descriptive statements. There are only two alternative responses for each statement. From each pair of statements, the person trying to identify the organism chooses the statement that describes the organism. Either the chosen statement identifies the organism or the person is directed to another pair of statements. By working through the statements in the key in order, the person can eventually identify the organism. Using the simple dichotomous key in **Figure 5,** try to identify the two animals shown.

dichotomous key an aid that is used to identify organisms and that consists of the answers to a series of questions

✓ **Reading Check** What is a dichotomous key?

Figure 5 *A dichotomous key can help you identify organisms.*

Dichotomous Key to 10 Common Mammals in the Eastern United States

1. a. This mammal flies. Its "hand" forms a wing.	**little brown bat**
b. This mammal does not fly. It's "hand" does not form a wing.	**Go to step 2.**
2. a. This mammal has no hair on its tail.	**Go to step 3.**
b. This mammal has hair on its tail.	**Go to step 4.**
3. a. This mammal has a short, naked tail.	**eastern mole**
b. This mammal has a long, naked tail.	**Go to step 5.**
4. a. This mammal has a black mask across its face.	**raccoon**
b. This mammal does not have a black mask across its face.	**Go to step 6.**
5. a. This mammal has a tail that is flat and paddle shaped.	**beaver**
b. This mammal has a tail that is not flat or paddle shaped.	**opossum**
6. a. This mammal is brown and has a white underbelly.	**Go to step 7.**
b. This mammal is not brown and does not have a white underbelly.	**Go to step 8.**
7. a. This mammal has a long, furry tail that is black on the tip.	**longtail weasel**
b. This mammal has a long tail that has little fur.	**white-footed mouse**
8. a. This mammal is black and has a narrow white stripe on its forehead and broad white stripes on its back.	**striped skunk**
b. This mammal is not black and does not have white stripes.	**Go to step 9.**
9. a. This mammal has long ears and a short, cottony tail.	**eastern cottontail**
b. This mammal has short ears and a medium-length tail.	**woodchuck**

A Growing System

You may think that all of the organisms on Earth have already been classified. But people are still discovering and classifying organisms. Some newly discovered organisms fit into existing categories. But sometimes, someone discovers new evidence or an organism that is so different from other organisms that it does not fit existing categories. For example, in 1995, scientists studied an organism named *Symbion pandora* (SIM bee AHN pan DAWR uh). Scientists found *S. pandora* living on lobster lips! Scientists learned that *S. pandora* had some characteristics that no other known organism had. In fact, scientists trying to classify *S. pandora* found that it didn't fit in any existing phylum. So, taxonomists created a new phylum for *S. pandora*.

SECTION Review

Summary

- Classification refers to the arrangement of living things into orderly groups based on their similarities.

- Today's living things are classified by using a seven-level system of organization. The seven levels are kingdom, phylum, class, order, family, genus, and species.

- An organism has only one correct scientific name.

- Dichotomous keys are tools for identifying organisms.

Using Key Terms

1. In your own words, write a definition for each of the following terms: *classification* and *taxonomy*.

Understanding Key Ideas

2. The two parts of a scientific name are the names of the genus and the

   a. species.   **c.** family.
   b. phylum.   **d.** order.

3. Why do scientists use scientific names for organisms?

4. List the seven levels of classification.

5. Describe how a dichotomous key helps scientists identify organisms.

Critical Thinking

6. **Analyzing Processes** Biologists think that millions of species are not classified yet. Why do you think so many species have not been classified yet?

7. **Applying Concepts** Both dolphins and sharks have a tail and fins. How can you determine if dolphins and sharks are closely related?

Interpreting Graphics

Use the figure below to answer the questions that follow.

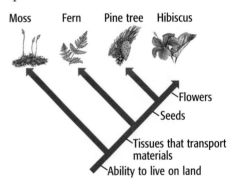

Moss   Fern   Pine tree   Hibiscus

Flowers
Seeds
Tissues that transport materials
Ability to live on land

8. Which plant is most similar to the hibiscus?

9. Which plant is least similar to the hibiscus?

The Six Kingdoms

What do you call an organism that is green, makes its own food, lives in pond water, and moves? Is it a plant, an animal, or something in between?

For hundreds of years, all living things were classified as either plants or animals. But over time, scientists discovered species that did not fit easily into these two kingdoms. For example, an organism of the genus *Euglena*, such as the one shown in **Figure 1,** has characteristics of both plants and animals. How would you classify such an organism?

What Is It?

Organisms are classified by their characteristics. For example, organisms of the genus *Euglena* are

- single celled and live in pond water
- green and make their own food through photosynthesis

These two characteristics might lead you to conclude that the genus of *Euglena* are plants. However, you should consider the following other characteristics before you form your conclusion:

- Members of the genus *Euglena* move by whipping their "tails," which are called *flagella*.
- *Euglena* can feed on other organisms.

Plants don't move themselves around and usually do not eat other organisms. So, are organisms of the genus *Euglena* animals? As you can see, *Euglena* does not fit into the category of plants or animals. Scientists solved this classification problem by adding another kingdom, the kingdom Protista, to classify organisms such as *Euglena*.

As scientists continued to learn about living things, they added kingdoms that account for the characteristics of different organisms. Currently, most scientists agree that the six-kingdom classification system works best. However, scientists will continue to adjust the system as they learn more.

READING WARM-UP

Objectives

- Explain how classification schemes for kingdoms developed as greater numbers of different organisms became known.
- Describe each of the six kingdoms.

Terms to Learn

Archaebacteria	Fungi
Eubacteria	Plantae
Protista	Animalia

READING STRATEGY

Reading Organizer As you read this section, make a table comparing the six classification kingdoms to each other.

Figure 1 *How would you classify this organism? This member of the genus* Euglena, *which is shown here highly magnified, has characteristics of both plants and animals.*

Figure 2 *The Grand Prismatic Spring in Yellowstone National Park contains water that is about 90°C (194°F). The spring is home to archaebacteria that thrive in its hot water.*

Archaebacteria a kingdom made up of bacteria that live in extreme environments

Eubacteria a kingdom that contains all prokaryotes except archaebacteria

The Two Kingdoms of Bacteria

Bacteria are extremely small, single-celled organisms that differ from all other living things. Bacteria are *prokaryotes* (proh KAYR ee OHTS), organisms that lack nuclei. Many biologists divide bacteria into two kingdoms: Archaebacteria (AHR kee bak TEER ee uh) and Eubacteria (YOO bak TEER ee uh).

Archaebacteria

Prokaryotes that can live in extreme environments are in the kingdom **Archaebacteria.** The prefix *archae-* comes from a Greek word meaning "ancient." Today, most archaebacteria can be found living in places where most organisms could not survive. **Figure 2** shows a hot spring in Yellowstone National Park. The yellow and orange rings around the edge of the hot spring are made up of the billions of archaebacteria that live there.

Eubacteria

Bacteria that are not in the kingdom Archaebacteria are in the kingdom **Eubacteria.** Eubacteria are prokaryotes that live in the soil, in water, and even on and inside the human body! For example, *Escherichia coli,* pictured in **Figure 3,** is present in large numbers in human intestines, where it produces vitamin K. One kind of eubacterium converts milk into yogurt. Another kind of eubacterium causes pneumonia.

Reading Check Name a type of eubacterium that lives in your body. (*See the Appendix for answers to Reading Checks.*)

Figure 3 *Specimens of* E. coli *are shown on the point of a pin under a scanning electron microscope. These eubacteria live in the intestines of animals and decompose undigested food.*

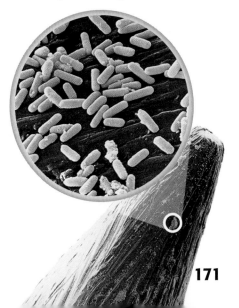

171

Kingdom Protista

Members of the kingdom **Protista** (proh TIST uh), commonly called *protists* (PROH tists), are single-celled or simple multicellular organisms that don't fit into any other kingdom. Unlike bacteria, protists are *eukaryotes,* organisms whose cells have a nucleus and membrane-bound organelles. The kingdom Protista contains all eukaryotes that are not plants, animals, or fungi. Scientists think the first protists evolved from ancient bacteria about 2 billion years ago. Much later, protists gave rise to plants, fungi, and animals as well as to modern protists.

The kingdom Protista contains many kinds of organisms. Animal-like protists are called *protozoans.* Plantlike protists are called *algae.* Slime molds, such as the one shown in **Figure 4,** and water molds are fungus-like protists. Members of *Euglena* are also members of the kingdom Protista.

Figure 4 *This slime mold is a protist.*

Protista a kingdom of mostly one-celled eukaryotic organisms that are different from plants, animals, bacteria, and fungi

Fungi a kingdom made up of nongreen, eukaryotic organisms that have no means of movement, reproduce by using spores, and get food by breaking down substances in their surroundings and absorbing the nutrients

Kingdom Fungi

Molds and mushrooms are examples of the complex multicellular members of the kingdom Fungi (FUHN JIE). Unlike plants, fungi do not perform photosynthesis, and unlike animals, fungi do not eat food. Instead, members of the kingdom **Fungi** absorb nutrients from substances in their surroundings. Fungi use digestive juices to break down the substances. **Figure 5** shows a very poisonous fungus. Never eat wild fungi.

Figure 5 *This beautiful fungus of the genus* Amanita *is poisonous.*

Figure 6 *Giant sequoias can measure 30 m around at the base and can grow to more than 91.5 m tall.*

▲ **Figure 7** *Plants such as these are common in the Tropics.*

Kingdom Plantae

Although plants vary remarkably in size and form, most people easily recognize the members of the kingdom Plantae. **Plantae** consists of organisms that are eukaryotic, have cell walls, and make food through photosynthesis. For photosynthesis to occur, plants must be exposed to sunlight. Plants can therefore be found on land and in water that light can penetrate.

The food that plants make is important not only for the plants but also for all of the organisms that get nutrients from plants. Most life on Earth is dependent on plants. For example, some members of the kingdoms Fungi, Protista, and Eubacteria consume plants. When these organisms digest the plant material, they get energy and nutrients made by the plants.

Plants also provide habitat for other organisms. The giant sequoias in **Figure 6** and the flowering plants in **Figure 7** provide birds, insects, and other animals with a place to live.

✓ **Reading Check** How do members of the kingdom Plantae provide energy and nutrients to members of other kingdoms?

Plantae a kingdom made up of complex, multicellular organisms that are usually green, have cell walls made of cellulose, cannot move around, and use the sun's energy to make sugar by photosynthesis

Ring-Around-the-Sequoia

How many students would have to join hands to form a human chain around a giant sequoia that is 30 m in circumference? Assume for this calculation that the average student can extend his or her arms about 1.3 m.

Kingdom Animalia

Animalia a kingdom made up of complex, multicellular organisms that lack cell walls, can usually move around, and quickly respond to their environment

The kingdom **Animalia** contains complex, multicellular organisms that don't have cell walls, are usually able to move around, and have specialized sense organs. These sense organs help most animals quickly respond to their environment. Organisms in the kingdom Animalia are commonly called *animals*. You probably recognize many of the organisms in the kingdom Animalia. All of the organisms in **Figure 8** are animals.

Animals depend on the organisms from other kingdoms. For example, animals depend on plants for food. Animals also depend on bacteria and fungi to recycle the nutrients found in dead organisms.

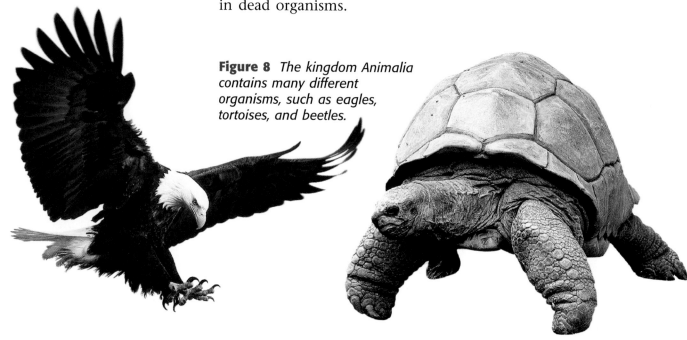

Figure 8 *The kingdom Animalia contains many different organisms, such as eagles, tortoises, and beetles.*

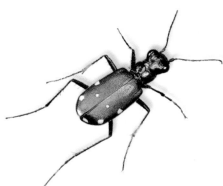

CONNECTION TO Social Studies

WRITING SKILL **Animals That Help** Humans have depended on animals for thousands of years. Many people around the world still use oxen to farm. Camels, horses, donkeys, goats, and llamas are all still used as pack animals. Dogs still help herd sheep, protect property, and help people hunt. Scientists are even discovering new ways that animals can help us. For example, scientists are training bees to help find buried land mines. Using the library or the Internet, research an animal that helps people. Make a poster describing the animal and the animal's scientific name. The poster should show who uses the animal, how the animal is used, and how long people have depended on the animal. Find or draw pictures to put on your poster.

ACTIVITY

Simple Animals

When you think of an animal, what do you imagine? You may think of a dog, a cat, or a parrot. All of those organisms are animals. But the animal kingdom also includes some members that might surprise you, such as worms, insects, and corals.

The red cup sponge shown in **Figure 9** is also an animal. Sponges are usually thought of as the simplest animals. They don't have sense organs. Most sponges cannot move. Sponges used to be considered plants. But sponges cannot make food. They must eat other organisms to get nutrients, which is one reason that sponges are classified as animals.

✓ Reading Check Why were sponges once thought to be plants?

Figure 9 *This red cup sponge is a simple animal.*

SECTION Review

Summary

- Most biologists recognize six kingdoms: Archaebacteria, Eubacteria, Protista, Fungi, Plantae, and Animalia.

- Archaebacteria live in extreme environments. Eubacteria live almost everywhere else.

- Plants, animals, fungi, and protists are eukaryotic organisms. Plants perform photosynthesis. Animals eat food and digest it inside their body. Fungi absorb nutrients from material that they break down outside of their body. Protists are organisms that don't fit in other kingdoms.

Using Key Terms

For each pair of terms, explain how the meanings of the terms differ.

1. *Archaebacteria* and *Eubacteria*

2. *Plantae* and *Fungi*

Understanding Key Ideas

3. Biological classification schemes change
   a. as new evidence and more kinds of organisms are discovered.
   b. every 100 years.
   c. when scientists disagree.
   d. only once.

4. Explain the different ways in which plants, fungi, and animals obtain nutrients.

5. Why are protists placed in their own kingdom?

6. Describe the six kingdoms.

Math Skills

7. A certain eubacterium can divide every 30 min. If you begin with 1 eubacterium, when will you have more than 1,000 eubacteria?

Critical Thinking

8. **Identifying Relationships** How are bacteria similar to fungi? How are fungi similar to animals?

9. **Analyzing Methods** Why do you think Linnaeus did not include classification kingdoms for categories of bacteria?

10. **Applying Concepts** The Venus' flytrap does not move around. It can make its own food by using photosynthesis. It can also trap insects and digest the insects to get nutrients. The flytrap also has a cell wall. Into which kingdom would you place the Venus' flytrap? What makes this organism unusual in the kingdom you chose?

SCiLINKS® NSTA
Developed and maintained by the National Science Teachers Association

For a variety of links related to this chapter, go to www.scilinks.org

Topic: The Six Kingdoms
SciLinks code: HSM1397

Skills Practice Lab

Shape Island

You are a biologist exploring uncharted parts of the world to look for new animal species. You sailed for days across the ocean and finally found Shape Island hundreds of miles south of Hawaii. Shape Island has some very unusual organisms. The shape of each organism is a variation of a geometric shape. You have spent more than a year collecting and classifying specimens. You have been able to assign a two-part scientific name to most of the species that you have collected. Now, you must assign a two-part scientific name to each of the last 12 specimens collected before you begin your journey home.

Procedure

1. Draw each of the organisms pictured on the facing page. Beside each organism, draw a line for its name, as shown on the top left of the following page. The first organism pictured has already been named, but you must name the remaining 12. Use the glossary of Greek and Latin prefixes, suffixes, and root words in the table to help you name the organisms.

Greek and Latin roots, prefixes, and suffixes	Meaning
ankylos	angle
antennae	external sense organs
bi-	two
cyclo-	circular
macro-	large
micro-	small
mono-	one
peri-	around
-plast	body
-pod	foot
quad-	four
stoma	mouth
tri-	three
uro-	tail

Analyze Results

1. **Analyzing Results** If you gave species 1 a common name, such as *round-face-no-nose*, would any other scientist know which of the newly discovered organisms you were referring to? Explain. How many others have a round face and no nose?

2. **Organizing Data** Describe two characteristics that are shared by all of your newly discovered specimens.

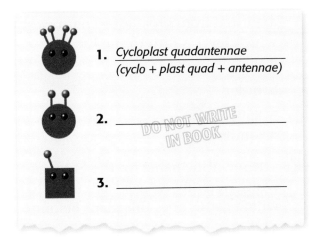

1. *Cycloplast quadantennae*
   (cyclo + plast quad + antennae)

2. _____
   DO NOT WRITE IN BOOK

3. _____

Draw Conclusions

3 **Applying Conclusions** One more organism exists on Shape Island, but you have not been able to capture it. However, your supplies are running out, and you must start sailing for home. You have had a good look at the unusual animal and can draw it in detail. Draw an animal that is different from all of the others, and give it a two-part scientific name.

Applying Your Data

Look up the scientific names *Mertensia virginica* and *Porcellio scaber.* Answer the following questions as they apply to each organism: Is the organism a plant or an animal? How many common names does the organism have? How many scientific names does it have?

Think of the name of your favorite fruit or vegetable. Find out if it has other common names, and find out its two-part scientific name.

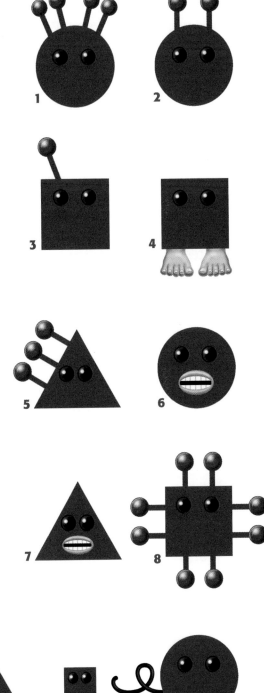

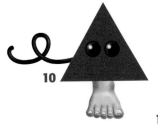

Chapter Review

USING KEY TERMS

Complete each of the following sentences by choosing the correct term from the word bank.

Animalia   Protista
Eubacteria   Plantae
Archaebacteria   classification
taxonomy

1 Linnaeus founded the science of ___.

2 Bacteria that live in extreme environments are in the kingdom ___.

3 Complex multicellular organisms that can usually move around and respond to their environment are in the kingdom ___.

4 A system of ___ can help group animals into categories.

5 Prokaryotes that are not archaebacteria are in the kingdom ___.

UNDERSTANDING KEY IDEAS

Multiple Choice

6 Scientists classify organisms by
a. arranging the organisms in orderly groups.
b. giving the organisms many common names.
c. deciding whether the organisms are useful.
d. using only existing categories of classification.

7 When the seven levels of classification are listed from broadest to narrowest, which level is fifth in the list?
a. class
b. order
c. genus
d. family

8 The scientific name for the European white waterlily is *Nymphaea alba*. To which genus does this plant belong?
a. *Nymphaea*   c. water lily
b. *alba*   d. alba lily

9 *Animalia, Protista, Fungi, Archaebacteria, Eubacteria,* and *Plantae* are the
a. scientific names of different organisms.
b. names of kingdoms.
c. levels of classification.
d. scientists who organized taxonomy.

10 Bacteria that live in your intestines are classified in the kingdom
a. Protista.   c. Archaebacteria.
b. Eubacteria.   d. Fungi.

11 What kind of organism thrives in hot springs and other extreme environments?
a. fungus   c. archaebacterium
b. eubacterium   d. protist

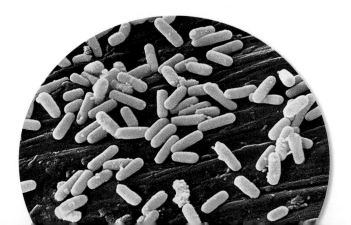

Short Answer

12 Why is the use of scientific names important in biology?

13 What kind of evidence is used by modern taxonomists to classify organisms based on evolutionary relationships?

14 Is a eubacterium a type of eukaryote? Explain your answer.

15 Scientists used to classify organisms as either plants or animals. Why doesn't that classification system work?

CRITICAL THINKING

16 **Concept Mapping** Use the following terms to create a concept map: *kingdom, fern, lizard, Animalia, Fungi, algae, Protista, Plantae,* and *mushroom*.

17 **Analyzing Methods** Explain how the levels of classification depend on the similarities and differences between organisms.

18 **Making Inferences** Explain why two species that belong to the same genus, such as white oak (*Quercus alba*) and cork oak (*Quercus suber*), also belong to the same family.

19 **Identifying Relationships** What characteristic do the members of all six kingdoms have in common?

INTERPRETING GRAPHICS

Use the branching diagram of selected primates below to answer the questions that follow.

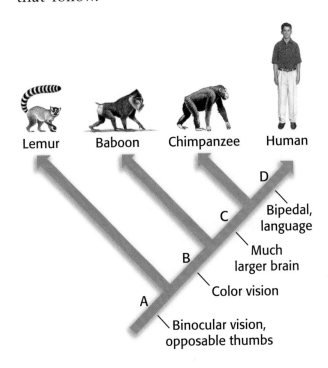

20 Which primate is the closest relative to the common ancestor of all primates?

21 Which primate shares the most traits with humans?

22 Do both lemurs and humans have the characteristics listed at point D? Explain your answer.

23 What characteristic do baboons have that lemurs do not have? Explain your answer.

Standardized Test Preparation

Read each of the passages below. Then, answer the questions that follow each passage.

Passage 1 When organizing life on Earth into categories, we must remember that organisms are not equally <u>distributed</u> throughout the categories of our classification system. We often think of Earth's living things as only the plants and animals that live on Earth's surface. However, the largest kingdoms in terms of the number of individuals and total mass are the kingdoms Archaebacteria and Eubacteria. And a common home of bacteria may be deep within the Earth's crust.

1. In the passage, what does *distributed* mean?
   - **A** divided
   - **B** important
   - **C** visible
   - **D** variable

2. According to the passage, what are most of the organisms living on Earth?
   - **F** plants
   - **G** animals
   - **H** fungi
   - **I** bacteria

3. Which of the following statements is a fact according to the passage?
   - **A** All organisms are equally distributed over Earth's surface.
   - **B** Plants are the most important organisms on Earth.
   - **C** Many bacteria may live deep within Earth's crust.
   - **D** Bacteria are equally distributed over Earth's surface.

Passage 2 When you think of an animal, what do you imagine? You may think of a dog, a cat, or a parrot. All of those organisms are animals. But the animal kingdom also includes some <u>members</u> that might surprise you, such as worms, insects, <u>corals</u>, and sponges.

1. In the passage, what is coral?
   - **A** a kind of animal
   - **B** a kind of insect
   - **C** a color similar to pink
   - **D** an organism found in lakes and streams

2. What can you infer from the passage?
   - **F** All members of the animal kingdom are visible.
   - **G** Parrots make good pets.
   - **H** Not all members of the animal kingdom have DNA.
   - **I** Members of the animal kingdom come in many shapes and sizes.

3. Which of the following can you infer from the passage?
   - **A** Worms and corals make good pets.
   - **B** Corals and cats have some traits in common.
   - **C** All organisms are animals.
   - **D** Worms, corals, insects, and sponges are in the same family.

4. In the passage, what does *members* mean?
   - **F** teammates
   - **G** limbs
   - **H** individuals admitted to a club
   - **I** components

The Venn diagrams below show two classification systems. Use the diagrams to answer the questions that follow.

Classification system A

Classification system B

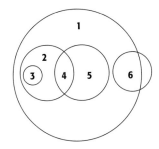

1. For Classification system A, which of the following statements is true?

   A All organisms in group 6 are in group 7.
   B All organisms in group 5 are in group 4.
   C All organisms in group 6 are in group 1.
   D All organisms in group 2 are in group 1.

2. For Classification system A, which of the following statements is true?

   F All organisms in group 3 are in group 2.
   G All organisms in group 3 are in group 4.
   H All organisms in group 3 are in group 1.
   I All organisms in group 3 are in every other group.

3. For Classification system B, which of the following statements is true?

   A All organisms in group 1 are in group 6.
   B All organisms in group 6 are in group 1.
   C All organisms in group 3 are in group 1.
   D All organisms in group 2 are in group 5.

4. For Classification system B, which of the following statements is true?

   F All organisms in group 4 are in group 1, 2, and 5.
   G All organisms in group 4 are in groups 3 and 5.
   H All organisms in group 4 are in groups 5 and 6.
   I All organisms in group 4 are in groups 1, 5, and 6.

5. In Classification system B, which group contains organisms that are not in group 1?

   A 2
   B 4
   C 5
   D 6

MATH

Read each question below, and choose the best answer.

1. Scientists estimate that millions of species have not yet been discovered and classified. About 1.8 million species have been discovered and classified. If scientists think that this 1.8 million makes up only 10% of the total number of species on Earth, how many species do scientists think exist on Earth?

   A 180 million
   B 18 million
   C 1.8 million
   D 180,000

2. Sequoia trees can grow to more than 90 m in height. There are 3.28 feet in 1 meter. How many feet are in 90 m?

   F 27.4 ft
   G 95.2 ft
   H 270 ft
   I 295.2 ft

Science in Action

Scientific Debate

Birds and Dinosaurs

Did birds evolve from dinosaurs? Some scientists think that birds evolved from small, carnivorous dinosaurs such as *Velociraptor* about 115 million to 150 million years ago. This idea is based on similarities of modern birds and these small dinosaurs. These similarities include the size, shape, and number of toes and "fingers," the location and shape of the breastbone and shoulder, and the presence of a hollow bone structure. Many scientists find this evidence convincing.

However, some scientists think that birds developed 100 million years before *Velociraptor* and its relatives did. These scientists point out that *Velociraptor* and its relatives were ground dwellers and were the wrong shape and size for flying.

Scientific Discovery

A New Insect Order

In 2001, Oliver Zompro was studying a fossil insect preserved in amber. Although the fossil insect resembled a grasshopper or a walking stick, it was unique and could not be classified in the same group as either one. Zompro wondered if he might be seeing a new type of insect or an insect that was now thought to be extinct. The fossil insect was less than 4 cm long. Its spiny appearance earned the insect the nickname "gladiator." The gladiator bug that Zompro discovered is so unusual that it cannot be classified in any of the 30 existing orders of insects. Instead, the gladiator bug constitutes its own new order, which has been named *Mantophasmatodea*.

Math ACTIVITY

Velociraptor lived between 115 million and 150 million years ago. Find the average of these two numbers. Use that average to answer the following questions: How many weeks ago did *Velociraptor* live on Earth? How many days ago did *Velociraptor* live on Earth?

Language Arts ACTIVITY

WRITING SKILL Give the gladiator bug a new nickname. Write a short essay about why you chose that particular name for the insect.

Michael Fay

Crossing Africa Finding and classifying wild animals takes a great deal of perseverance. Just ask Michael Fay, who spent 15 months crossing 2,000 miles of uninhabited rain forest in the Congo River Basin of West Africa. He used video, photography, and old-fashioned note taking to record the types of animals and vegetation that he encountered along the way.

To find and classify wild animals, Fay often had to think like an animal. When coming across a group of monkeys swinging high above him in the emerald green canopy, Fay would greet the monkeys with his imitation of the crowned eagle's high-pitched, whistling cry. When the monkeys responded with their own distinctive call, Fay could identify exactly what species they were and would jot it down in one of his 87 waterproof notebooks. Fay also learned other tricks, such as staying downwind of an elephant to get as close to the elephant as possible. He could then identify its size, its age, and the length of its tusks.

Social Studies ACTIVITY

WRITING SKILL Many organizations around the world are committed to helping preserve biodiversity. Conduct some Internet and library research to find out about an organization that works to keep species safe from extinction. Create a poster that describes the organization and some of the species that the organization protects.

To learn more about these Science in Action topics, visit **go.hrw.com** and type in the keyword **HL5CLSF.**

Current Science

Check out Current Science® articles related to this chapter by visiting go.hrw.com. Just type in the keyword **HL5CS09.**

Skills Practice Lab

Cells Alive!

You have probably used a microscope to look at single-celled organisms such as those shown below. They can be found in pond water. In the following exercise, you will look at *Protococcus*—algae that form a greenish stain on tree trunks, wooden fences, flowerpots, and buildings.

Euglena

Amoeba

Paramecium

Procedure

1. Locate some *Protococcus*. Scrape a small sample into a container. Bring the sample to the classroom, and make a wet mount of it as directed by your teacher. If you can't find *Protococcus* outdoors, look for algae on the glass in an aquarium. Such algae may not be *Protococcus*, but it will be a very good substitute.

2. Set the microscope on low power to examine the algae. On a separate sheet of paper, draw the cells that you see.

3. Switch to high power to examine a single cell. Draw the cell.

4. You will probably notice that each cell contains several chloroplasts. Label a chloroplast on your drawing. What is the function of the chloroplast?

5. Another structure that should be clearly visible in all the algae cells is the nucleus. Find the nucleus in one of your cells, and label it on your drawing. What is the function of the nucleus?

6. What does the cytoplasm look like? Describe any movement you see inside the cells.

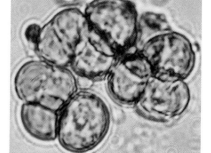

Protococcus

Analyze the Results

1. Are *Protococcus* single-celled organisms or multicellular organisms?

2. How are *Protococcus* different from amoebas?

Skills Practice Lab

Stayin' Alive!

Every second of your life, your body's trillions of cells take in, use, and store energy. They repair themselves, reproduce, and get rid of waste. Together, these processes are called *metabolism.* Your cells use the food that you eat to provide the energy you need to stay alive.

Your Basal Metabolic Rate (BMR) is a measurement of the energy that your body needs to carry out all the basic life processes while you are at rest. These processes include breathing, keeping your heart beating, and keeping your body's temperature stable. Your BMR is influenced by your gender, your age, and many other things. Your BMR may be different from everyone else's, but it is normal for you. In this activity, you will find the amount of energy, measured in Calories, you need every day in order to stay alive.

MATERIALS
- bathroom scale
- tape measure

Procedure

1. Find your weight on a bathroom scale. If the scale measures in pounds, you must convert your weight in pounds to your mass in kilograms. To convert your weight in pounds (lb) to mass in kilograms (kg), multiply the number of pounds by 0.454.

   Example: If Carlos weighs 125 lb, his mass in kilograms is:

   $$\begin{array}{r} 125 \text{ lb} \\ \times\ 0.454 \\ \hline 56.75 \text{ kg} \end{array}$$

2. Use a tape measure to find your height. If the tape measures in inches, convert your height in inches to height in centimeters. To convert your height in inches (in.) to your height in centimeters (cm), multiply the number of inches by 2.54.

   If Carlos is 62 in. tall, his height in centimeters is:

   $$\begin{array}{r} 62 \text{ in.} \\ \times\ 2.54 \\ \hline 157.48 \text{ cm} \end{array}$$

3 Now that you know your height and mass, use the appropriate formula below to get a close estimate of your BMR. Your answer will give you an estimate of the number of Calories your body needs each day just to stay alive.

Calculating Your BMR	
Females	**Males**
65 + (10 × your mass in kilograms)	66 + (13.5 × your mass in kilograms)
+ (1.8 × your height in centimeters)	+ (5 × your height in centimeters)
− (4.7 × your age in years)	− (6.8 × your age in years)

4 Your metabolism is also influenced by how active you are. Talking, walking, and playing games all take more energy than being at rest. To get an idea of how many Calories your body needs each day to stay healthy, select the lifestyle that best describes yours from the table at right. Then multiply your BMR by the activity factor.

Activity Factors	
Activity lifestyle	**Activity factor**
Moderately inactive (normal, everyday activities)	1.3
Moderately active (exercise 3 to 4 times a week)	1.4
Very active (exercise 4 to 6 times a week)	1.6
Extremely active (exercise 6 to 7 times a week)	1.8

Analyze the Results

1 In what way could you compare your whole body to a single cell? Explain.

2 Does an increase in activity increase your BMR? Does an increase in activity increase your need for Calories? Explain your answers.

Draw Conclusions

3 If you are moderately inactive, how many more Calories would you need if you began to exercise every day?

Applying Your Data

The best energy sources are those that supply the correct amount of Calories for your lifestyle and also provide the nutrients you need. Research in the library or on the Internet to find out which kinds of foods are the best energy sources for you. How does your list of best energy sources compare with your diet?

List everything you eat and drink in 1 day. Find out how many Calories are in each item, and find the total number of Calories you have consumed. How does this number of Calories compare with the number of Calories you need each day for all your activities?

Inquiry Lab

Tracing Traits

Have you ever wondered about the traits you inherited from your parents? Do you have a trait that neither of your parents has? In this project, you will develop a family tree, or pedigree, similar to the one shown in the diagram below. You will trace an inherited trait through a family to determine how it has passed from generation to generation.

Procedure

1. The diagram at right shows a family history. On a separate piece of paper, draw a similar diagram of the family you have chosen. Include as many family members as possible, such as grandparents, parents, children, and grandchildren. Use circles to represent females and squares to represent males. You may include other information, such as the family member's name, birth date, or picture.

2. Draw a table similar to the one on the next page. Survey each of the family members shown in your family tree. Ask them if they have hair on the middle segment of their fingers. Write each person's name in the appropriate square. Explain to each person that it is normal to have either trait. The presence of hair on the middle segment is the dominant form of this trait.

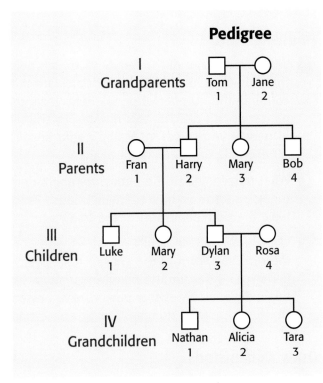

Pedigree

I Grandparents — Tom 1, Jane 2

II Parents — Fran 1, Harry 2, Mary 3, Bob 4

III Children — Luke 1, Mary 2, Dylan 3, Rosa 4

IV Grandchildren — Nathan 1, Alicia 2, Tara 3

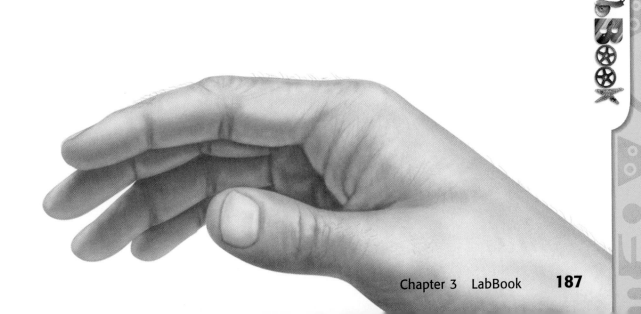

Dominant trait	Recessive trait	Family members with the dominant trait	Family members with the recessive trait
Hair present on the middle segment of fingers (*H*)	Hair absent on the middle segment of fingers (*h*)	DO NOT WRITE IN BOOK	

3 Trace this trait throughout the family tree you diagrammed in step 1. Shade or color the symbols of the family members who demonstrate the dominant form of this trait.

Analyze the Results

1 What percentage of the family members demonstrate the dominant form of the trait? Calculate this by counting the number of people who have the dominant trait and dividing this number by the total number of people you surveyed. Multiply your answer by 100. An example has been done at right.

Example: Calculating percentage

$$\frac{10 \text{ people with trait}}{20 \text{ people surveyed}} = \frac{1}{2}$$

$$\frac{1}{2} = 0.50 \times 100 = 50\%$$

2 What percentage of the family members demonstrate the recessive form of the trait? Why doesn't every family member have the dominant form of the trait?

3 Choose one of the family members who demonstrates the recessive form of the chosen trait. What is this person's genotype? What are the possible genotypes for the parents of this individual? Does this person have any brothers or sisters? Do they show the dominant or recessive trait?

Draw Conclusions

4 Draw a Punnett square like the one at right. Use this to determine the genotypes of the parents of the person you chose in step 3. Write this person's genotype in the bottom right-hand corner of your Punnett square. **Hint:** There may be more than one possible genotype for the parents. Don't forget to consider the genotypes of the person's brothers and sisters.

Father

	?	?
?		
?		

Mother

Skills Practice Lab

The Half-life of Pennies

Carbon-14 is a special unstable element used in the absolute dating of material that was once alive, such as fossil bones. Every 5,730 years, half of the carbon-14 in a fossil specimen decays or breaks down into a more stable element. In the following experiment you will see how pennies can show the same kind of "decay."

Procedure

1 Place 100 pennies in a large, covered container. Shake the container several times, and remove the cover. Carefully empty the container on a flat surface making sure the pennies don't roll away.

2 Remove all the coins that have the "head" side of the coin turned upward. Record the number of pennies removed and the number of pennies remaining in a data table similar to the one at right.

3 Repeat the process until no pennies are left in the container. Remember to remove only the coins showing "heads."

4 Draw a graph similar to the one at right. Label the *x*-axis "Number of shakes," and label the *y*-axis "Pennies remaining." Using data from your data table, plot the number of coins remaining at each shake on your graph.

Analyze the Results

1 Examine the Half-life of Carbon-14 graph at right. Compare the graph you have made for pennies with the one for carbon-14. Explain any similarities that you see.

2 Recall that the probability of landing "heads" in a coin toss is 1/2. Use this information to explain why the remaining number of pennies is reduced by about half each time they are shaken and tossed.

Shake number	Number of coins remaining	Number of coins removed
1		
2	*DO NOT WRITE IN BOOK*	
3		

Half-life of Pennies

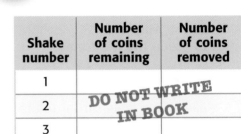

Half-life of Carbon-14

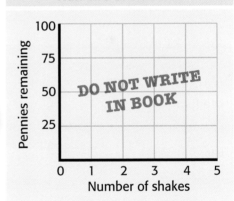

Skills Practice Lab

Voyage of the USS *Adventure*

You are a crew member on the USS *Adventure*. The *Adventure* has been on a 5-year mission to collect life-forms from outside the solar system. On the voyage back to Earth, your ship went through a meteor shower, which ruined several of the compartments containing the extraterrestrial life-forms. Now it is necessary to put more than one life-form in the same compartment.

You have only three undamaged compartments in your starship. You and your crewmates must stay in one compartment, and that compartment should be used for extraterrestrial life-forms only if absolutely necessary. You and your crewmates must decide which of the life-forms could be placed together. It is thought that similar life-forms will have similar needs. You can use only observable characteristics to group the life-forms.

Life-form 1

Life-form 2

Life-form 3

Procedure

1 Make a data table similar to the one below. Label each column with as many characteristics of the various life-forms as possible. Leave enough space in each square to write your observations. The life-forms are pictured on this page.

Life-form 4

Life-form Characteristics			
	Color	Shape	Legs	Eyes
Life-form 1				
Life-form 2				
Life-form 3	*DO NOT WRITE IN BOOK*			
Life-form 4				

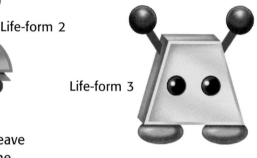

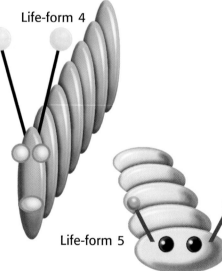

Life-form 5

2 Describe each characteristic as completely as you can. Based on your observations, determine which of the life-forms are most alike.

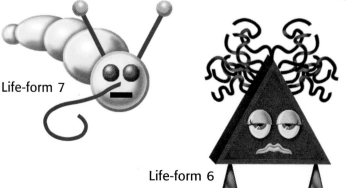

Life-form 7

Life-form 6

3 Make a data table like the one below. Fill in the table according to the decisions you made in step 2. State your reasons for the way you have grouped your life-forms.

Life-form Room Assignments		
Compartment	Life-forms	Reasons
1		
2		DO NOT WRITE IN BOOK
3		

4 The USS *Adventure* has to make one more stop before returning home. On planet X437 you discover the most interesting life-form ever found outside of Earth—the CC9, shown at right. Make a decision, based on your previous grouping of life-forms, about whether you can safely include CC9 in one of the compartments for the trip to Earth.

CC9

Analyze the Results

1 Describe the life-forms in compartment 1. How are they similar? How are they different?

2 Describe the life-forms in compartment 2. How are they similar? How do they differ from the life-forms in compartment 1?

3 Are there any life-forms in compartment 3? If so, describe their similarities. In which compartment will you and your crewmates remain for the journey home?

Draw Conclusions

4 Are you able to transport life-form CC9 safely back to Earth? If so, in which compartment will it be placed? How did you decide?

Applying Your Data

In 1831, Charles Darwin sailed from England on a ship called the HMS *Beagle*. You have studied the finches that Darwin observed on the Galápagos Islands. What were some of the other unusual organisms he found there? For example, find out about the Galápagos tortoise.

Contents

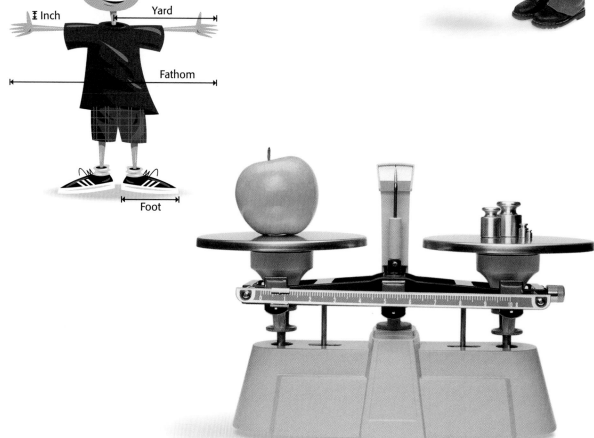

✓ *Reading Check* Answers

Chapter 1 Cells: The Basic Units of Life

Section 1

Page 5: Sample answer: All organisms are made of one or more cells, the cell is the basic unit of all living things, and all cells come from existing cells.

Page 6: If a cell's volume gets too large, the cell's surface area will not be able to take in enough nutrients or get rid of wastes fast enough to keep the cell alive.

Page 7: Organelles are structures within a cell that perform specific functions for the cell.

Page 9: One difference between eubacteria and archaea is that bacterial ribosomes are different from archaebacterial ribosomes.

Page 10: The main difference between prokaryotes and eukaryotes is that eukaryotic cells have a nucleus and membrane-bound organelles and prokaryotic cells do not.

Section 2

Page 12: Plant, algae, and fungi cells have cell walls.

Page 13: A cell membrane encloses the cell and separates and protects the cell's contents from the cell's environment. The cell wall also controls the movement of materials into and out of the cell.

Page 14: The cytoskeleton is a web of proteins in the cytoplasm. It gives the cell support and structure.

Page 16: Most of a cell's ATP is made in the cell's mitochondria.

Page 18: Lysosomes destroy worn-out organelles, attack foreign invaders, and get rid of waste material from inside the cell.

Section 3

Page 20: Sample answer: larger size, longer life, and cell specialization

Page 21: An organ is a structure of two or more tissues working together to perform a specific function in the body.

Page 22: cell, tissue, organ, organ system

Chapter 2 The Cell in Action

Section 1

Page 35: Red cells would burst in pure water because water particles move from outside, where particles were dense, to inside the cell, where particles were less dense. This movement of water would cause red cells to fill up and burst.

Page 37: Exocytosis is the process by which a cell moves large particles to the outside of the cell.

Section 2

Page 39: Cellular respiration is a chemical process by which cells produce energy from food. Breathing supplies the body with the raw materials needed for cellular respiration.

Page 41: the kind that happens in the muscle cells of animals and the kind that occurs in bacteria

Section 3

Page 43: No, the number of chromosomes is not always related to the complexity of organisms.

Page 44: During mitosis in plant cells, a cell plate is formed. During mitosis in animal cells, a cell plate does not form.

Chapter 3   Heredity

Section 1

Page 58:   the passing of traits from parents to offspring

Page 61:   During his second set of experiments, Mendel allowed the first-generation plants, which resulted from his first set of experiments, to self-pollinate.

Page 62:   A ratio is a relationship between two different numbers that is often expressed as a fraction.

Section 2

Page 64:   A gene contains the instructions for an inherited trait. The different versions of a gene are called *alleles*.

Page 66:   Probability is the mathematical chance that something will happen.

Page 68:   In incomplete dominance, one trait is not completely dominant over another.

Section 3

Page 71:   23 chromosomes

Page 72:   During meiosis, one parent cell makes four new cells.

Chapter 4   Genes and DNA

Section 1

Page 89:   Guanine and cytosine are always found in DNA in equal amounts, as are adenine and thymine.

Page 91:   every time a cell divides

Section 2

Page 92:   a string of nucleotides that give the cell information about how to make a specific trait

Page 95:   They transfer amino acids to the ribosome.

Page 96:   a physical or chemical agent that can cause a mutation in DNA

Page 97:   Sickle cell anemia is caused by a mutation in a single nucleotide of DNA, which then causes a different amino acid to be assembled in a protein used in blood cells.

Page 98:   a near-identical copy of another organism, created with the original organism's genes

Chapter 5 The Evolution of Living Things

Section 1

Page 110: if they mate with each other and produce more of the same type of organism

Page 112: by their estimated ages and physical similarities

Page 114: a four-legged land mammal

Page 116: that they have common ancestry

Section 2

Page 119: 965 km (600 mi) west of Ecuador

Page 121: that Earth had been formed by natural processes over a long period of time

Page 122: *On the Origin of Species by Means of Natural Selection*

Section 3

Page 125: because they often produce many offspring and have short generation times

Page 126: Sample answer: A newly formed canyon, mountain range, or lake could divide the members of a population.

Chapter 6 The History of Life on Earth

Section 1

Page 139: absolute dating

Page 141: periods of sudden extinction of many species

Page 142: the idea that the Earth's continents once formed a single landmass surrounded by ocean

Section 2

Page 144: The early Earth was very different from today—there were violent events and a harsh atmosphere.

Page 147: a mass extinction

Page 148: "recent life"

Section 3

Page 151: the hominid family

Page 152: Africa

Page 155: Paleontologists will review their ideas about the evolution of hominids.

Chapter 7 Classification

Section 1

Page 166: Sample answer: How many known species are there? What are the defining characteristics of each species? and What are the relationships between these species?

Page 169: genus and species

Page 170: A dichotomous key is an identification aid that uses a series of descriptive statements.

Section 2

Page 173: *Escherichia coli*

Page 175: Sample answer: Plants make energy through photosynthesis. Some members of the kingdoms Fungi, Protista, and Eubacteria consume plants. When these organisms digest the plant material, they get energy and nutrients made by the plants.

Page 177: Sponges don't have sense organs, and they usually can't move around.

Study Skills

FoldNote Instructions

Have you ever tried to study for a test or quiz but didn't know where to start? Or have you read a chapter and found that you can remember only a few ideas? Well, FoldNotes are a fun and exciting way to help you learn and remember the ideas you encounter as you learn science!

FoldNotes are tools that you can use to organize concepts. By focusing on a few main concepts, FoldNotes help you learn and remember how the concepts fit together. They can help you see the "big picture." Below you will find instructions for building 10 different FoldNotes.

Pyramid

1. Place a sheet of paper in front of you. Fold the lower left-hand corner of the paper diagonally to the opposite edge of the paper.

2. Cut off the tab of paper created by the fold (at the top).

3. Open the paper so that it is a square. Fold the lower right-hand corner of the paper diagonally to the opposite corner to form a triangle.

4. Open the paper. The creases of the two folds will have created an X.

5. Using scissors, cut along one of the creases. Start from any corner, and stop at the center point to create two flaps. Use tape or glue to attach one of the flaps on top of the other flap.

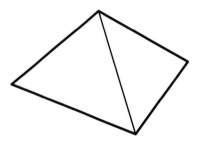

Double Door

1. Fold a sheet of paper in half from the top to the bottom. Then, unfold the paper.

2. Fold the top and bottom edges of the paper to the crease.

Booklet

1. Fold a sheet of paper in half from left to right. Then, unfold the paper.

2. Fold the sheet of paper in half again from the top to the bottom. Then, unfold the paper.

3. Refold the sheet of paper in half from left to right.

4. Fold the top and bottom edges to the center crease.

5. Completely unfold the paper.

6. Refold the paper from top to bottom.

7. Using scissors, cut a slit along the center crease of the sheet from the folded edge to the creases made in step 4. Do not cut the entire sheet in half.

8. Fold the sheet of paper in half from left to right. While holding the bottom and top edges of the paper, push the bottom and top edges together so that the center collapses at the center slit. Fold the four flaps to form a four-page book.

Layered Book

1. Lay one sheet of paper on top of another sheet. Slide the top sheet up so that 2 cm of the bottom sheet is showing.

2. Hold the two sheets together, fold down the top of the two sheets so that you see four 2 cm tabs along the bottom.

3. Using a stapler, staple the top of the FoldNote.

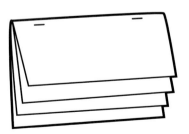

Key-Term Fold

1. Fold a sheet of lined notebook paper in half from left to right.

2. Using scissors, cut along every third line from the right edge of the paper to the center fold to make tabs.

Four-Corner Fold

1. Fold a sheet of paper in half from left to right. Then, unfold the paper.

2. Fold each side of the paper to the crease in the center of the paper.

3. Fold the paper in half from the top to the bottom. Then, unfold the paper.

4. Using scissors, cut the top flap creases made in step 3 to form four flaps.

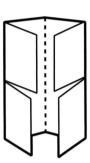

Three-Panel Flip Chart

1. Fold a piece of paper in half from the top to the bottom.

2. Fold the paper in thirds from side to side. Then, unfold the paper so that you can see the three sections.

3. From the top of the paper, cut along each of the vertical fold lines to the fold in the middle of the paper. You will now have three flaps.

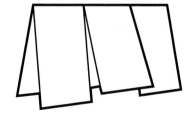

Table Fold

1. Fold a piece of paper in half from the top to the bottom. Then, fold the paper in half again.

2. Fold the paper in thirds from side to side.

3. Unfold the paper completely. Carefully trace the fold lines by using a pen or pencil.

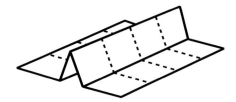

Two-Panel Flip Chart

1. Fold a piece of paper in half from the top to the bottom.

2. Fold the paper in half from side to side. Then, unfold the paper so that you can see the two sections.

3. From the top of the paper, cut along the vertical fold line to the fold in the middle of the paper. You will now have two flaps.

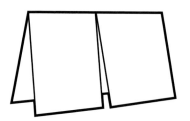

Tri-Fold

1. Fold a piece a paper in thirds from the top to the bottom.

2. Unfold the paper so that you can see the three sections. Then, turn the paper sideways so that the three sections form vertical columns.

3. Trace the fold lines by using a pen or pencil. Label the columns "Know," "Want," and "Learn."

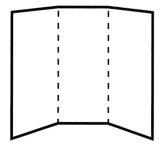

Graphic Organizer Instructions

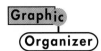 Have you ever wished that you could "draw out" the many concepts you learn in your science class? Sometimes, being able to *see* how concepts are related really helps you remember what you've learned. Graphic Organizers do just that! They give you a way to draw or map out concepts.

All you need to make a Graphic Organizer is a piece of paper and a pencil. Below you will find instructions for four different Graphic Organizers designed to help you organize the concepts you'll learn in this book.

Spider Map

1. Draw a diagram like the one shown. In the circle, write the main topic.

2. From the circle, draw legs to represent different categories of the main topic. You can have as many categories as you want.

3. From the category legs, draw horizontal lines. As you read the chapter, write details about each category on the horizontal lines.

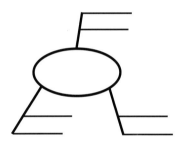

Comparison Table

1. Draw a chart like the one shown. Your chart can have as many columns and rows as you want.

2. In the top row, write the topics that you want to compare.

3. In the left column, write characteristics of the topics that you want to compare. As you read the chapter, fill in the characteristics for each topic in the appropriate boxes.

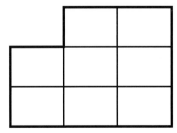

Chain-of-Events-Chart

1. Draw a box. In the box, write the first step of a process or the first event of a timeline.

2. Under the box, draw another box, and use an arrow to connect the two boxes. In the second box, write the next step of the process or the next event in the timeline.

3. Continue adding boxes until the process or timeline is finished.

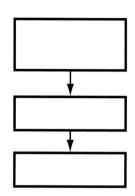

Concept Map

1. Draw a circle in the center of a piece of paper. Write the main idea of the chapter in the center of the circle.

2. From the circle, draw other circles. In those circles, write characteristics of the main idea. Draw arrows from the center circle to the circles that contain the characteristics.

3. From each circle that contains a characteristic, draw other circles. In those circles, write specific details about the characteristic. Draw arrows from each circle that contains a characteristic to the circles that contain specific details. You may draw as many circles as you want.

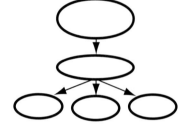

SI Measurement

The International System of Units, or SI, is the standard system of measurement used by many scientists. Using the same standards of measurement makes it easier for scientists to communicate with one another.

SI works by combining prefixes and base units. Each base unit can be used with different prefixes to define smaller and larger quantities. The table below lists common SI prefixes.

SI Prefixes

Prefix	Symbol	Factor	Example
kilo-	k	1,000	kilogram, 1 kg = 1,000 g
hecto-	h	100	hectoliter, 1 hL = 100 L
deka-	da	10	dekameter, 1 dam = 10 m
		1	meter, liter, gram
deci-	d	0.1	decigram, 1 dg = 0.1 g
centi-	c	0.01	centimeter, 1 cm = 0.01 m
milli-	m	0.001	milliliter, 1 mL = 0.001 L
micro-	μ	0.000 001	micrometer, 1 μm = 0.000 001 m

SI Conversion Table

SI units	From SI to English	From English to SI
Length		
kilometer (km) = 1,000 m	1 km = 0.621 mi	1 mi = 1.609 km
meter (m) = 100 cm	1 m = 3.281 ft	1 ft = 0.305 m
centimeter (cm) = 0.01 m	1 cm = 0.394 in.	1 in. = 2.540 cm
millimeter (mm) = 0.001 m	1 mm = 0.039 in.	
micrometer (μm) = 0.000 001 m		
nanometer (nm) = 0.000 000 001 m		
Area		
square kilometer (km^2) = 100 hectares	1 km^2 = 0.386 mi^2	1 mi^2 = 2.590 km^2
hectare (ha) = 10,000 m^2	1 ha = 2.471 acres	1 acre = 0.405 ha
square meter (m^2) = 10,000 cm^2	1 m^2 = 10.764 ft^2	1 ft^2 = 0.093 m^2
square centimeter (cm^2) = 100 mm^2	1 cm^2 = 0.155 in.^{2}	1 in.^{2} = 6.452 cm^2
Volume		
liter (L) = 1,000 mL = 1 dm^3	1 L = 1.057 fl qt	1 fl qt = 0.946 L
milliliter (mL) = 0.001 L = 1 cm^3	1 mL = 0.034 fl oz	1 fl oz = 29.574 mL
microliter (μL) = 0.000 001 L		
Mass		
kilogram (kg) = 1,000 g	1 kg = 2.205 lb	1 lb = 0.454 kg
gram (g) = 1,000 mg	1 g = 0.035 oz	1 oz = 28.350 g
milligram (mg) = 0.001 g		
microgram (μg) = 0.000 001 g		

Measuring Skills

Using a Graduated Cylinder

When using a graduated cylinder to measure volume, keep the following procedures in mind:

1. Place the cylinder on a flat, level surface before measuring liquid.

2. Move your head so that your eye is level with the surface of the liquid.

3. Read the mark closest to the liquid level. On glass graduated cylinders, read the mark closest to the center of the curve in the liquid's surface.

Using a Meterstick or Metric Ruler

When using a meterstick or metric ruler to measure length, keep the following procedures in mind:

1. Place the ruler firmly against the object that you are measuring.

2. Align one edge of the object exactly with the 0 end of the ruler.

3. Look at the other edge of the object to see which of the marks on the ruler is closest to that edge. (Note: Each small slash between the centimeters represents a millimeter, which is one-tenth of a centimeter.)

Using a Triple-Beam Balance

When using a triple-beam balance to measure mass, keep the following procedures in mind:

1. Make sure the balance is on a level surface.

2. Place all of the countermasses at 0. Adjust the balancing knob until the pointer rests at 0.

3. Place the object you wish to measure on the pan. **Caution:** Do not place hot objects or chemicals directly on the balance pan.

4. Move the largest countermass along the beam to the right until it is at the last notch that does not tip the balance. Follow the same procedure with the next-largest countermass. Then, move the smallest countermass until the pointer rests at 0.

5. Add the readings from the three beams together to determine the mass of the object.

6. When determining the mass of crystals or powders, first find the mass of a piece of filter paper. Then, add the crystals or powder to the paper, and remeasure. The actual mass of the crystals or powder is the total mass minus the mass of the paper. When finding the mass of liquids, first find the mass of the empty container. Then, find the combined mass of the liquid and container. The mass of the liquid is the total mass minus the mass of the container.

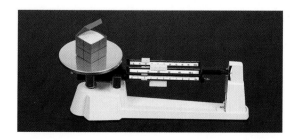

Scientific Methods

The ways in which scientists answer questions and solve problems are called **scientific methods.** The same steps are often used by scientists as they look for answers. However, there is more than one way to use these steps. Scientists may use all of the steps or just some of the steps during an investigation. They may even repeat some of the steps. The goal of using scientific methods is to come up with reliable answers and solutions.

Six Steps of Scientific Methods

Ask a Question
Good questions come from careful **observations.** You make observations by using your senses to gather information. Sometimes, you may use instruments, such as microscopes and telescopes, to extend the range of your senses. As you observe the natural world, you will discover that you have many more questions than answers. These questions drive investigations.

Questions beginning with *what, why, how,* and *when* are important in focusing an investigation. Here is an example of a question that could lead to an investigation.

Question: How does acid rain affect plant growth?

Form a Hypothesis
After you ask a question, you need to form a **hypothesis.** A hypothesis is a clear statement of what you expect the answer to your question to be. Your hypothesis will represent your best "educated guess" based on what you have observed and what you already know. A good hypothesis is testable. Otherwise, the investigation can go no further. Here is a hypothesis based on the question, "How does acid rain affect plant growth?"

Hypothesis: Acid rain slows plant growth.

The hypothesis can lead to predictions. A prediction is what you think the outcome of your experiment or data collection will be. Predictions are usually stated in an if-then format. Here is a sample prediction for the hypothesis that acid rain slows plant growth.

Prediction: If a plant is watered with only acid rain (which has a pH of 4), then the plant will grow at half its normal rate.

Test the Hypothesis
After you have formed a hypothesis and made a prediction, your hypothesis should be tested. One way to test a hypothesis is with a controlled experiment. A **controlled experiment** tests only one factor at a time. In an experiment to test the effect of acid rain on plant growth, the **control group** would be watered with normal rain water. The **experimental group** would be watered with acid rain. All of the plants should receive the same amount of sunlight and water each day. The air temperature should be the same for all groups. However, the acidity of the water will be a variable. In fact, any factor that is different from one group to another is a **variable.** If your hypothesis is correct, then the acidity of the water and plant growth are *dependant variables.* The amount a plant grows is dependent on the acidity of the water. However, the amount of water each plant receives and the amount of sunlight each plant receives are *independent variables.* Either of these factors could change without affecting the other factor.

Sometimes, the nature of an investigation makes a controlled experiment impossible. For example, the Earth's core is surrounded by thousands of meters of rock. Under such circumstances, a hypothesis may be tested by making detailed observations.

Analyze the Results
After you have completed your experiments, made your observations, and collected your data, you must analyze all the information you have gathered. Tables and graphs are often used in this step to organize the data.

Draw Conclusions

After analyzing your data, you can determine if your results support your hypothesis. If your hypothesis is supported, you (or others) might want to repeat the observations or experiments to verify your results. If your hypothesis is not supported by the data, you may have to check your procedure for errors. You may even have to reject your hypothesis and make a new one. If you cannot draw a conclusion from your results, you may have to try the investigation again or carry out further observations or experiments.

Communicate Results

After any scientific investigation, you should report your results. By preparing a written or oral report, you let others know what you have learned. They may repeat your investigation to see if they get the same results. Your report may even lead to another question and then to another investigation.

Scientific Methods in Action

Scientific methods contain loops in which several steps may be repeated over and over again. In some cases, certain steps are unnecessary. Thus, there is not a "straight line" of steps. For example, sometimes scientists find that testing one hypothesis raises new questions and new hypotheses to be tested. And sometimes, testing the hypothesis leads directly to a conclusion. Furthermore, the steps in scientific methods are not always used in the same order. Follow the steps in the diagram, and see how many different directions scientific methods can take you.

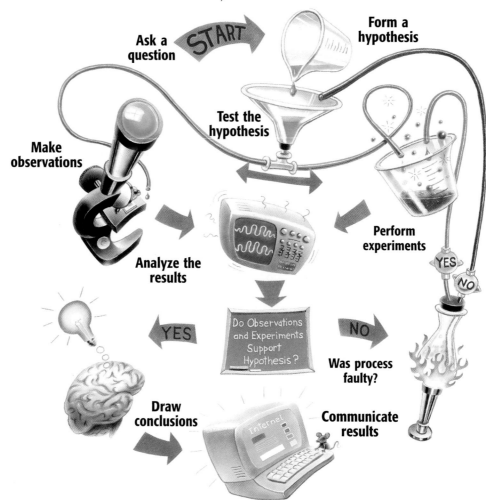

Temperature Scales

Temperature can be expressed by using three different scales: Fahrenheit, Celsius, and Kelvin. The SI unit for temperature is the kelvin (K).

Although 0 K is much colder than 0°C, a change of 1 K is equal to a change of 1°C.

Three Temperature Scales		

	Fahrenheit	Celsius	Kelvin
Water boils	212°	100°	373
Body temperature	98.6°	37°	310
Room temperature	68°	20°	293
Water freezes	32°	0°	273

Temperature Conversions Table		
To convert	**Use this equation:**	**Example**
Celsius to Fahrenheit °C → °F	$°F = \left(\dfrac{9}{5} \times °C \right) + 32$	Convert 45°C to °F. $°F = \left(\dfrac{9}{5} \times 45°C \right) + 32 = 113°F$
Fahrenheit to Celsius °F → °C	$°C = \dfrac{5}{9} \times (°F - 32)$	Convert 68°F to °C. $°C = \dfrac{5}{9} \times (68°F - 32) = 20°C$
Celsius to Kelvin °C → K	$K = °C + 273$	Convert 45°C to K. $K = 45°C + 273 = 318\ K$
Kelvin to Celsius K → °C	$°C = K - 273$	Convert 32 K to °C. $°C = 32K - 273 = -241°C$

Making Charts and Graphs

Pie Charts

A pie chart shows how each group of data relates to all of the data. Each part of the circle forming the chart represents a category of the data. The entire circle represents all of the data. For example, a biologist studying a hardwood forest in Wisconsin found that there were five different types of trees. The data table at right summarizes the biologist's findings.

Wisconsin Hardwood Trees	
Type of tree	Number found
Oak	600
Maple	750
Beech	300
Birch	1,200
Hickory	150
Total	3,000

How to Make a Pie Chart

1 To make a pie chart of these data, first find the percentage of each type of tree. Divide the number of trees of each type by the total number of trees, and multiply by 100.

$$\frac{600 \text{ oak}}{3,000 \text{ trees}} \times 100 = 20\%$$

$$\frac{750 \text{ maple}}{3,000 \text{ trees}} \times 100 = 25\%$$

$$\frac{300 \text{ beech}}{3,000 \text{ trees}} \times 100 = 10\%$$

$$\frac{1,200 \text{ birch}}{3,000 \text{ trees}} \times 100 = 40\%$$

$$\frac{150 \text{ hickory}}{3,000 \text{ trees}} \times 100 = 5\%$$

2 Now, determine the size of the wedges that make up the pie chart. Multiply each percentage by 360°. Remember that a circle contains 360°.

20% × 360° = 72°   25% × 360° = 90°

10% × 360° = 36°   40% × 360° = 144°

5% × 360° = 18°

3 Check that the sum of the percentages is 100 and the sum of the degrees is 360.

20% + 25% + 10% + 40% + 5% = 100%

72° + 90° + 36° + 144° + 18° = 360°

4 Use a compass to draw a circle and mark the center of the circle.

5 Then, use a protractor to draw angles of 72°, 90°, 36°, 144°, and 18° in the circle.

6 Finally, label each part of the chart, and choose an appropriate title.

A Community of Wisconsin Hardwood Trees

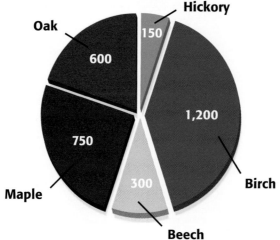

Line Graphs

Line graphs are most often used to demonstrate continuous change. For example, Mr. Smith's students analyzed the population records for their hometown, Appleton, between 1900 and 2000. Examine the data at right.

Because the year and the population change, they are the *variables*. The population is determined by, or dependent on, the year. Therefore, the population is called the **dependent variable,** and the year is called the **independent variable.** Each set of data is called a **data pair.** To prepare a line graph, you must first organize data pairs into a table like the one at right.

Population of Appleton, 1900–2000	
Year	Population
1900	1,800
1920	2,500
1940	3,200
1960	3,900
1980	4,600
2000	5,300

How to Make a Line Graph

1 Place the independent variable along the horizontal (*x*) axis. Place the dependent variable along the vertical (*y*) axis.

2 Label the *x*-axis "Year" and the *y*-axis "Population." Look at your largest and smallest values for the population. For the *y*-axis, determine a scale that will provide enough space to show these values. You must use the same scale for the entire length of the axis. Next, find an appropriate scale for the *x*-axis.

3 Choose reasonable starting points for each axis.

4 Plot the data pairs as accurately as possible.

5 Choose a title that accurately represents the data.

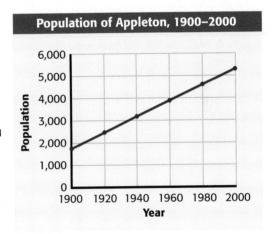

How to Determine Slope

Slope is the ratio of the change in the *y*-value to the change in the *x*-value, or "rise over run."

1 Choose two points on the line graph. For example, the population of Appleton in 2000 was 5,300 people. Therefore, you can define point *a* as (2000, 5,300). In 1900, the population was 1,800 people. You can define point *b* as (1900, 1,800).

2 Find the change in the *y*-value.
(*y* at point *a*) − (*y* at point *b*) =
5,300 people − 1,800 people =
3,500 people

3 Find the change in the *x*-value.
(*x* at point *a*) − (*x* at point *b*) =
2000 − 1900 = 100 years

4 Calculate the slope of the graph by dividing the change in *y* by the change in *x*.

$$slope = \frac{change\ in\ y}{change\ in\ x}$$

$$slope = \frac{3,500\ people}{100\ years}$$

$$slope = 35\ people\ per\ year$$

In this example, the population in Appleton increased by a fixed amount each year. The graph of these data is a straight line. Therefore, the relationship is **linear.** When the graph of a set of data is not a straight line, the relationship is **nonlinear.**

Using Algebra to Determine Slope

The equation in step 4 may also be arranged to be

$$y = kx$$

where y represents the change in the y-value, k represents the slope, and x represents the change in the x-value.

$$slope = \frac{change\ in\ y}{change\ in\ x}$$

$$k = \frac{y}{x}$$

$$k \times x = \frac{y \times x}{x}$$

$$kx = y$$

Bar Graphs

Bar graphs are used to demonstrate change that is not continuous. These graphs can be used to indicate trends when the data cover a long period of time. A meteorologist gathered the precipitation data shown here for Hartford, Connecticut, for April 1–15, 1996, and used a bar graph to represent the data.

Precipitation in Hartford, Connecticut April 1–15, 1996			
Date	Precipitation (cm)	Date	Precipitation (cm)
April 1	0.5	April 9	0.25
April 2	1.25	April 10	0.0
April 3	0.0	April 11	1.0
April 4	0.0	April 12	0.0
April 5	0.0	April 13	0.25
April 6	0.0	April 14	0.0
April 7	0.0	April 15	6.50
April 8	1.75		

How to Make a Bar Graph

1 Use an appropriate scale and a reasonable starting point for each axis.

2 Label the axes, and plot the data.

3 Choose a title that accurately represents the data.

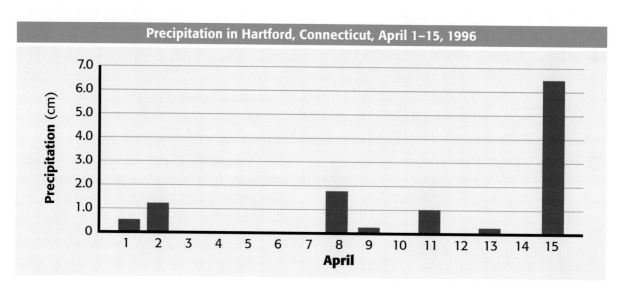

Precipitation in Hartford, Connecticut, April 1–15, 1996

Math Refresher

Science requires an understanding of many math concepts. The following pages will help you review some important math skills.

Averages

An **average,** or **mean,** simplifies a set of numbers into a single number that *approximates* the value of the set.

> **Example:** Find the average of the following set of numbers: 5, 4, 7, and 8.

Step 1: Find the sum.
$$5 + 4 + 7 + 8 = 24$$

Step 2: Divide the sum by the number of numbers in your set. Because there are four numbers in this example, divide the sum by 4.

$$\frac{24}{4} = 6$$

The average, or mean, is **6.**

Ratios

A **ratio** is a comparison between numbers, and it is usually written as a fraction.

> **Example:** Find the ratio of thermometers to students if you have 36 thermometers and 48 students in your class.

Step 1: Make the ratio.
$$\frac{36 \text{ thermometers}}{48 \text{ students}}$$

Step 2: Reduce the fraction to its simplest form.

$$\frac{36}{48} = \frac{36 \div 12}{48 \div 12} = \frac{3}{4}$$

The ratio of thermometers to students is **3 to 4,** or $\frac{3}{4}$. The ratio may also be written in the form 3:4.

Proportions

A **proportion** is an equation that states that two ratios are equal.

$$\frac{3}{1} = \frac{12}{4}$$

To solve a proportion, first multiply across the equal sign. This is called *cross-multiplication.* If you know three of the quantities in a proportion, you can use cross-multiplication to find the fourth.

> **Example:** Imagine that you are making a scale model of the solar system for your science project. The diameter of Jupiter is 11.2 times the diameter of the Earth. If you are using a plastic-foam ball that has a diameter of 2 cm to represent the Earth, what must the diameter of the ball representing Jupiter be?

$$\frac{11.2}{1} = \frac{x}{2 \text{ cm}}$$

Step 1: Cross-multiply.
$$\frac{11.2}{1} \diagtimes \frac{x}{2}$$
$$11.2 \times 2 = x \times 1$$

Step 2: Multiply.
$$22.4 = x \times 1$$

Step 3: Isolate the variable by dividing both sides by 1.
$$x = \frac{22.4}{1}$$
$$x = 22.4 \text{ cm}$$

You will need to use a ball that has a diameter of **22.4 cm** to represent Jupiter.

Percentages

A **percentage** is a ratio of a given number to 100.

Example: What is 85% of 40?

Step 1: Rewrite the percentage by moving the decimal point two places to the left.

0.85

Step 2: Multiply the decimal by the number that you are calculating the percentage of.

0.85 × 40 = 34

85% of 40 is **34.**

Decimals

To **add** or **subtract decimals,** line up the digits vertically so that the decimal points line up. Then, add or subtract the columns from right to left. Carry or borrow numbers as necessary.

Example: Add the following numbers: 3.1415 and 2.96.

Step 1: Line up the digits vertically so that the decimal points line up.

$$\begin{array}{r} 3.1415 \\ + 2.96 \\ \hline \end{array}$$

Step 2: Add the columns from right to left, and carry when necessary.

$$\begin{array}{r} {}^{1}\ {}^{1}\quad\ \\ 3.1415 \\ + 2.96 \\ \hline 6.1015 \end{array}$$

The sum is **6.1015.**

Fractions

Numbers tell you how many; **fractions** tell you *how much of a whole.*

Example: Your class has 24 plants. Your teacher instructs you to put 5 plants in a shady spot. What fraction of the plants in your class will you put in a shady spot?

Step 1: In the denominator, write the total number of parts in the whole.

$$\frac{?}{24}$$

Step 2: In the numerator, write the number of parts of the whole that are being considered.

$$\frac{5}{24}$$

So, $\frac{5}{24}$ of the plants will be in the shade.

Reducing Fractions

It is usually best to express a fraction in its simplest form. Expressing a fraction in its simplest form is called *reducing* a fraction.

Example: Reduce the fraction $\frac{30}{45}$ to its simplest form.

Step 1: Find the largest whole number that will divide evenly into both the numerator and denominator. This number is called the *greatest common factor* (GCF).

Factors of the numerator 30:
1, 2, 3, 5, 6, 10, **15,** 30

Factors of the denominator 45:
1, 3, 5, 9, **15,** 45

Step 2: Divide both the numerator and the denominator by the GCF, which in this case is 15.

$$\frac{30}{45} = \frac{30 \div 15}{45 \div 15} = \frac{2}{3}$$

Thus, $\frac{30}{45}$ reduced to its simplest form is $\frac{2}{3}$.

Adding and Subtracting Fractions

To **add** or **subtract fractions** that have the **same denominator,** simply add or subtract the numerators.

Examples:

$$\frac{3}{5} + \frac{1}{5} = ? \quad \text{and} \quad \frac{3}{4} - \frac{1}{4} = ?$$

Step 1: Add or subtract the numerators.

$$\frac{3}{5} + \frac{1}{5} = \frac{4}{} \quad \text{and} \quad \frac{3}{4} - \frac{1}{4} = \frac{2}{}$$

Step 2: Write the sum or difference over the denominator.

$$\frac{3}{5} + \frac{1}{5} = \frac{4}{5} \quad \text{and} \quad \frac{3}{4} - \frac{1}{4} = \frac{2}{4}$$

Step 3: If necessary, reduce the fraction to its simplest form.

$\frac{4}{5}$ cannot be reduced, and $\frac{2}{4} = \frac{1}{2}$.

To **add** or **subtract fractions** that have **different denominators,** first find the least common denominator (LCD).

Examples:

$$\frac{1}{2} + \frac{1}{6} = ? \quad \text{and} \quad \frac{3}{4} - \frac{2}{3} = ?$$

Step 1: Write the equivalent fractions that have a common denominator.

$$\frac{3}{6} + \frac{1}{6} = ? \quad \text{and} \quad \frac{9}{12} - \frac{8}{12} = ?$$

Step 2: Add or subtract the fractions.

$$\frac{3}{6} + \frac{1}{6} = \frac{4}{6} \quad \text{and} \quad \frac{9}{12} - \frac{8}{12} = \frac{1}{12}$$

Step 3: If necessary, reduce the fraction to its simplest form.

The fraction $\frac{4}{6} = \frac{2}{3}$, and $\frac{1}{12}$ cannot be reduced.

Multiplying Fractions

To **multiply fractions,** multiply the numerators and the denominators together, and then reduce the fraction to its simplest form.

Example:

$$\frac{5}{9} \times \frac{7}{10} = ?$$

Step 1: Multiply the numerators and denominators.

$$\frac{5}{9} \times \frac{7}{10} = \frac{5 \times 7}{9 \times 10} = \frac{35}{90}$$

Step 2: Reduce the fraction.

$$\frac{35}{90} = \frac{35 \div 5}{90 \div 5} = \frac{7}{18}$$

Dividing Fractions

To **divide fractions,** first rewrite the divisor (the number you divide by) upside down. This number is called the *reciprocal* of the divisor. Then multiply and reduce if necessary.

Example:

$$\frac{5}{8} \div \frac{3}{2} = ?$$

Step 1: Rewrite the divisor as its reciprocal.

$$\frac{3}{2} \rightarrow \frac{2}{3}$$

Step 2: Multiply the fractions.

$$\frac{5}{8} \times \frac{2}{3} = \frac{5 \times 2}{8 \times 3} = \frac{10}{24}$$

Step 3: Reduce the fraction.

$$\frac{10}{24} = \frac{10 \div 2}{24 \div 2} = \frac{5}{12}$$

Scientific Notation

Scientific notation is a short way of representing very large and very small numbers without writing all of the place-holding zeros.

Example: Write 653,000,000 in scientific notation.

Step 1: Write the number without the place-holding zeros.

653

Step 2: Place the decimal point after the first digit.

6.53

Step 3: Find the exponent by counting the number of places that you moved the decimal point.

6.53000000

The decimal point was moved eight places to the left. Therefore, the exponent of 10 is positive 8. If you had moved the decimal point to the right, the exponent would be negative.

Step 4: Write the number in scientific notation.

$$6.53 \times 10^8$$

Area

Area is the number of square units needed to cover the surface of an object.

Formulas:

area of a square = side × side
area of a rectangle = length × width
area of a triangle = $\frac{1}{2}$ × base × height

Examples: Find the areas.

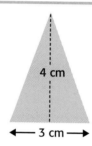

Triangle

$area = \frac{1}{2} \times base \times height$

$area = \frac{1}{2} \times 3 \text{ cm} \times 4 \text{ cm}$

$area = \textbf{6 cm}^2$

4 cm

← 3 cm →

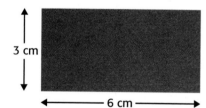

Rectangle

$area = length \times width$
$area = 6 \text{ cm} \times 3 \text{ cm}$
$area = \textbf{18 cm}^2$

3 cm

← 6 cm →

Square

$area = side \times side$
$area = 3 \text{ cm} \times 3 \text{ cm}$
$area = \textbf{9 cm}^2$

3 cm

← 3 cm →

Volume

Volume is the amount of space that something occupies.

Formulas:

volume of a cube = side × side × side

volume of a prism = area of base × height

Examples:

Find the volume of the solids.

Cube

$volume = side \times side \times side$
$volume = 4 \text{ cm} \times 4 \text{ cm} \times 4 \text{ cm}$
$volume = \textbf{64 cm}^3$

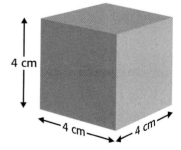

4 cm

← 4 cm → ← 4 cm →

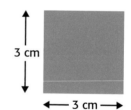

3 cm

4 cm

5 cm

Prism

$volume = area \ of \ base \times height$
$volume = (area \ of \ triangle) \times height$
$volume = (\frac{1}{2} \times 3 \text{ cm} \times 4 \text{ cm}) \times 5 \text{ cm}$
$volume = 6 \text{ cm}^2 \times 5 \text{ cm}$
$volume = \textbf{30 cm}^3$

Glossary

A

absolute dating any method of measuring the age of an event or object in years (137)

active transport the movement of substances across the cell membrane that requires the cell to use energy (36)

adaptation a characteristic that improves an individual's ability to survive and reproduce in a particular environment (108)

allele (uh LEEL) one of the alternative forms of a gene that governs a characteristic, such as hair color (62)

Animalia a kingdom made up of complex, multicellular organisms that lack cell walls, can usually move around, and quickly respond to their environment (174)

Archaebacteria (AHR kee bak TEER ee uh) a kingdom made up of bacteria that live in extreme environments (171)

C

cell in biology, the smallest unit that can perform all life processes; cells are covered by a membrane and contain DNA and cytoplasm (4)

cell cycle the life cycle of a cell (42)

cell membrane a phospholipid layer that covers a cell's surface and acts as a barrier between the inside of a cell and the cell's environment (7)

cellular respiration the process by which cells use oxygen to produce energy from food (39)

cell wall a rigid structure that surrounds the cell membrane and provides support to the cell (12)

Cenozoic era (SEN uh ZOH ik ER uh) the most recent geologic era, beginning 65 million years ago; also called the *Age of Mammals* (146)

chromosome in a eukaryotic cell, one of the structures in the nucleus that are made up of DNA and protein; in a prokaryotic cell, the main ring of DNA (42)

classification the division of organisms into groups, or classes, based on specific characteristics (164)

cytokinesis the division of the cytoplasm of a cell (44)

D

dichotomous key (die KAHT uh muhs KEE) an aid that is used to identify organisms and that consists of the answers to a series of questions (168)

diffusion (di FYOO zhuhn) the movement of particles from regions of higher density to regions of lower density (34)

DNA **d**eoxyribo**n**ucleic **a**cid, a molecule that is present in all living cells and that contains the information that determines the traits that a living thing inherits and needs to live (86)

dominant trait the trait observed in the first generation when parents that have different traits are bred (59)

E

endocytosis (EN doh sie TOH sis) the process by which a cell membrane surrounds a particle and encloses the particle in a vesicle to bring the particle into the cell (36)

endoplasmic reticulum (EN doh PLAZ mik ri TIK yuh luhm) a system of membranes that is found in a cell's cytoplasm and that assists in the production, processing, and transport of proteins and in the production of lipids (15)

Eubacteria (YOO bak TEER ee uh) a kingdom that contains all prokaryotes except archaebacteria (171)

eukaryote an organism made up of cells that have a nucleus enclosed by a membrane; eukaryotes include animals, plants, and fungi but not archaebacteria or eubacteria (10)

evolution the process in which inherited characteristics within a population change over generations such that new species sometimes arise (109)

exocytosis (EK soh sie TOH sis) the process in which a cell releases a particle by enclosing the particle in a vesicle that then moves to the cell surface and fuses with the cell membrane (37)

extinct describes a species that has died out completely (139)

F

fermentation the breakdown of food without the use of oxygen (39)

fossil the remains or physical evidence of an organism preserved by geological processes (110, 136)

fossil record a historical sequence of life indicated by fossils found in layers of the Earth's crust (110)

function the special, normal, or proper activity of an organ or part (22)

Fungi (FUHN JIE) a kingdom made up of nongreen, eukaryotic organisms that have no means of movement, reproduce by using spores, and get food by breaking down substances in their surroundings and absorbing the nutrients (172)

G

gene one set of instructions for an inherited trait (62)

generation time the period between the birth of one generation and the birth of the next generation (123)

genotype the entire genetic makeup of an organism; also the combination of genes for one or more specific traits (63)

geologic time scale the standard method used to divide the Earth's long natural history into manageable parts (138)

Golgi complex (GOHL jee KAHM PLEKS) cell organelle that helps make and package materials to be transported out of the cell (17)

H

heredity the passing of genetic traits from parent to offspring (56)

hominid a type of primate characterized by bipedalism, relatively long lower limbs, and lack of a tail; examples include humans and their ancestors (149)

homologous chromosomes (hoh MAHL uh guhs KROH muh SOHMZ) chromosomes that have the same sequence of genes and the same structure (43, 68)

Homo sapiens (HOH moh SAY pee UHNZ) the species of hominids that includes modern humans and their closest ancestors and that first appeared about 100,000 to 150,000 years ago (152)

L

lysosome (LIE suh SOHM) a cell organelle that contains digestive enzymes (18)

M

meiosis (mie OH sis) a process in cell division during which the number of chromosomes decreases to half the original number by two divisions of the nucleus, which results in the production of sex cells (gametes or spores) (68)

Mesozoic era (MES oh ZOH ik ER uh) the geologic era that lasted from 248 million to 65 million years ago; also called the *Age of Reptiles* (145)

mitochondrion (MIET oh KAHN dree uhn) in eukaryotic cells, the cell organelle that is surrounded by two membranes and that is the site of cellular respiration (16)

mitosis in eukaryotic cells, a process of cell division that forms two new nuclei, each of which has the same number of chromosomes (43)

mutation a change in the nucleotide-base sequence of a gene or DNA molecule (94)

N

natural selection the process by which individuals that are better adapted to their environment survive and reproduce more successfully than less well adapted individuals do; a theory to explain the mechanism of evolution (120)

nucleotide in a nucleic-acid chain, a subunit that consists of a sugar, a phosphate, and a nitrogenous base (86)

nucleus in a eukaryotic cell, a membrane-bound organelle that contains the cell's DNA and that has a role in processes such as growth, metabolism, and reproduction (7)

O

organ a collection of tissues that carry out a specialized function of the body (21)

organelle one of the small bodies in a cell's cytoplasm that are specialized to perform a specific function (7)

organism a living thing; anything that can carry out life processes independently (22)

organ system a group of organs that work together to perform body functions (22)

osmosis (ahs MOH sis) the diffusion of water through a semipermeable membrane (35)

P

Paleozoic era (PAY lee OH ZOH ik ER uh) the geologic era that followed Precambrian time and that lasted from 543 million to 248 million years ago (244)

passive transport the movement of substances across a cell membrane without the use of energy by the cell (36)

pedigree a diagram that shows the occurrence of a genetic trait in several generations of a family (74)

phenotype (FEE noh TIEP) an organism's appearance or other detectable characteristic (62)

photosynthesis (FOHT oh SIN thuh sis) the process by which plants, algae, and some bacteria use sunlight, carbon dioxide, and water to make food (38)

Plantae a kingdom made up of complex, multicellular organisms that are usually green, have cell walls made of cellulose, cannot move around, and use the sun's energy to make sugar by photosynthesis (173)

plate tectonics the theory that explains how large pieces of the Earth's outermost layer, called *tectonic plates*, move and change shape (140)

Precambrian time (pree KAM bree uhn TIEM) the period in the geologic time scale from the formation of the Earth to the beginning of the Paleozoic era, from about 4.6 billion to 543 million years ago (142)

primate a type of mammal characterized by opposable thumbs and binocular vision (148)

probability the likelihood that a possible future event will occur in any given instance of the event (64)

prokaryote (pro KAR ee OHT) an organism that consists of a single cell that does not have a nucleus (8)

Protista (proh TIST uh) a kingdom of mostly one-celled eukaryotic organisms that are different from plants, animals, bacteria, and fungi (172)

R

recessive trait a trait that is apparent only when two recessive alleles for the same characteristic are inherited (59)

relative dating any method of determining whether an event or object is older or younger than other events or objects (137)

ribosome a cell organelle composed of RNA and protein; the site of protein synthesis (15, 93)

RNA ribonucleic acid, a molecule that is present in all living cells and that plays a role in protein production (92)

S

selective breeding the human practice of breeding animals or plants that have certain desired characteristics (118)

sex chromosome one of the pair of chromosomes that determine the sex of an individual (73)

speciation (SPEE shee AY shuhn) the formation of new species as a result of evolution (124)

species a group of organisms that are closely related and can mate to produce fertile offspring (108)

structure the arrangement of parts in an organism (22)

T

taxonomy (taks AHN uh mee) the science of describing, naming, and classifying organisms (165)

tissue a group of similar cells that perform a common function (21)

trait a genetically determined characteristic (118)

V

vesicle (VES i kuhl) a small cavity or sac that contains materials in a eukaryotic cell; forms when part of the cell membrane surrounds the materials to be taken into the cell or transported within the cell (17)

Spanish Glossary

A

absolute dating/datación absoluta cualquier método que sirve para determinar la edad de un suceso u objeto en años (137)

active transport/transporte activo el movimiento de substancias a través de la membrana celular que requiere que la célula gaste energía (36)

adaptation/adaptación una característica que mejora la capacidad de un individuo para sobrevivir y reproducirse en un determinado ambiente (108)

allele/alelo una de las formas alternativas de un gene que rige un carácter, como por ejemplo, el color del cabello (62)

Animalia/Animalia un reino formado por organismos pluricelulares complejos que no tienen pared celular, normalmente son capaces de moverse y reaccionan rápidamente a su ambiente (174)

Archaebacteria/arqueobacteria un reino formado por bacterias que viven en ambientes extremos (171)

C

cell/célula en biología, la unidad más pequeña que puede realizar todos los procesos vitales; las células están cubiertas por una membrana y tienen ADN y citoplasma (4)

cell cycle/ciclo celular el ciclo de vida de una célula (42)

cell membrane/membrana celular una capa de fosfolípidos que cubre la superficie de la célula y funciona como una barrera entre el interior de la célula y el ambiente de la célula (7)

cellular respiration/respiración celular el proceso por medio del cual las células utilizan oxígeno para producir energía a partir de los alimentos (39)

cell wall/pared celular una estructura rígida que rodea la membrana celular y le brinda soporte a la célula (12)

Cenozoic era/era Cenozoica la era geológica más reciente, que comenzó hace 65 millones de años; también llamada *Edad de los Mamíferos* (146)

chromosome/cromosoma en una célula eucariótica, una de las estructuras del núcleo que está hecha de ADN y proteína; en una célula procariótica, el anillo principal de ADN (42)

classification/clasificación la división de organismos en grupos, o clases, en función de características específicas (164)

cytokinesis/citoquinesis la división del citoplasma de una célula (44)

D

dichotomous key/clave dicotómica una ayuda para identificar organismos, que consiste en las respuestas a una serie de preguntas (168)

diffusion/difusión el movimiento de partículas de regiones de mayor densidad a regiones de menor densidad (34)

DNA/ADN ácido desoxirribonucleico, una molécula que está presente en todas las células vivas y que contiene la información que determina los caracteres que un ser vivo hereda y necesita para vivir (86)

dominant trait/carácter dominante el carácter que se observa en la primera generación cuando se cruzan progenitores que tienen caracteres diferentes (59)

E

endocytosis/endocitosis el proceso por medio del cual la membrana celular rodea una partícula y la encierra en una vesícula para llevarla al interior de la célula (36)

endoplasmic reticulum/retículo endoplásmico un sistema de membranas que se encuentra en el citoplasma de la célula y que tiene una función en la producción, procesamiento y transporte de proteínas y en la producción de lípidos (15)

Eubacteria/Eubacteria un reino que agrupa a todos los procariotes, excepto a las arqueobacterias ni las eubacterias (171)

eukaryote/eucariote un organismo cuyas células tienen un núcleo rodeado por una membrana; entre los eucariotes se encuentran los animales, las plantas y los hongos, pero no las arqueobacterias (10)

evolution/evolución el proceso por medio del cual las características heredadas dentro de una población cambian con el transcurso de las generaciones de manera tal que a veces surgen nuevas especies (109)

exocytosis/exocitosis el proceso por medio del cual una célula libera una partícula encerrándola en una vesícula que luego se traslada a la superficie de la célula y se fusiona con la membrana celular (37)

extinct/extinto término que describe a una especie que ha desaparecido por completo (139)

F

fermentation/fermentación la descomposición de los alimentos sin utilizar oxígeno (39)

fossil/fósil los restos o las pruebas físicas de un organismo preservados por los procesos geológicos (110, 136)

fossil record/registro fósil una secuencia histórica de la vida indicada por fósiles que se han encontrado en las capas de la corteza terrestre (110)

function/función la actividad especial, normal o adecuada de un órgano o parte (22)

Fungi/Fungi un reino formado por organismos eucarióticos no verdes que no tienen capacidad de movimiento, se reproducen por esporas y obtienen alimento al descomponer substancias de su entorno y absorber los nutrientes (172)

G

gene/gene un conjunto de instrucciones para un carácter heredado (62)

generation time/tiempo de generación el período entre el nacimiento de una generación y el nacimiento de la siguiente generación (123)

genotype/genotipo la constitución genética completa de un organismo; *también* la combinación genes para uno o más caracteres específicos (63)

geologic time scale/escala de tiempo geológico el método estándar que se usa para dividir la larga historia natural de la Tierra en partes razonables (138)

Golgi complex/aparato de Golgi un organelo celular que ayuda a hacer y a empacar los materiales que serán transportados al exterior de la célula (17)

H

heredity/herencia la transmisión de caracteres genéticos de padres a hijos (56)

hominid/homínido un tipo de primate caracterizado por ser bípedo, tener extremidades inferiores relativamente largas y no tener cola; incluye a los seres humanos y sus ancestros (149)

homologous chromosomes/cromosomas homólogos cromosomas con la misma secuencia de genes y la misma estructura (43, 68)

Homo sapiens/Homo sapiens la especie de homínidos que incluye a los seres humanos modernos y a sus ancestros más cercanos; apareció hace entre 100,000 y 150,000 años (152)

L

lysosome/lisosoma un organelo celular que contiene enzimas digestivas (18)

M

meiosis/meiosis un proceso de división celular durante el cual el número de cromosomas disminuye a la mitad del número original por medio de dos divisiones del núcleo, lo cual resulta en la producción de células sexuales (gametos o esporas) (68)

Mesozoic era/era Mesozoica la era geológica que comenzó hace 248 millones de años y terminó hace 65 millones de años; también llamada *Edad de los Reptiles* (145)

mitochondrion/mitocondria en las células eucarióticas, el organelo celular rodeado por dos membranas que es el lugar donde se lleva a cabo la respiración celular (16)

mitosis/mitosis en las células eucarióticas, un proceso de división celular que forma dos núcleos nuevos, cada uno de los cuales posee el mismo número de cromosomas (43)

mutation/mutación un cambio en la secuencia de la base de nucleótidos de un gene o de una molécula de ADN (94)

N

natural selection/selección natural el proceso por medio del cual los individuos que están mejor adaptados a su ambiente sobreviven y se reproducen con más éxito que los individuos menos adaptados; una teoría que explica el mecanismo de la evolución (120)

nucleotide/nucleótido en una cadena de ácidos nucleicos, una subunidad formada por un azúcar, un fosfato y una base nitrogenada (86)

nucleus/núcleo en una célula eucariótica, un organelo cubierto por una membrana, el cual contiene el ADN de la célula y participa en procesos tales como el crecimiento, metabolismo y reproducción (7)

O

organ/órgano un conjunto de tejidos que desempeñan una función especializada en el cuerpo (21)

organelle/organelo uno de los cuerpos pequeños del citoplasma de una célula que están especializados para llevar a cabo una función específica (7)

organism/organismo un ser vivo; cualquier cosa que pueda llevar a cabo procesos vitales independientemente (22)

organ system/aparato (o sistema) de órganos un grupo de órganos que trabajan en conjunto para desempeñar funciones corporales (22)

osmosis/ósmosis la difusión del agua a través de una membrana semipermeable (35)

P

Paleozoic era/era Paleozoica la era geológica que vino después del período Precámbrico; comenzó hace 543 millones de años y terminó hace 248 millones de años (244)

passive transport/transporte pasivo el movimiento de substancias a través de una membrana celular sin que la célula tenga que usar energía (36)

pedigree/pedigrí un diagrama que muestra la incidencia de un carácter genético en varias generaciones de una familia (74)

phenotype/fenotipo la apariencia de un organismo u otra característica perceptible (62)

photosynthesis/fotosíntesis el proceso por medio del cual las plantas, las algas y algunas bacterias utilizan la luz solar, el dióxido de carbono y el agua para producir alimento (38)

Plantae/Plantae un reino formado por organismos pluricelulares complejos que normalmente son verdes, tienen una pared celular de celulosa, no tienen capacidad de movimiento y utilizan la energía del Sol para producir azúcar mediante la fotosíntesis (173)

plate tectonics/tectónica de placas la teoría que explica cómo se mueven y cambian de forma las placas tectónicas, que son grandes porciones de la capa más externa de la Tierra (140)

Precambrian time/tiempo Precámbrico el período en la escala de tiempo geológico que abarca desde la formación de la Tierra hasta el comienzo de la era Paleozoica; comenzó hace aproximadamente 4.6 mil millones de años y terminó hace 543 millones de años (142)

primate/primate un tipo de mamífero caracterizado por tener pulgares oponibles y visión binocular (148)

probability/probabilidad la probabilidad de que ocurra un posible suceso futuro en cualquier caso dado del suceso (64)

prokaryote/procariote un organismo que está formado por una sola célula y que no tiene núcleo (8)

Protista/Protista un reino compuesto principalmente por organismo eucarióticos unicelulares que son diferentes de las plantas, animales, bacterias y hongos (172)

R

recessive trait/carácter recesivo un carácter que se hace aparente sólo cuando se heredan dos alelos recesivos de la misma característica (59)

relative dating/datación relativa cualquier método que se utiliza para determinar si un acontecimiento u objeto es más viejo o más joven que otros acontecimientos u objetos (137)

ribosome/ribosoma un organelo celular compuesto de ARN y proteína; el sitio donde ocurre la síntesis de proteínas (15, 93)

RNA/ARN ácido ribonucleico, una molécula que está presente en todas las células vivas y que juega un papel en la producción de proteínas (92)

S

selective breeding/reproducción selectiva la práctica humana de cruzar animales o plantas que tienen ciertas características deseadas (118)

sex chromosome/cromosoma sexual uno de los dos cromosomas que determinan el sexo de un individuo (73)

speciation/especiación la formación de especies nuevas como resultado de la evolución (124)

species/especie un grupo de organismos que tienen un parentesco cercano y que pueden aparearse para producir descendencia fértil (108)

structure/estructura el orden y distribución de las partes de un organismo (22)

T

taxonomy/taxonomía la ciencia de describir, nombrar y clasificar organismos (165)

tissue/tejido un grupo de células similares que llevan a cabo una función común (21)

trait/carácter una característica determinada genéticamente (118)

V

vesicle/vesícula una cavidad o bolsa pequeña que contiene materiales en una célula eucariótica; se forma cuando parte de la membrana celular rodea los materiales que van a ser llevados al interior la célula o transportados dentro de ella (17)

Index

Boldface page numbers refer to illustrative material, such as figures, tables, margin elements, photographs, and illustrations.

Index

Index

Credits

Abbreviations used: (t) top, (c) center, (b) bottom, (l) left, (r) right, (bkgd) background

PHOTOGRAPHY

Front Cover Dennis Kunkel/Phototake

Skills Practice Lab Teens Sam Dudgeon/HRW

Connection to Astrology Corbis Images; **Connection to Biology** David M. Phillips/Visuals Unlimited; **Connection to Chemistry** Digital Image copyright © 2005 PhotoDisc; **Connection to Environment** Digital Image copyright © 2005 PhotoDisc; **Connection to Geology** Letraset Phototone; **Connection to Language Arts** Digital Image copyright © 2005 PhotoDisc; **Connection to Meteorology** Digital Image copyright © 2005 PhotoDisc; **Connection to Oceanography** © ICONOTEC; **Connection to Physics** Digital Image copyright © 2005 PhotoDisc

Table of Contents iv (tr), James Beveridge/Visuals Unlimited; iv (bl), ©National Geographic Image Collection/Ned M. Seidler; v (tr), Sam Dudgeon/HRW; x (bl), Sam Dudgeon/HRW; xi (tl), John Langford/HRW; xi (b), Sam Dudgeon/HRW; xii (tl), Victoria Smith/HRW; xii (bl), Stephanie Morris/HRW; xii (br), Sam Dudgeon/HRW; xiii (tl), Patti Murray/Animals, Animals; xiii (tr), Jana Birchum/HRW; xiii (b), Peter Van Steen/HRW

Chapter One 2–3, Dennis Kunkel/Phototake; 4 (l), Visuals Unlimited/Kevin Collins; 4 (r), Leonard Lessin/Peter Arnold; 5 (r), T.E. Adams/Visuals Unlimited; 5 (cl), Roland Birke/Peter Arnold, Inc.; 5 (bkgd), Jerome Wexler/Photo Researchers; 5 (cr), Biophoto Associates/Photo Researchers, Inc.; 5 (l), M.I. Walker/Photo Researchers, Inc.; 6 Photodisc, Inc.; 7 (t), William Dentler/BPS/Stone; 7 (b), Dr. Gopal Murti/Science Photo Library/Photo Researchers, Inc.; 9 Wolfgang Baumeister/Science Photo Library/Photo Researchers, Inc.; 10 (l), Biophoto Associates/Photo Researchers, Inc.; 14 (bl), Don Fawcett/Visuals Unlimited; 14 (t), Dr. Peter Dawson/Science Photo Library/Photo Researchers, Inc.; 15 (r), R. Bolender–D. Fawcett/Visuals Unlimited; 16 (cl), Don Fawcett/Visuals Unlimited; 16 (bl), Newcomb & Wergin/BPS/Tony Stone Images; 17 (br), Garry T Cole/BPS/Stone; 18 (tl), Dr. Gopal Murti/Science Photo Library/Photo Researchers, Inc.; 18 (cl), Dr. Jeremy Burgess/Science PhotoLibrary/Science Source/Photo Researchers; 76 Quest/Science Photo Library/Photo Researchers, Inc.; 77 Manfred Kage/Peter Arnold, Inc. ; 24 (b), Sam Dudgeon/HRW; 30 (r), Photo Researchers, Inc.; 30 (l), Science Photo Library/Photo Researchers, Inc.; 31 (b), Digital Image copyright © 2005 Artville; 31 (t), Courtesy Caroline Schooley

Chapter Two 32–33 © Michael & Patricia Fogden/CORBIS; 34 Sam Dudgeon/HRW; 36 (br), Photo Researchers; 37 (tr), Birgit H. Satir; 38 (l), Runk/Schoenberger/Grant Heilman; 39 (r), John Langford/HRW Photo; 41 Corbis Images; 42 CNRI/Science Photo Library/Photo Researchers, Inc.; 43 (l), L. Willatt, East Anglian Regional Genetics Service/Science Photo Library/Photo Researchers, Inc. ; 43 (b), Biophoto Associates/Photo Researchers; 44 (b), Visuals Unlimited/R. Calentine; 44 (cl), Ed Reschke/Peter Arnold, Inc.; 44 (c), Ed Reschke/Peter Arnold, Inc.; 44 (cr), Ed Reschke/Peter Arnold, Inc.; 45 (cl), Ed Reschke/Peter Arnold, Inc.; 45 (c), Biology Media/Photo Researchers, Inc.; 45 (cr), Biology Media/Photo Researchers, Inc.; 46 Sam Dudgeon/HRW; 47 Sam Dudgeon/HRW; 48 (l), Runk/Schoenberger/Grant Heilman; 49 (cl), Biophoto Associates/Science Source/Photo Researchers; 49 (cr), Biophoto Associates/Science Source/Photo Researchers; 49 (br), John Langford/HRW Photo; 52 (l), Lee D. Simons/Science Souce/Photo Researchers; 53 (tr), Courtesy Dr. Jarrel Yakel; 53 (tr), David McCarthy/SPL/Photo Researchers, Inc.

Chapter Three 54–55 © Maximilian Weinzierl/Alamy Photos; 56 Ned M. Seidler/National Geographic Society Image Collection; 61 © Andrew Brookes/CORBIS; 62 © Joe McDonald/Visuals Unlimited; 63 (b), Sam Dudgeon/HRW; 65 Digital Image copyright © 2005 PhotoDisc; 66 (b), © Mervyn Rees/Alamy Photos; 67 (b), Image Copyright ©2001 Photodisc, Inc.; 67 (tl), Sam Dudgeon/HRW; 67 (tr), Sam Dudgeon/HRW; 68 (br), Biophoto Associates/Photo Researchers; 68 (b), Phototake/CNRI/Phototake NYC; 73 (b), © Rob vanNostrand; 74 (b), © ImageState; 75 © ImageState; 76 (b), Sam Dudgeon/HRW; 77 (b), Sam Dudgeon/HRW; 79 (r), © Mervyn Rees/Alamy Photos; 79 (l), © Rob vanNostrand; 82 (c), Dr. F. R. Turner, Biology Dept., Indiana University; 82 (r), Dr. F. R. Turner, Biology Dept., Indiana University; 82 (l), Hank Morgan/Rainbow; 83, Courtesy of Stacey Wong

Chapter Four 84–85 US Department of Energy/Science Photo Library/Photo Researchers, Inc.; 87 (r), Science Photo Library/Photo Researchers, Inc.; 87 (l), Hulton Archive/Getty Images; 90 (l), Sam Dudgeon/HRW; 90 (l), Sam Dudgeon/HRW; 91 (bl), David M. Phillips/Visuals Unlimited; 91 (cl), J.R. Paulson & U.K. Laemmli/University of Geneva; 95 (br), Jackie Lewin/Royal Free Hospital/Science Photo Library/Photo Researchers, Inc.; 95 (tr), Jackie Lewin/Royal Free Hospital/Science Photo Library/Photo Researchers, Inc.; 96 (t), Visuals Unlimited/Science Visuals Unlimited/Keith Wood ; 96 (b), Volker Steger/Peter Arnold; 97 Sam Dudgeon/HRW; 99 Victoria Smith/HRW; 104 (l), Robert Brook/Science Photo Library/Photo Researchers, Inc.; 105 (r), Photo courtesy of the Whitehead Institute for Biomedical Research at MIT; 105 (l), Garry Watson/Science Photo Library/Photo Researchers, Inc.106–107 (t), © Stuart Westmorland/CORBIS; 108 (bl), James Beveridge/Visuals Unlimited; 108 (tc), © Gail Shumway/Getty Images/FPG International; 108 (br), Doug Wechsler/Animals Animals

Chapter Five 110 (l), Ken Lucas; 110 (r), John Cancalosi/Tom Stack & Associates; 111 (cl), © SuperStock; 111 (bl), © Martin Ruegner/Alamy Photos; 111 (br), © James D. Watt/Stephen Frink Collection/Alamy Photos; 111 (tl), © Ron Kimball/Ron Kimball Stock; 111 (tr), © Carl & Ann Purcell/CORBIS; 111 (cr), © Martin B. Withers/Frank Lane Picture Agency/CORBIS; 112 (tr), Illustration by Carl Buell, and taken from http://www.neoucom.edu/Depts/Anat/Pakicetid.html. ; 112 (tl), Courtesy of Research Casting International and Dr. J. G. M. Thewissen; 112 (b), Courtesy of Research Casting International and Dr. J. G. M. Thewissen; 113 (t), © 1998 Philip Gingerich/Courtesy of the Museum of Paleontology, The University of Michigan; 113 (c), Courtesy of Betsy Webb, Pratt Museum, Homer, Alaska; 113 (b), Courtesy of Betsy Webb, Pratt Museum, Homer, Alaska; 115 (b), Visuals Unlimited/H.W. Robison; 115 (t), James Beveridge/Visuals Unlimited; 116 (t), Christopher Ralling; 116 (r), © William E. Ferguson; 118 (b), Carolyn A. McKeone/Photo Researchers, Inc. ; 122 (b), Getty Images/Stone; 125 (r), Zig Leszczynski/Animals Animals/Earth Scenes; 125 (l), Gary Mezaros/Visuals Unlimited; 127 Victoria Smith/HRW; 128 (t), James Beveridge/Visuals Unlimited; 129 Courtesy of Betsy Webb, Pratt Museum, Homer, Alaska; 132 (l), Doug Wilson/Westlight; 133 (r), Wally Emerson/Courtesy of Raymond Pierotti; 133 (l), George D. Lepp/Photo Researchers, Inc.; 134–135 © Reuters NewMedia Inc./CORBIS

Chapter Six 148 (r), © Daniel J. Cox/Getty Images/Stone; 150 (b), John Reader/Science Photo Library/Photo Researchers; 150 (t), © Partick Robert/CORBIS; 151 John Gurche; 152 (tr), John Reader/Science Photo Library/Photo Researchers; 152 (tl & tc), E.R. Degginger/Bruce Coleman; 152 (bl), Neanderthal Museum; 152 (br), Volker Steger/Nordstar–4 Million Years, of Man/Science Photo Library/Photo Researchers, Inc.; 160 (r), Rikki Larma/AP/Wide World Photos; 160 (l), Copyright M. Ponce de León and Christoph Zollikofer, Zurich; 161 (r), © Robert Campbell/CORBIS; 161 (l), John Reader/Science Photo Library/Photo Researchers, Inc.; 162–163 Frans Lanting/Minden Pictures

Chapter Seven 164 Gerry Ellis/ENP Images; 170 Biophoto Associates/Photo Researchers; 171 (t), Sherrie Jones/Photo Researchers; 171 (br), Dr. Tony Brian & David Parker/Science Photo Library/Photo Researchers; 171 (inset), Dr. Tony Brian & David Parker/Science Photo Library/Photo Researchers; 172 (t), Visuals Unlimited/Stanley Flegler; 172 (b), © Phil A. Dotson/Photo Researchers, Inc.; 173 (l), © Royalty–free/CORBIS; 173 (r), David R. Frazier/Photo Researchers; 174 (tl), SuperStock; 174 (tr), © G. Randall/Getty Images/FPG International; 174 (bl), SuperStock; 175, Corbis Images; 175 Dr. Tony Brian & David Parker/Science Photo Library/Photo Researchers; 178 (b), Dr. Tony Brian & David Parker/Science Photo Library/Photo Researchers; 179 (b), SuperStock; 182 (r), Piotr Naskrecki/Conservation International; 183 (r), © National Geographic Image Collection/Michael Nichols; 183 (l), © National Geographic Image Collection/Michael Fay

Lab Book/Appendix "LabBook Header", "L", Corbis Images; "a", Letraset Phototone; "b", and "B", HRW; "o", and "k", images ©2006 PhotoDisc/HRW; 184 (tl), Runk/Schoenberger/Grant Heilman; 184 (tc), Runk/Schoenberger/Grant Heilman; 184 (tr), Michael Abbey/Photo Researchers, Inc.; 184 (tr), Sam Dudgeon/HRW; 184 (br), Runk/Schoenberger/Grant Heilman; 185 (b), Sam Dudgeon/HRW; 185 (c), Sam Dudgeon/HRW; 186 HRW; 189 (all), Sam Dudgeon/HRW; 198 Sam Dudgeon/HRW; 199 Sam Dudgeon/HRW; 204 (t), Peter Van Steen/HRW; 204 (b), Sam Dudgeon/HRW